THE MILITARY SIDE OF JAPANESE LIFE

THE MILITARY SIDE OF JAPANESE LIFE

BY

CAPTAIN M. D. KENNEDY

LATE THE CAMERONIANS (SCOTTISH RIFLES)

GREENWOOD PRESS, PUBLISHERS

WESTPORT, CONNECTICUT

The Library of Congress has catalogued this publication as follows:

Library of Congress Cataloging in Publication Data

Kennedy, Malcolm Duncan, 1895-
The military side of Japanese life.

Reprint of the 1924 ed.
1. Japan. Rikugun--Military life. I. Title.
U773.K4 1973 355'.00952 72-9091
ISBN 0-8371-6574-1

Originally published in 1924 by Constable & Co., Ltd., London

Reprinted in 1973 by Greenwood Press, Inc., 51 Riverside Avenue, Westport, Conn. 06880

Library of Congress catalog card number 72-9091
ISBN 0-8371-6574-1

Printed in the United States of America

10 9 8 7 6 5 4 3 2

TO THE MEMORY OF
THOSE FORMER BRITISH OFFICERS WHO
SERVED IN JAPAN AND FELL IN
THE GREAT WAR; AND
IN MEMORY OF

MAJOR JIRO KAWASE,

IMPERIAL JAPANESE ARMY,

WHO DIED AT HIS POST, MAY 8TH, 1922, WHILE
HOLDING THE APPOINTMENT OF ASSISTANT
MILITARY ATTACHÉ TO HIS IMPERIAL
JAPANESE MAJESTY'S EMBASSY,
LONDON, THESE PAGES
ARE RESPECTFULLY
DEDICATED.

UNIVERSITY LIBRARIES
CARNEGIE-MELLON UNIVERSITY
PITTSBURGH, PENNSYLVANIA 15213

TO THE GLORY OF GOD
AND IN HONOURED MEMORY OF THOSE
BRITISH OFFICERS
WHO FORMERLY SERVED IN JAPAN AND
LAID DOWN THEIR LIVES
FOR KING AND COUNTRY IN
THE GREAT WAR, 1914-1919.

MAJOR CHARLES ALLIX LAVINGTON YATE, V.C.
THE KING'S OWN YORKSHIRE LIGHT INFANTRY. 20.9.14.

CAPTAIN REGINALD WICKHAM HARLAND,
THE HAMPSHIRE REGIMENT. 30.10.14.

LIEUTENANT-COLONEL EVERARD FERGUSON CALTHROP,
ROYAL ARTILLERY, MILITARY ATTACHÉ TO H.B.M.EMBASSY. 19.12.15.

MAJOR JAMES LAWSON MITCHELL,
ROYAL ARTILLERY. 16.3.16.

CAPTAIN PHILIP WOOD,
89TH PUNJABIS. 5.4.16.

MAJOR WILLIAM HUGH SIMPSON,
93RD BURMA INFANTRY. 17.4.16.

CAPTAIN PERCY MONTAGUE CLIFTON WILDE,
ROYAL MARINE ARTILLERY. 31.5.16.

MAJOR GUY BERTRAM OLIVER,
ROYAL ARTILLERY. 29.9.16.

LIEUTENANT-COLONEL HERBERT FRANCIS GEORGE CARTER, M.C.
THE KING'S OWN YORKSHIRE LIGHT INFANTRY. 28.2.19.

ERECTED BY THEIR RELATIVES AND BROTHER OFFICERS.

Inscription on the tablet unveiled by H.R.H. The Prince of Wales, at S. Andrew's Church, Tokyo, on April 14th, 1922.

PREFACE

TOWARDS the end of last century a book entitled *Bibliography of Japan* made its appearance, the author being Herr von Wenckstern. I will admit straight away that I have never seen a copy of this work, but the late Mrs. Hugh Fraser puts it on record in her introduction to *A Diplomat's Wife in Japan* that the volume in question gives "four hundred pages in recording and classifying the mere titles of the books which have been written about the Island Empire."

Whether or no this bibliography has ever been revised I cannot say, but he would be a bold man who laid himself out now to record faithfully the name of every book dealing with this subject, as it is probably no exaggeration to say that the number of publications must have increased to twice, or even three times, as many as there were at the time when Herr von Wenckstern set to work to classify those which were then in existence.

The only excuse that can be made for adding yet another to the large number already existing is that, to the best of my knowledge, no other British officer sent to Japan to study the language and the military system of that country has ever attempted to describe the life led or the impressions gained by him during the period spent "seconded" in Japan. Some, it is true, have placed their impressions on record in articles which have appeared from time to time in military and other magazines, but none, so far as I know, have given anything like a full account of their doings either during their periods of attachment to Japanese military units or during any other portion of their stay in Japan. These, therefore, are the extenuating circumstances under which it is hoped that the reader's indulgence will be given to one who lays no claim to literary skill or to any special knowledge not held by at least a portion of his fellow beings.

Another apology which seems called for in regard to the following pages, is the frequent recurrence of the first person singular, which is apt to bring to mind the comment said to have been passed on the photograph of a certain well-known lady writer, when the gentleman to whom it was being shown was asked what he thought of it. His reply was that he considered that the lady's face had the same defect as her writings, namely, that " her ' eyes ' were too close ! " The pages which follow may well call forth some such remark, and the only excuse that can be given is that, taken on the whole, the contents are essentially a personal account and it is, therefore, difficult to do away with the egoistic pronoun. The reader is, however, asked to remember that, although it is in the nature of a personal account, it records doings such as are the lot of any British officer who may be sent to Japan, and that, if " the ' I's ' are too close " at times, he may, of his own accord, substitute the words " The Language Officer " or " The Writer " for the monosyllabic " I."

These pages, however, are not meant so much to show the life of a Language Officer in Japan as to describe what may be called the human side of the Japanese Army as seen by him during his periods of attachment to that fine body of men—what is meant by " the human side " being the type of officer and man in it, the life they lead, the various customs obtaining, and the traditions held by them. Technical details as to organisation, training, numbers, weapons, or tactics are scarcely mentioned, as much of the matter of that description is, of necessity, of a confidential nature and, therefore, cannot be included in a book of this scope or, for that matter, in any publication intended for general circulation.

In regard to the comments on Japan and her Army there may be those who think that too much " fulsome praise " has been written. Sir Ian Hamilton is reputed to have been hoodwinked on certain occasions by the Japanese military authorities, and it may be thought, therefore, that if a distinguished soldier like Sir Ian could be deluded into believing just what the Japanese wished him to believe, it would be still easier to make a young junior officer obtain wrong impressions. Those who take this view base their reasoning on a false surmise. An important military commander, such as Sir Ian, is greatly handicapped by his position, which restricts his movements and necessitates his being attended by those who can be instructed what to tell him and what to keep from him; moreover, his inability to speak the language likewise acts as a handicap. On the other hand, the British subaltern or captain sent to Japan for study of the language and military system is free to move about as he likes, and has the advantage of knowing the language and, therefore, of being able to discuss matters with whomsoever he will. It stands to reason, therefore, that there is less chance of his being imposed upon than there is for a distinguished, but closely attended, officer such as Sir Ian Hamilton. The latter can be made to see and hear just what the authorities wish, but the former is not so easily restricted.

In this book, therefore, an attempt has been made to apportion praise where praise is due, but, at the same time, to criticise freely what are considered to be the weak points of the Japanese military system. If these criticisms are disliked by such Japanese officers and others who may read them, it is hoped that they will be taken in the spirit in which they are given, as they are made with no unfriendly intentions, but, on the contrary, with the same idea as they themselves deliver their *kōhyō*[1] on the conclusion of manœuvres or training in the field.

[1] "Kōhyō" literally means "criticism," or "conference." In Japanese military circles it normally refers to the "pow-wow" held on the conclusion of each field operation carried out by troops in the course of their training, when their commander or an umpire gives a criticism of the operation carried out—see pp. 145 and 354.

In regard to the criticisms made, and other points raised, it must be remembered that more than two years have elapsed since I completed my tour of duty with the Japanese Army, and that I write of conditions as they were at the time of my attachment. Events have occurred since then, however, which have brought about certain changes. Where these are of special importance the information given has been modified so as to bring it more up to date ; but, where only small points of detail are concerned, it has been thought best to rest content with merely recording things as they were at the end of 1920, as it is meant rather to show the impressions left on a British officer during periods of attachment than to present a carefully-compiled treatise on the Japanese Army as it is now in 1923. It is, in fact, a personal record rather than a serious study.

Another point which should be mentioned by way of apology is that the somewhat disjointed method in which the pages are written is mainly due to the fact that they have had to be compiled in the few leisure moments at my disposal during the last year or so, an hour one day and a couple of hours the next, and then perhaps a lapse of two or three weeks in which nothing at all was written. Anyone who has ever tried to write a book under such conditions will readily understand the difficulty of giving anything like a clear and well-connected account. It is hoped, therefore, that due allowance will be made for the numerous imperfections, of which I am only too painfully aware. Were these pages to be rewritten they would certainly not be shown in their present form, but, in place of recording impressions and other matters in the chronological order of their happening, as has been done in Part I., the material contained would be split up into chapters under definite headings. This is but one of the many obvious faults and has been partly remedied in Parts II. and III. ; and, were it not that the material is already becoming out of date in many ways, the whole book would be rewritten before publication. Under the circumstances, however, it has been thought best to leave things as they are, as leisure moments are too few and far between to ensure the rearranging of the material within a sufficiently short space of time.

Finally, be it said, I wish to record my gratitude towards all those who have been so generous in their advice and constructive criticism during the writing of these pages and to those who have helped in proof-reading and in other ways. The book may be badly written, but there is a certain amount of satisfaction in the fact that it is better than it would have been if it had not been for the invaluable help of this kind received from friends who prefer to remain anonymous, and to all of whom I feel most grateful.

TOKYO, *June*, 1923.

CONTENTS

PART I

WITH THE JAPANESE ARMY IN THEIR HOME COUNTRY

CHAPTER I

CHAPTER II

CHAPTER III

CHAPTER XXIX

CHAPTER XXX

CHAPTER XXXI

CHAPTER XXXII

MAPS.

PART I

WITH THE JAPANESE ARMY IN THEIR HOME COUNTRY

CHAPTER I

PRELIMINARY PERIOD

In 1903 a system of sending British officers to Japan to study the language and to be attached to Japanese regiments in order to study the military system of our, then, new ally was begun.

From that year onwards up to the outbreak of the World War, a succession of "Language Officers," the term by which they were known, were sent out to Japan, the period of their stay in the country varying from one to four years. During those eleven years some fifty or sixty officers of the British and Indian armies were seconded for this purpose When, however, the War broke out in August, 1914, the half-dozen or so "Language Officers" then in Japan were recalled to their regiments, and for the next three years there were no British officers out there except the Military Attaché himself. One result of this was that the General Staff began to lose touch with current affairs in the army of our Far Eastern ally, and, therefore, after a lapse of over two years, they decided to re-start the "Language Officer" system, selecting only officers who had been too badly wounded to be passed "fit G.S."

Six of us were selected to do a preliminary course in Japanese at the School of Oriental Studies, and, as a result of an examination held on the conclusion of the course, two of us were selected to go to Japan, for which country we sailed early in September, 1917.

For the first year of our stay in Japan, our time was chiefly spent in studying the language, and, though we were duly presented to the heads of the various military departments and from time to time attended military functions, it was not till December, 1918, that we were attached for the first time to an army unit, Capt. B. . . . going to the 3rd Infantry Regiment stationed at Azabu in Tokyo, while I was sent to the 34th Infantry Regiment at Shizuoka, a hundred and twenty miles or so to the south-west.

As the first year of our stay in Japan was concerned but little with matters of purely military interest, nothing more than a rough summary of it need be given—no more, in fact, than is necessary, as it were, to get the reader into the picture. Probably the best way to do this will be to jot down one or two anecdotes and some of the impressions received. The reader who is only interested in the military side of these pages is advised, therefore, to leave out this " preliminary canter " and begin straight away with Chapter III.

As the Language Officer who proceeds to Japan is attached to the British Embassy during his period of residence in the country, it probably goes without saying that he comes in for a certain number of diplomatic functions if he happens to settle down in Tokyo. As both B. . . . and I spent a large part of our first year in that city, it came about that we took part in several such entertainments, and as some of them are essentially Japanese, it may be of interest to some who read these pages if a brief outline of the chief ones is given.

One of the first of these functions which took place after our arrival in Japan was the Imperial Chrysanthemum Garden Party, an annual event given by the Emperor and Empress. Some six weeks later the New Year came in, and with it the ceremony for which all the members of the various embassies and legations go to the palace to pay their respects to the Emperor and Empress and to the Princes of the Blood. Though both these functions were interesting in their way, they have little to do with the army, and no details need therefore be given.

One of the first military functions which we attended

was the parade held in front of the Imperial Palace on January 9th, 1918. This is the annual ceremony known as the Rikugun Hajime which marks the beginning of the army year. All units of the Japanese army hold a special parade on that day, whilst those in Tokyo are reviewed by the Emperor himself, the foreign military attachés, and such diplomats as wish to do so, attending.

It being the first time that I had seen Japanese troops on parade, it came as a surprise to find that the infantry used the German "goose-step" when marching past. As, however, one came to realise later, most of their drill, as well as their organisation and tactics, is still based on that of Germany, owing to officers of the German army having been employed formerly as instructors (1885-1894).

What struck one more than anything else in this parade, however, were the regimental colours, which in some cases consisted of nothing more than a bare pole with a ragged strip of purple cloth swinging from it. Though one became accustomed to colours of this kind later, it was a point which impressed itself on one very much at the time. Japanese regiments even at the present day carry their colours into action and take them wherever they go, manœuvres included; the more tattered they are the more proud are their owners, as it helps to show the amount of service seen by the unit. To return, however, to the subject of functions.

Before going to Japan we had been warned that we should need a large supply of cards, and it was not long after our arrival in Tokyo before we realised that this bit of advice, supplied by a thoughtful War Office, was good. Even prior to January 5th we had distributed a large number, but on that day the two of us, together with the new British Naval Attaché, must have created something of a record as regards "shooting" cards, for in one afternoon, with the able assistance of a car chartered for the occasion, we left cards at all the embassies and legations and wrote our names in the visiting-books of all the Imperial Princes in Tokyo, a total of twenty-nine calls.

A few days later B. . . and I were taken to the War Office, General Staff, and Military Education Bureau in the morning, to be presented to the heads of the military departments, and in the evening attended a *soirée* at the Foreign Office.

A *soirée* of this kind, when depicted on the musical comedy stage in London, at Daly's or some such place, is an interesting and amusing spectacle, but when you come to the real thing, it may be interesting in its way, but there is no "Berry" or "George Robey" to enliven proceedings in the guise of a comic count or other similar rôle, and one comes away breathing a prayer of thanks for having been born into the profession of arms rather than into that of Diplomacy. During the next year or two several functions of a like nature took place, and on each occasion one felt inclined to put up a similar prayer of thanks. No offence is meant by this to the members of the *Corps Diplomatique*; the sentiments expressed are merely that the life of the barrack-square or, better still, camp, is preferable to that of formal receptions and ballrooms. No doubt there are some among the diplomats themselves who share these feelings.

On the evening of January the 17th, the War Minister gave a dinner at his official residence to the members of the British Embassy in honour of the King, who had been made a Marshal in the Japanese army, and the Emperor, who had become a British Field-Marshal. Some twenty or thirty Japanese officers were present.

"The dinner was held in the War Minister's banqueting hall, a fine large building in beautiful grounds. The quarter mile or so of the grounds through which we had to pass in order to reach the building was lit by rows of Japanese lanterns, each of which had the crossed flags of Great Britain and Japan painted upon it. The actual dinner reminded one of a 'Guest Night' in a British regimental mess, as everyone was in uniform and a military band played throughout dinner.

"As we went in, the band struck up 'God save the King,' this being followed by 'Kimi ga yo,' the Japanese national anthem.

"Each guest was presented with a frosted silver box as a souvenir, the crossed flags of the two nations being on the lids in enamel.

"Towards the end of dinner speeches were made by the War Minister and Sir Connynghame-Greene, after which were drunk the healths of the two Sovereigns."[1]

It was at the dinner mentioned above that I first came to realise that, although Japanese music conveys little or nothing to the average foreigner, it is equally true that our own music is nothing more than a medley of noises to a great many Japanese. The realisation of this fact was brought about as follows :—

As recorded above, a military band dispensed music during dinner. By way of making conversation, therefore, I asked my right-hand neighbour, a tough old major-general with a large, flowing moustache, what he thought of European music. His reply was to the effect that he did not like it because it sounded like the howling of dogs.

It struck me as rather humorous, as it was just about the same answer that I myself would have been inclined to give if anyone had asked for my opinion of Japanese or Chinese music ; in fact an entry made in my diary, referring to a visit made with a Chinese merchant and some of his friends to a Chinese restaurant in Singapore on the way out to Japan, shows the impression left on me after hearing Chinese music for the first time, and it is not altogether unlike the first impression which one receives of Japanese music, though the latter is certainly rather less discordant.

"... The place was brilliantly lit up, and much beating of drums with discordant sounds of all kinds was proceeding from the restaurants round about. . . . Chinese singing-girls were called, and gave out the most ear-piercing and discordant shrieks (one could hardly call it music) throughout the evening, accompanied by an orchestra of three. One of these latter played an instrument shaped like a violin, but only possessing one string and about as many notes ! Another spent his time beating a kind of 'tom-tom,' while

[1] Extract from diary of that date.

the third whacked away at a piece of wood and at times used a kind of metal clapper—altogether a most ghastly row, but an interesting experience!"

While on the subject of music, it may not be out of place to say a few words about one side of Japanese life about which so much has been written in books dealing with Japan, namely the *geisha* or "singing-girl." As frequent references will be found later on in these pages to *geisha* dinners which I attended during periods of attachment to Japanese units, it may be stated once and for all that the *geisha* is not necessarily, as so many people seem to imagine, synonymous with the *joro* or inmate of the licensed quarters. No doubt the morals of some of them are not above reproach, but it is wrong to suppose that they are all lacking in morality.

As one *geisha* dinner is not unlike another, the impressions of the first one I attended may be quoted from the diary. The hosts on this particular occasion were two Japanese major-generals belonging to the War Office, whilst the guests consisted of four foreign and ten or twelve other Japanese officers. "... Cushions, on which we had to squat, were ranged in a semicircle round the room, and in front of each guest was a *hangyoku*—a girl learning to be a *geisha*. Their business is to see that each guest has everything he wants and that the *sake* cup is always full. When the actual feeding was over, the sliding doors of the room were opened and four *geisha* came in, two singing *geisha* and two dancing *geisha*, and proceeded to perform for our edification. I cannot say that I was very much taken by either their singing or their dancing, though it was very interesting in its way. They wore beautiful costumes, but there was very little actual dancing, the whole thing being a succession of poses. There was not enough 'go' in it.

"After their singing and dancing was over, things began to liven up a bit. Apparently the correct thing at this stage of the proceedings is to get out into the middle of the room and try to imitate the dancing of the *geisha*. One of the officers got up and pirouetted round and then tried to make me do likewise, and before I knew where I was I found myself being dragged out to give a performance of some kind. Being unable to dance on account of my 'game' leg I thought the most appropriate thing to do was to sing '*A wee deoch an doris*' to them. They cheered wildly, though I do not suppose they understood a word. S. . . . gave them a Japanese song, which one of the *geisha* subsequently tried to teach to me. In exchange she wanted me to teach her, '*If you were the only girl in the World,*' which she said she had heard on a gramophone! It struck me as a most appropriate song, so I endeavoured to comply with her request. Some of these *geisha* are very fascinating in their way, but taken on the whole they are too doll-like and empty-headed. One funny thing about a show of this kind is that the hosts crawl round on their knees to each guest in turn in order to exchange cups of *sake* with them."

Geisha dinners of the kind described above form a part of Japanese life, both military and civil, which has no real counterpart in the life of western nations. The Japanese, for instance, very seldom give dinner parties in their houses, but, instead, invite their friends to a local *geisha* restaurant.

Although this is true as a whole, especially in the case of foreign guests, the fact remains that a foreigner on a job such as that of Language Officer is, by virtue of living in constant touch with Japanese of his own profession, able to get to know them sufficiently well to be invited to their private houses—a privilege seldom accorded to the foreign business man or tourist unless by those who have been to Europe or America themselves.

My first invitation to a Japanese private house was some two or three months after my arrival in Japan, the host being a Japanese officer to whom I had received an introduction a week or two before. Later on, of course, while attached to a Japanese regiment, officers often invited me to their houses, and many a cheery evening have I spent with them; but this being my first experience of a meal in a proper Japanese house, everything was interesting, and I was much struck by the friendly manner of my host and his wife. The meal was an ordinary Japanese one taken squatting on the floor, there being no chairs or any other furniture of that kind in a Japanese house.

In Japan the women seldom eat with their men-folk when guests are present, but have their meals separately, and I remember being greatly surprised to find the lady of the house waiting on us instead of sitting down to eat with us.

A great deal more could be written on the subject of entertainments in Japan, but as it is not intended to do more than give a brief outline of the kind which one normally meets while carrying out an attachment to a unit of the Japanese army, no mention of the theatre, the *hanashi-ka* ("story-teller"), or any other form of entertainment need be made here. Before closing this chapter, however, reference may be made to one more essentially Japanese function, namely the "cherry-viewing garden party."

The first party of this kind which I attended was given by Prince Fushimi to the members of the various embassies and legations and to a number of the chief Japanese officials, in order to present them to Prince Yi, the Crown Prince of Korea, who was shortly to be married to one of the Japanese Princesses. "It was an interesting ceremony, though the 'cherry-viewing' part was rather spoiled by the weather, as it had been raining all the morning and was very misty and damp in the afternoon. Each guest was presented to the Prince in turn, after which we went into the grounds to see the cherry blossoms, which were very fine in spite of the weather. The grounds themselves were beautiful."

It was unfortunate having such bad weather that day, as Tokyo itself was looking its best just then—cherry blossom and flowering trees and shrubs of all kinds being in full bloom everywhere. Many of the main roads in Tokyo have cherry trees planted on both sides, and these trees, when their flowers are out, are a wonderful sight.

It is probably superfluous to mention what great store the Japanese set by their cherry blossoms, but as these pages are largely concerned with the Japanese army, it may not be out of place to quote two popular sayings to show how the soldier and the cherry blossom are connected in the minds of the people of these islands. One of these is an ancient proverb, "*Hana wa sakura ni, Hito wa Bushi,*" which Professor Chamberlain translates, "The cherry is the first among flowers, as the warrior is first among men." The second one reads, "*Shikishima no yamato gokoro wo, Hito towaba, Asahi ni niou Yamazakura bana.*" The same authority translates this, "If one should enquire of you concerning the spirit of the Japanese, point to the wild cherry blossom shining in the sun." The Japanese construe this to mean that death in action is as beautiful as the short life of the cherry blossom. These two sayings are much used in military circles in Japan, especially in the so-called "spiritual training," to which great attention is paid in the education of the soldier, and to which fuller reference will be found later on in these pages.

In most, if not all regiments, cherry trees are to be seen on the barrack-square. The reason for this is said to be that the military authorities endeavour to make the conscript regard his unit as his temporary home, the recruit being taught to look upon his corporal as his elder brother, the sergeant as his mother, and the company commander as his father. The part played by the cherry tree on the barrack-square is to remind the newly-joined soldier of the poems of the cherry blossom he learned in his childhood days, the idea being to make him feel more at home.

CHAPTER II

PRELIMINARY PERIOD (*Continued*)

HAVING now shown the reader something of the sort of entertainments for which the Language Officer in Japan comes in, and also their connection with Japanese military life, where such exists, it is time that something were said about some of the trips made prior to being properly attached to a Japanese military unit, as one can learn a considerable amount about the customs and characteristics of the people as a whole by one's own experiences during visits to places in the country districts.

In order to get into touch with the Japanese as much as possible, it is always as well to put up at the native inns, in preference to staying at foreign or semi-foreign hotels. A few words on the subject of Japanese inns may, therefore, be of interest to those who have never had experience of such establishments.

To anyone wishing to travel light, nothing better than a Japanese inn can be recommended as a resting-place for the night. You are supplied, as a matter of course, with a sleeping-suit, so you need not trouble to take pyjamas with you; you are lent *geta*, the Japanese wooden clogs, if you want to go out for a walk, so you need not bother to bring a spare pair of shoes; and you get the use of towels, umbrellas, and even tooth-brushes (if you want one), so you can dispense with a burberry, towels, and other such *impedimenta* if you wish to keep down the weight of your baggage.

In regard to what I have called the sleeping-suit, the actual kind of garment provided as such varies with the time of year. In summer you are given a *yukata,* that is to say a thin cotton *kimono,* whilst in winter you are provided with a wadded silk one, a beautifully warm, comfortable garment. In either case, though these clothes are provided mainly as sleeping kit, it is quite in order to change into them as soon as you enter the inn, and to sit in them for the rest of the day, or even to go out into the road with them, which could hardly be done if one were wearing their British counterpart, pyjamas.

On one occasion after stopping at a Japanese inn for a few days by the side of Hakone Lake, we had an amusing experience, which throws a certain amount of light on the Japanese attitude towards the War, which was still very much in full swing at the time. "On the way down from Hakone we passed through a small mountain village called Hata, and stopped at a tea-house for a drink. A girl came out to serve us, and, while we were having something to drink, kept up an animated conversation, during which F. . . . mentioned something about the War to her. Much to my surprise, she asked what war he was talking about, and when he explained that there was a war in progress at that very time, and that, moreover, it had been in full swing for some three and a half years, nothing would induce her to believe it! In fact, when F. . . . told her that her own country was one of the belligerents, she laughed and said '*uso yo*!'—a polite way of calling a man a liar! It so happened, however, that I was wearing 'shorts' at the time, so F. . . ., in order to convince her that there really was a war in progress, pointed to my 'game' leg, and explained that it had been 'knocked out of shape' as a result of being wounded. Even with that she still seemed a bit doubtful, though she at once called out to the old lady who owned the tea-house that there was a war on. The old lady, however, was equally incredulous, and maintained that there had been no war since Japan fought Russia, and that therefore I must have been wounded in that war!"

It seemed almost incredible that, even as late as 1918, there were people living who had never heard of the War, but for the veracity of this statement I am prepared to take my oath. People in England probably did not realise the comparatively little interest taken by the average Japanese in the War, though it is not meant to infer by this that there were many who had not even heard of it.[1] But when one comes to analyse the matter, it is not really so very surprising, for the War was brought about by a quarrel in which Japan, as a whole, had no part, situated as she was many thousands of miles away from it all.

"When F. . . . pointed out that I had been wounded, the girl was most sympathetic, and amused us very much by saying, 'How your wife and children must have cried when they heard the news!' When I replied that I was unmarried and therefore had neither wife nor children to cry, she was more convinced than ever that I was prevaricating. The Japanese from the country marry very young and cannot understand anyone over twenty being unmarried; hence her incredulity.

"When F. . . . insisted on the fact that neither he nor I were married she seemed quite distressed, and offered in all sincerity to do her best to get a wife for each of us! We assured her that we did not wish to put her to so much trouble, and that no doubt we should find wives for ourselves in due course![2]

"The old lady who owned the tea-house told us that she had been born and brought up in the village, and said that one of her earliest recollections was when, as a young girl, she and her parents had had to flee to the woods and hide themselves during the course of a battle which took place close by. She recalled how, whilst they were in hiding, they saw the victors returning from the fray carrying the heads of the vanquished on pieces of cloth and on the points of bamboo poles according to the rank of the slain, the former being the more important enemy dead, while those stuck on poles were the rank and file.

[1] When a Japanese talks of "the War," he means the Russo-Japanese War and not the War of 1914-18.

[2] It may be stated here that both of us since then have joined the ranks of the Benedicts!

" Having told us this somewhat grizzly story, she then proceeded to say that she herself was quite prepared to die, as she had lived long enough to see Japan change from the days when men fought and carried off the heads of the vanquished in this way, to the days when ' men walked in the clouds.' Thinking that the old lady must have had a dream of some sort in which she had seen this happening, F. . . . asked the girl if she could explain what she meant, and we found that the old lady's ' men walking in the clouds ' referred to an aeroplane which had flown over the village on a recent occasion."

One trip which is perhaps worth mentioning in more or less detail, as it was in connection with an event of historical interest, took place in the spring of 1918.

Every year, on May 30th, the Americans celebrate what they call Memorial Day, by holding special services for the dead and decorating the graves of their fellow-countrymen. In Japan the main ceremony is generally held in Yokohama, with the American Ambassador presiding. In this particular year, M'D. . . . of the American Embassy was deputed by his Ambassador to go to the village of Shimoda to lay wreaths on the graves of some of Commodore Perry's men who lie buried there. Knowing that I was always keen on seeing as much of the country as possible, he asked me to go with him, an invitation which I readily accepted.

Shimoda lies at the southern end of the Izu Peninsula, a hundred miles or so south of Tokyo, and it was in Shimoda Bay that the famous Perry anchored his fleet and demanded the opening of Japan some seventy odd years ago, the first treaty with the outside world being signed by Japan at a temple on the outskirts of the village, this temple being there to this day.

Stopping at Yokohama for the night of the 28th, we set off by car about seven next morning, laden with wreaths and flags for laying on the graves. It had been raining hard all night and was still drizzling a bit when we set out, but it soon cleared and ended in first-rate weather.

The scenery the whole way was beautiful, especially that

of the Izu Peninsula itself—a succession of beautifully wooded hills rising three and four thousand feet, with rugged valleys, steep ravines, mountain streams and waterfalls everywhere. The road for the most part was fairly good, but in several places we had trouble with pack-ponies which we were continually passing.

In all these country districts all transport is done by means of pack-ponies, as it is too hilly for wheeled traffic, except motors, which are still comparatively scarce outside the big towns.

" The Japanese pony is a very timid beast and gets frightened when he hears anything so uncommon as a motor. We had a great deal of trouble on this account all the way along and were constantly having to draw up in order to let the man in charge of these ponies pacify them. One thing that must be said for the Japanese peasant, is that he takes everything as it comes, and, instead of cursing and fuming at one for making his ponies bolt (as no doubt his good old British counterpart would do under similar circumstances), he puts himself to a great amount of trouble and runs considerable risk of being badly kicked by the beast in his endeavours to quieten it, and then, having successfully manœuvred it, turns round with his face wreathed in smiles as though he thoroughly enjoyed the whole thing and thought it a great joke ! Nothing seems to worry him in the least, and his women-folk are just the same. Several times when we were passing small children standing by the road-side, their mothers, on seeing the car approaching, dashed across in front of us to pick up their offsprings and, after being nearly run over themselves, stood holding the children in their arms, laughing as though the whole thing was a joke.

" It was close on 6.30 p.m. when we reached Shimoda, where we were met by the mayor and other officials, who had heard of our coming from the manager of the inn to whom we had previously wired for rooms. Owing to a misunderstanding they had got the idea that the British and American Ambassadors themselves were coming. They were somewhat overcome, therefore, on learning that neither of us were either of those dignitaries. To add to it, the village band had also turned out and was wheezing out a tune of sorts in a terrible succession of discords, though we found out subsequently that this was not for our special benefit, but was, in fact, merely the orchestra from a neighbouring cinema. The whole effect, however, was truly Gilbertian—the town council in full war-paint, the stately bowing and greeting of the same, and the painful sounds (no aspersions on the late Mr. Sullivan's art!) emanating from the orchestra, whilst the two central figures, somewhat overcome by so unexpected a greeting, clambered painfully out from the depths of a 'Ford' machine, pretty well smothered in dust."

The civic officials who had come to greet us were somewhat taken aback when it was explained to them that neither of us had as yet attained the dizzy heights of ambassadorial rank. With true Japanese courtesy, however, they laughed the matter over on learning their mistake, and, even though we were not such exalted personages as they had been led to believe, they treated us with great kindness and promised to make all the necessary arrangements for visiting the graves of Perry's men the next day.

The landlord of the inn at which we put up for the night was profuse in his apologies for being unable to supply us with European food, furniture, etc., and for the "dirty" state of the building. The "dirt," however, was only there in his imagination, everything being spotlessly clean, as is invariably the case with the better class Japanese houses and inns. But like all Orientals, the Japanese in their desire to show courtesy always depreciate themselves and their belongings, and on some occasions almost seem to apologise for their very existence.

After we had had something to eat, the local newspaper correspondent came in to make his bows and offered to show us round the village, an offer which we readily accepted. It is an interesting place and very pretty, boasting of a population of about four thousand, to most of whom the sight of a foreigner was something of a rarity. Many small islands are dotted about in the bay, while at the back of the village there are well-wooded hills. On the top of one of these is a tree with Perry's name carved on it, and near the inn is the temple in which Perry signed the first treaty with Japan.

On returning to our quarters, we were shown a photo of a group taken the previous year, the photo having been taken to commemorate the visit of the American Ambassador. A curious thing about this photo was that the face of one of those in the group had been deliberately scratched out. On enquiring the reason for this, we were told that the man had since died, and there is a superstition amongst Japanese country-folk that, if a group is taken and one of the group dies, the people on either side of him will do likewise unless his face is removed.

In regard to this it may be said, in passing, that I came across a somewhat similar superstition in Korea, while travelling through that country some two years later. I wished to obtain a photograph of an aged Korean peasant and asked the old gentleman to pose for me. Far from acquiescing, the man covered his face with his hands and tried to run away. Unable to understand the reason for this behaviour I made enquiries, and was told that it was because the old-fashioned Korean imagines that, if you take his photo, you extract his soul and he will then die.

The inn at which we were staying was of the ordinary Japanese type—no furniture of any kind, but spotlessly clean *tatami*—Japanese straw matting—and *zabuton*—Japanese cushions—on which to sit.

Sliding paper doors divided the rooms, and walls of a similar description separated the rooms from the outside world. Being summer, however, the latter were removed during the day-time, so we looked out on to the garden in which the orange trees were in full bloom, the perfume from which was blown into the house.

Our friendly newspaper correspondent having bade us good-night, we changed into *yukata* and were shown to the bathroom.

A Japanese bath is a very different kind of thing from that used in England. It is like a great wooden vat, the water being heated by means of a charcoal stove let in underneath. The same water is used throughout the day, no matter how many people bathe in it, but as you soap yourself and rinse it off thoroughly before you enter the bath, the water remains comparatively clean.

A somewhat disconcerting thing to a foreigner when first he goes to stay at a country inn in Japan is that, just as he is preparing to enjoy his bath and has arrayed himself in "Nature's own garment," he suddenly finds himself confronted by a smiling-faced *neesan*—the Japanese chambermaid—who has come in to see if the *danna san*—the master—wants his back scrubbed. Gentle reader, should you ever go to Japan and find yourself confronted in this way, show not your surprise, but smile benignly on the damsel and let her scrub away to her heart's content, as though you had been used to such proceedings all your life. It is all in accordance with Japanese custom, and seems no more unusual to a Japanese than it is for a European to have his boots cleaned.

As already mentioned, we had to live *à la Japonaise*, eating Japanese food with chop-sticks, and squatting and sleeping on the floor. It was in equally Japanese style that the ladies of the inn who "tended to our wants" walked in and out of the room while we were dressing, and even into the bath-room while we were in our "tubs," to make sure that we had everything that we wanted. One cannot help thinking that Master Adam had not much Japanese blood in him—either that, or else he did not get as big a bite out of the apple as he is reputed to have done. However much he really did bite off, it seems to have had very little effect on the country-folk of the "Land of the Rising Sun." In hot weather you see the children in the country running about clad in nothing but a smile, while their "fond" mammas and papas go about in even less clothing than a European "Society" lady in evening dress.

Next morning we were in the middle of our ablutions

when in walked our friends of the previous evening in full war-paint—frock-coats, brown boots, and straw hats. I tried to explain how pleased we were to see them and to look as if I meant it. Having finished our ablutions and clothed ourselves and had a hurried meal, we set out in solemn procession to the harbour, where a *sampan* was waiting to take us across to the temple at Kakkesaki, the other side of the bay.

One could not help being amused at our appearance—first, three or four men carrying the flowers for the graves, then M'D. . . . and I doing our best to look solemn, while behind us, clad in the aforesaid raiment, came the village "civic officials," followed by a nondescript crowd of villagers.

In the *sampan* were a couple of European chairs, raised from heaven knows where, on which M'D . . . and I had to sit, while the rest of those who came with us squatted in Japanese fashion in the bottom of the boat.

It took us about half an hour to cross over to Kakkesaki, which is a little bit of a fishing village, and here we were met by some of the local villagers and escorted to the temple.

The graves of Perry's men are in a row at one side of the temple, and it was to these that we went first, laying a basket of flowers and placing small American and Japanese flags on each. This done, two priests from the temple, in full-dress (curiously similar to "high church" vestments), led the way into the temple and held a kind of "Mass" for the souls of these men and for Townshend Harris, who, so far as one could make out, has been more or less deified by them.[1]

It was all very interesting in its way. The two priests stood before a kind of altar and drawled out some sort of chant, one of them, in addition, beating a gong from time to time. At the end of the chant they sprinkled incense on the little braziers in front of the altar and then got both of us to do likewise. That finished proceedings more or

[1] Townshend Harris, America's first diplomatic representative in Japan, originally lived at Kakkesaki in this temple, with a Dutch interpreter, who was afterwards assassinated when they moved to Tokyo.

less, except that we, of course, had to drink the ubiquitous tea, as is done on every possible occasion in Japan.

After the rendering of thanks, we returned to our *sampan* and across to our "pub," and a little later, after more tea-drinking, set off for Tokyo.

M'D. . . . went the whole way back by car, but as I had to attend a dinner that evening given by General Oshima, the War Minister, I only motored as far as Numazu, the nearest station, some fifty or sixty miles north of Shimoda, and returned from there to Tokyo by train.

Reference has already been made to the somewhat curious (to a European) dress worn by the civic officials at Shimoda. It is not, as other people who have lived in Japan will admit, by any means unusual to see Japanese dressed in this way. The frock-coat is the recognised garment for official ocasions, and so long as he has that on his back, the average official in the country districts does not worry very much about the rest of his attire. Japan is a wonderful country for dress, and it is doubtful if any other country in the world boasts of so many styles—men in Japanese attire, others in European kit; many wearing a mixture of both; students in their blue uniforms; soldiers, police, and other officials each in theirs; men in coolie dress; men in frock-coats and tweed trousers; men in clothes designed by themselves, and a hundred and one other forms of garment. The combined effect of this curious mixture is, as may well be imagined, a phenomenon which one cannot forget. The variety in headgear, it may be added, is equally noteworthy.

One more event which took place during these first twelve months in Japan, and which cannot be left out, was the visit of Prince Arthur of Connaught, who arrived in Japan on June 18th, 1918, in order to present the Emperor with the batôn of a British Field-Marshal. During his stay in the country several interesting ceremonies took place, including that of the actual presentation of the batôn and a banquet given by General Oshima, the War Minister, in honour of that event.

The presentation of the batôn took place at the Palace on

the 19th, and, though only certain members of the Embassy were invited to attend the ceremony, the two Language Officers, being military officers, had the good fortune to be amongst those invited, it being primarily a military affair.

On arriving at the Palace we were shown to the Assembly Room, where we were presented to the various high officials, some twenty in all, who had also been ordered to attend, these including Marshals Yamagata, Terauchi, and Kawamura, and Admirals of the Fleet Togo and Ijuin, the first named being, at that time, the most powerful man in Japan and the real "power behind the throne" for many years past.

Some ten minutes later we were all ushered into the Throne Room, and shortly afterwards the Emperor, followed by the Imperial Princes, came in through a door to the right of the throne, the former ascending to the top step. A minute or so later an unseen band struck up 'God Save the King,' very slowly and impressively, as Prince Arthur and his suite were seen coming towards the Throne Room.

"Captain St. Clair entered first, passing through a door immediately in front of the throne, advancing slowly towards it, and, after bowing, backed to the right of the throne and halted facing inwards. Major the Earl of Pembroke came next, being followed by General Pulteney carrying the batôn, the latter falling back to the left of the throne. Last of all came Prince Arthur himself. Halting in front of the throne, he read a message from the King, asking the Emperor to honour the British Army by accepting the rank of Field-Marshal in it. This having been translated into Japanese by Prince Ito, the Emperor himself then read out a speech of thanks, this being translated, in like manner, into English by the Court Chamberlain. Prince Arthur then took over the batôn from General Pulteney and presented it to the Emperor, after which he retired from the room, the hidden band again striking up 'God Save the King.' The other three followed, and the ceremony came to an end."

The actual ceremony was quite short, but the solemnity of it all was very impressive, and it is mentioned here as being of military interest inasmuch as such a ceremony as the investing of an Emperor of Japan with the insignia of a British Field-Marshal is without precedent in history.

The banquet given by the War Minister took place on the 22nd, and, after it was over, we were given an exhibition of *Sumo*, the Japanese form of wrestling. It is one of the favourite forms of amusement in Japan, and attracts enormous crowds, much the same as the cup-tie finals do in England. On this occasion, of course, no one was admitted except the guests, about seventy or eighty in all. Onishi, Tochigiyama, Nishinoumi, and Kyushuzan, the four champion wrestlers of Japan, were amongst those who performed.

Japanese wrestlers wear their hair long and knot it in a " bun " at the back. They are enormously fat and hugely developed in every way and probably weigh, on an average, eighteen to twenty stone. It is not, however, all fat, but chiefly pretty hard muscle. They are extraordinarily powerful, as may be judged by the fact that, in the battle of Mukden in 1905, one of them, who had become a soldier, is reputed to have carried away on his shoulders by himself a mountain gun which was in danger of falling into the hands of the Russians.

Before beginning, the wrestlers go through a kind of religious ceremony. They start by marching in, two at a time, with a third man walking in front. The latter holds a large sword above his head with both hands. After bowing to the audience they half squat on their haunches, and the leader claps his hands, and slaps his chest and thighs, and goes through various movements with his arms and legs, after which all three solemnly walk out, to be followed by the next couple with their sword-bearer, who go through the same sort of ritual, and so on till all have been introduced, the introducer being the " umpire," who is dressed in sort of " vestments " somewhat similar to those of a Shinto priest.

The champions themselves wear a thick rope like a three-inch hawser tied round their stomachs (one cannot say " waists ") when they come in the first time to be introduced, though of course they divest themselves of this *impedimenta* when they prepare for the fray.

After all have been introduced, the first pair comes in together with the umpire, and a couple of men squat on either side of the "ring" and call out the names of the wrestlers. The two wrestlers then squat on their haunches, facing each other, after which they get up, each one clapping his hands and invoking the gods for victory. Each then throws a handful of salt into the "ring" (for luck), and, after slapping his thighs, again squats himself on his haunches and throws himself forward in a half crouching position on to his hands, waiting for the umpire to give the word. The word being given, they hurl themselves at each other and try to come to grips. The winner is the man who either throws his opponent out of the "ring," or throws him on the ground first. The way they go for each other rather reminds one of a "Rugger" scrum, as at times they push each other in much the same way as do the "forwards" in a scrimmage. The winner then renders thanks to the gods and receives a kind of blessing from the umpire.

A longish account of Japanese wrestling has been given, as, besides being a national sport, it is a form of pastime much indulged in by Japanese soldiers and, to a lesser degree, by the officers as well.

Various other functions took place during Prince Arthur's stay in Japan, but as none of them were exclusively military, no mention need be made of them here, and the next event of a military nature was the arrival in Japan of a British tank about the end of October—the first tank ever seen in Japan.

On October 30th, Major Bruce, the officer who had brought the tank from England, gave an exhibition of its capabilities on the Aoyama Parade Ground in Tokyo. The crowds were greatly impressed, and when the tank went over a specially prepared "obstacle course," they broke into loud cheers, a very unusual thing for Japanese. Other tanks have been brought to Japan since then, but further remarks on this subject will be reserved for a subsequent chapter.

A week later the War Minister gave a dinner to those of the foreign attachés who were going to attend Grand Manœuvres, in order to introduce us to our "bear-leaders," the chief of whom was Lt.-Col. Terauchi, eldest son of the late Marshal of that name, and a week after that—November 13th, to be exact—we set off for the Grand Manœuvres and I had my first real insight into the Japanese Army. Incidentally, it is interesting to note, in passing, that these " Grand Manœuvres " began just two days after the successful completion of certain " Very Grand Manœuvres " which we and our Allies had been carrying out for more than four years without rest day or night. As, however, the main object of this book is to throw some light on to the everyday life of the Japanese army as seen by a British officer attached to it, no more mention of the War and other events which took place during that officer's stay in Japan will be made in this chapter, which has already been filled up with too much of an irrelevant nature. Before closing it, however, a few words must be added on the subject of the Language Officer's principal work.

Anyone reading these pages might, if he, or she, did not know otherwise, imagine that a British officer in Japan has a very slack time and spends his days sight-seeing and " poodle-faking." If this is so he, or she, will be more or less in harmony with that cheery humourist (history does not relate his name) who was responsible for the Language Officer course in Japan being originally " dubbed " in official regulations as " Language Leave." The latter word in this expression has been known to mislead more than one otherwise well-meaning C.O. into believing that an officer of his unit, on completing such a course, would require no further " leave " of any kind for many a long day to come.

The three years which one spends in Japan as a Language Officer can hardly be termed " leave " in any sense. One is certainly very much more one's own master on a course of this kind than one is when carrying out ordinary regimental duty ; but in order to pass the required examinations, which have to be taken at the end of each year, one has to work, for the study of the Japanese language requires considerable mental application and patience.

In regard to the actual language study it may be pointed out that, although trips to Kyushu, Shikoku, Hokkaido, Korea, Manchuria, Siberia, Shantung, or any other such places as recounted later on in these pages, may sound rather after the style of "joy-riding," they are nevertheless invaluable, especially if carried out by oneself, or at any rate without the company of another foreigner. Not only does a trip of this kind increase one's knowledge of the country and the people inhabiting it, but it also gives one an excellent opportunity of tuning the ear to the different dialects, whilst the fact of being unaccompanied by another foreigner makes it necessary to talk nothing but Japanese —a necessity which naturally helps very considerably towards the mastering of the language and towards obtaining a better understanding of the national customs and characteristics. Admittedly there are times when one almost longs for the company of a fellow-countryman, and for that reason, amongst others, I personally would never advocate a Language Officer cutting himself off for any great length of time from all intercourse with foreigners. At the same time it is useless for anyone to attempt to master the language if he spends all his spare time with other members of the foreign community. Let him live by himself, for the most part, when not carrying out periods of attachment to military units, within reasonable distance of other foreigners, and merely cut himself off entirely from them from time to time for periods of about three or four weeks each in order to go off on up-country trips.

Most Language Officers in Japan work on this or some similar principle, so it should be seen from this that "Language Leave" is not quite such a "cushie" job as at first it might appear. Not only must one work, but it is necessary to keep away, up to a certain point, from one's fellow-countrymen also, and even to change one's diet at times and accustom oneself to living on the native food, as, for instance, when on manœuvres or when travelling about up-country. On ordinary manœuvres or in barracks the diet is, as will be shown later on, very Spartan-like and becomes excessively monotonous after a few days. It is during his periods of attachment that the Language Officer is mostly thrown on his own resources, and, unless he is attached to a unit in Tokyo, he is likely to find himself cut off for weeks on end from his fellow-countrymen and from anyone with whom he can discuss matters in English either connected or unconnected with his work. Until one has had experience of this sort for himself, it is difficult to realise that there is any special hardship involved. The fact nevertheless remains that there are times when one longs for the company of a fellow-countryman with whom to discuss matters of mutual interest and to take one's mind off one's work for a time and return to the normal life to which one was formerly accustomed. No offence is meant thereby to the Japanese, who, when one lives amongst them in this way, are always eager to help in every way and to make one feel at home with them. It is simply the call of one's own civilisation as compared to that of Japan, which, though just as good as our own in its own way, is, nevertheless, different. The Japanese who goes to England or any other country for language study experiences a similar longing for his home country and his own particular civilisation at times, and is, in many ways, affected even more strongly, as his own countrymen abroad are usually even fewer and more scattered than are those of the British Language Officer in Japan.

In regard to the study of the language itself, one needs to put in from six to eight hours concentrated work per day during the first year or so and to mix as much as possible with Japanese in order to train the ear and to practise oneself in speaking. The Language Officer's first period of attachment to a military unit usually commences early in the second year of his stay in Japan, and this involves additional work in that it is necessary to study the military system as well as the language.

From what has been written above, it will be seen that, however interesting and enjoyable the life of a Language Officer in Japan may be, the job, if carried out conscientiously, is not by any means a sinecure. Hard work, isolation from one's own countrymen, change of diet and habits—all these, and a hundred things besides, fall to his lot and make his three years in Japan a period of anything but "Leave" in the usually understood sense.[1]

The Japanese, though not good linguists, are generally anxious to learn foreign languages, so one can very often find officers or students who are only too glad to come to one's house during their spare time in order to exchange lessons in Japanese for lessons in English. I was lucky enough to get into touch with two or three such officers soon after my arrival in Tokyo, and they used frequently to drop in in the evening for an exchange in languages.

During my time in Tokyo, in order to combine business with pleasure, I used to go out most Saturday afternoons with one of my teachers to see places of interest in the neighbourhood, and it was on one of these occasions that I went to see the burial-place of the forty-seven *Ronin*, mentioned elsewhere in this book.

On another occasion this same teacher, who was an excellent fellow and very good company, took me to see another place of historical interest to the Japanese, namely the house in which Count Nogi, the hero of Port Arthur, committed *hara-kiri*, together with his wife, on the occasion of the late Emperor's funeral, in order that he might join his Imperial master in the next world. By this act he raised himself still further in the estimation of his countrymen, who now look on him almost as a god. To the Japanese mind, Nogi, with his sterling fighting qualities, his simplicity of living, his love for his men and, finally, his great loyalty to his Emperor and country, is the personification of all that a soldier should be, and probably few names in Japanese history are more honoured than his. As an example of his

[1] Since the above remarks were written I have been shown an article entitled "The Language Officer in Japan" which appeared in the *United Service Magazine* in the summer of 1914. Under the *nom-de-plume* of "James Weymouth," the writer of this article, himself a Language Officer at that time, expresses himself in a manner similar to that which has just been written.

simplicity of living, it is said that his staff-officers, much as they loved and honoured him, were sometimes rather annoyed at this particular characteristic of his, and thought he was carrying it to rather an extreme when, for instance, he was travelling, for he always insisted on going third-class, which meant that they had to do likewise.

The house in which he lived and died will stand for ever as a memorial to his belief in simplicity of living, for, unlike what one might imagine the house of so famous a man to be, it is a small unpretentious building with nothing special to distinguish it from any other. A small shrine to his memory now stands in the garden, and on the day on which we went to see it, even in the short time we were there, half a dozen or more Japanese walked up to it and, having rinsed their hands and mouths in a pool of running water close by and clapped their hands three times in order to attract Nogi's spirit, offered up prayers before the shrine. Whatever religion one might profess, one could not but be impressed by the simplicity of this act of faith; and, after all, though we do not offer up prayers to our dead, the ceremonies which take place at the Cenotaph and the grave of the "Unknown Warrior," and, for that matter, at any of our War memorials throughout the country, are not unlike this.

CHAPTER III

1918 GRAND MANŒUVRES

WHEN I arrived in Japan in 1917, the Grand Manœuvres for that year were just about to take place, and I was invited to attend. Unfortunately, however, the after effects of some odd bits of scrap-iron picked up in the early days of 1915 were still such as to prevent my riding a horse, so, much to my regret, I was unable to go. On that occasion (1917) the manœuvres had been held in the neighbourhood of Kyoto and Hikone, four divisions—3rd, 4th, 19th and 16th—having taken part. This is about the usual number of divisions employed in the annual Grand Manœuvres in Japan, but in 1918 the number was increased to seven divisions, together with two cavalry corps (each of two brigades) and two independent artillery brigades, plus the usual auxiliary units —cable, aviation, wireless, etc.

The area chosen for the latter operations was a hundred miles or so north of Tokyo, in Tochigi Province, the country in this district being comparatively level—not unlike parts of Flanders, except that paddy-fields take the place of the beet fields common to those parts. This area was crossed by two rivers and a number of small streams.

Though the main manœuvre area was comparatively level, the country all round it was rough and hilly, and one division, in crossing these hills, met with difficulties in the form of having their guns bogged in the muddy mountain tracks by which they had to move.

Leaving Tokyo on the morning of November 13th, the foreign attachés taking part went by train to Tochigi, where quarters had been prepared for us in a large school building.

In the afternoon of the same day our "bear-leaders" explained in detail the scheme of the manœuvres, after which we were taken to the General Headquarters to be presented to Prince Kanin, and then went to the station to meet the Emperor, who arrived about 4 p.m.

There were, in all, fourteen foreign attachés, representing ten different countries. Six Japanese officers were attached to the party as "bear-leaders," the leader of them being Lt.-Col. Terauchi, and nothing could have exceeded the kindness shown to us by them throughout the period of the manœuvres and also by the numerous other Japanese officers we met.

In addition to our own party of foreign attachés, there was also a batch of Chinese officers and a mixed Chilean and Bolivian military mission on these manœuvres, but they were quartered elsewhere, so we did not see very much of them. It may be mentioned in passing, however, that the head of this Chinese mission was General Hsu, who made himself famous two years later, after the fall of the Anfu Party in Pekin. There being a price on his head on that occasion, he fled to the Japanese Legation for protection, and later effected his escape—smuggled out of China by the Japanese, it is said, in a packing-case labelled "Military Supplies."

To return, however, to November 1918. The divisions taking part in these manœuvres were the Guards, 2nd, 8th, and 15th, representing the Eastern Force (Red Army), the Commander of this force being General Matsukawa, with Major-General Onodera as his Chief of Staff. Opposed to them was a Western Force (Blue) consisting of the 1st, 13th, and 14th divisions under the command of General Nitawara with Major-General Yamada as Chief of Staff. In addition, each side had a cavalry corps and an independent artillery brigade together with the usual auxiliary troops. Most of these troops had just completed their annual brigade and divisional manœuvres and had marched the whole way to their appointed places of assembly in the Tochigi area, carrying out other manœuvres *en route*. Many of the units taking part came from places nearly two hundred miles away, covering the whole distance on foot, averaging twenty-five miles a day, and all were as fit as could be. The Japanese cavalry is poor and their artillery nothing very special, but their infantry is excellent. To the casual observer this may not appear so, for they are untidy in their appearance compared with our own troops ; but their discipline is very good and their marching powers excellent.

So far as the foreign attachés were concerned our usual procedure was to set off each day about 7 or 8 a.m. and go by train up or down the line to some point near which the most activity was expected to take place. Horses would be waiting at the station, and we would then get mounted and ride round to see various items of interest in different phases of the fighting.

Though much impressed with the toughness of the troops, one could not but be surprised at the lack of modern material and also at the " out-of-dateness " of the tactical formations employed ; in fact, the manœuvres were little, if any, different from such as were carried out at Aldershot and elsewhere in pre-War days. The troops, basing their tactics no doubt on those of their former German instructors, had a great tendency towards adopting mass formations, and the small number of machine-guns and aircraft seemed almost incredible in view of lessons taught by the War. Such things as bombs, light trench-mortars, and tanks were non-existent, and camouflage of any kind was chiefly conspicuous by its absence.

Though I had unfortunately been knocked out in the early stages of the War too severely to return to the front line, and, therefore, had had no personal experience of war as fought in the later periods, I had endeavoured to keep pace with developments as much as possible by reading. It came, therefore, as a revelation to find a great military power such as Japan so far behind in the matter of tactics and equipment, both of which had undergone so great a change in the last few years.

But though the material was sadly lacking from the point of view of recent developments, nothing better could have been wanted than the personnel, and, after all, it is the personnel with high *moral*, efficient training, and good discipline, provided the leaders themselves are good, that is the backbone of an army, and, unless these are present, no amount of modern material will make up the deficiency.

During the time that has elapsed since the Grand Manœuvres of 1918, Japan has begun to make good her lack of modern material and has, to a certain extent, modified her system of tactics, though she is still some way behind the great European powers in both these respects. The reason for this, however, is probably not far to seek, and the following explanation is very likely something near the mark.

Japan is a poor country, and, even as it is, her army and navy cost a sum out of all proportion to the other items of her expenditure.[1] She cannot, therefore, afford to spend large sums on equipping herself with all the latest instruments of war, especially as even the most modern war material is still subject to supersession by something better, and such supersession is likely to continue for some time yet, in fact, until all the lessons of the War have been thoroughly digested.

Japan, therefore, is biding her time and is purposely playing a cautious game, refusing to invest her money in new armaments until she is satisfied that nothing better is procurable. A special branch of the General Staff has been established for the purpose of studying all the lessons of the War both in regard to material required and to the development of tactics, and it is this special branch which is to be responsible for the re-moulding of the Japanese army.[2]

During the War a certain number of Japanese officers were attached to the various Allied armies, and, since the

[1] For the financial year 1921-2, the army and navy together accounted for fifty per cent. of the total Budget.

[2] This branch has now been abolished and the results of its investigations are being put into practice, though experimental and research work is still being carried out.

termination of the War, large numbers have been despatched to Europe for the purpose of studying, at first hand, the post-War conditions existing in the former belligerent armies. The reports sent in by these officers are duly sifted and studied by the branch of the Japanese General Staff mentioned above, as also are the numerous revised training manuals which the British, French, and other armies are gradually bringing out, based on their own experiences. In addition to this, all histories and personal accounts of the War, both German and Allied, are likewise studied and their " meat " extracted.

In this way Japan has, metaphorically, sat down and set to work to suck the brains of the late belligerents, and, while the latter squabble and quibble amongst themselves, she quietly and unostentatiously sets her military house in order ; and, after all, is this not a case of history repeating itself ? Did not Japan, when forced out of her self-imposed seclusion of two hundred and fifty odd years, adopt much the same attitude ? Finding herself far behind other countries in matters of war and learning at that time, she sent out the pick of her men to study the armies and navies, the methods of law and administration, the police and parliamentary systems, the medical and other professions, besides a hundred and one other matters of importance, and, having carefully sifted the good and bad points of everything, proceeded to base her own institutions on those which she considered to be the best. Her navy and her constitution she copied from Great Britain, her army from France and later from Germany ; her medical science was likewise copied from Germany—and so on. Taken all in all, one cannot but approve of her choice, not excepting that she chose the German army as her model, for, however much one may dislike German methods, one cannot but admire her ability for organisation as exemplified in her former " war-machine."

There are those who regard as a weakness this habit of copying other nations, and in some respects this may be so, as it practically means that Japan will always be one point behind those whom she copies, as she must wait till they give the lead before she herself advances. This contention, however, is superficial, as it is not one country only that she copies but the best points of all. Moreover, it is not entirely a case of copying but rather is it a tendency for assimilation and adaptation of the strength of others as best suited to her own particular needs. It is, in fact, a case of applying the principles of "*jujutsu*" to the problems of scientific efficiency, no matter whether military, mechanical, medical, or whatever else it may be.

In this Japanese art the whole idea is to turn the strength of your opponent to your own advantage whilst expending the minimum amount of one's own strength to gain the victory. This is just what Japan does in her everyday life. She watches the other nations and, instead of worrying too much about bringing out new inventions or new systems herself, adapts the strength of others to her own advantage and saves up her own for the crucial moment when it is most needed.

Japan has now set herself to study the lessons of the late War and to collect all the possible information she can in order to help her in her self-set task. When she considers she has learnt all she needs, she will select the best teachings of each nation and train and equip her army accordingly. It will require a number of years yet to complete fully the somewhat ambitious schemes for improvement which have been drawn up by her military authorities, but she will achieve her purpose all right and raise the standard of her army to the highest level required by her.[1] This process will go on slowly, provided no war breaks out in the meantime, for the Japanese are a methodical race and are at their best when they are not hurried. Meantime, not only are they studying the lessons of the War, but they are also carrying

[1] The present programme for the improvement of the Army, including the Army Air Force, was to have been completed by 1935, but in December 1922, owing to the retrenchment policy now in force, it was decided to extend the time to 1940. The main improvements will, of course, have been carried out long before this latter date.

out certain experiments at Chiba and elsewhere, Chiba being the site of their Infantry School and the place where most of her experiments in new weapons and new formations are carried out. As I had the good fortune to be attached to that institution for six months during my third year in Japan, further information concerning it will be left till later on in these pages.

To return, however, to the 1918 Grand Manœuvres. From the military point of view one of the main items of interest was that two of the divisions (Guards and 1st) each had a *Kobi* (2nd Reserve) Brigade attached, the organisation of these two divisions being different from the normal in that they each had three infantry brigades instead of only two. There was much talk at that time of changing the divisional organisation, and, on certain inter-divisional manœuvres which had taken place shortly before, experiments had been made of abolishing brigades entirely. Instead of having two infantry brigades (each of two regiments), the divisions taking part in these manœuvres had been organised into three regiments with no intermediate formation between regiment and division. It will be noticed, therefore, that whereas in the case of the inter-divisional manœuvres the two divisions employed had only three regiments each—that is to say, one less than the normal—the Guards and 1st Divisions in the Grand Manœuvres each had an organisation of six infantry regiments, or two more than ordinarily. In both cases the experiments gave good results, but, up to the time of writing, the old organisation of two brigades each of two regiments still holds good, though other reorganisations have taken place and are to take place. It is not impossible, however, that this may one day be dropped in favour of one or other of the two organisations tried in the autumn of 1918.

Another point of military interest in the 1918 Grand Manœuvres, and, moreover, a point which was noted also in those of 1919 and 1920 which I subsequently attended, was the total lack of second line transport, nothing but first line transport being used. Considering the great importance of second line transport in these days, and the essential need and difficulty of controlling it, one would imagine that no manœuvres of any importance would be carried out without it, owing to the good practice it affords. The Japanese are fully awake to this fact, but they say, when questioned on this point, that the reason it is not used is that it costs too much to collect the necessary vehicles and to pay for the damage which is bound to be done to the country roads and bridges by the use of heavy transport on a large scale. This is undoubtedly one of the main reasons, and, moreover, it brings out an interesting fact, that, until road communication in Japan is very greatly improved, it will be impossible for the Japanese to make much headway in regard to the use of motor transport.[1] There are but few roads in Japan at the present time capable of withstanding the wear and tear of heavy traffic. But to remedy this, large sums of money must be expended, and this at present is not obtainable. It will be of interest to see whether the reduction of armaments brought about by the decisions of the Washington Conference will release the amount required for this and other improvements. The estimates for the financial year 1923-24 do not indicate much improvement in this respect, although large sums have been voted for construction work of various kinds.

Having read so far the reader may ask himself, " What then is the use of the Japanese carrying out expensive manœuvres on a large scale ? " In the case of those under review, the " tactics were out of date, modern *materiel* was chiefly conspicuous by its absence, and commanders were not even afforded the opportunity of practising the moving of such important parts of a modern army as its second line transport." Briefly the answer is this : Japanese Grand Manœuvres are carried out partly by way of an endurance test and partly for the purpose of giving commanders

[1] It is also probable that the military authorities realise that the Japanese army is unlikely ever to fight anywhere but in China or Siberia, and that it is not therefore necessary to develop their motor transport to such an extent as would be required for a war in Europe where road communications are good.

practice in the employment of larger bodies of troops than are normally concentrated in one place. Due consideration is also given to the fact that manœuvres on a large scale afford an excellent opportunity of showing the army to the civil population, and, by so doing, raising their latent military ardour.

To the foreign military observer who attends these manœuvres, there is really very little to be learnt from the point of view either of tactics or of equipment, but they afford him the opportunity of seeing for himself the personnel, and of forming his own conclusions as to their state of *moral*, their powers of endurance, their physique and their discipline. Whatever one may think of the out-of-dateness of the *materiel* and tactics, no one who has once seen for himself the conduct of the troops can doubt that the men themselves are the best possible material for which any army commander could wish and are little, if at all, inferior to those which won immortal fame by their exploits in Manchuria in 1904 and 1905.

Although one may learn a certain amount about the Japanese army by attending the annual Grand Manœuvres, no one can hope to gauge its true fighting value unless he actually carries out a period of attachment to one of its units. By virtue of the erstwhile Anglo-Japanese Alliance, British officers gain this privilege, and, later on in these pages, an attempt will be made to show something of the everyday life of the army in Japan as seen by one who has had the good fortune to be so privileged.

Foreign officers attending Grand Manœuvres do not come into proper touch with Japanese army life, for, instead of being attached to, and living with, units taking part in the operations, they are kept to themselves and shown round by the "bear-leaders," of whom mention has already been made, and much of their time is spent in being "dined and wined" and in sight-seeing.

On the first and second days of the 1918 Manœuvres (November 14th and 15th) we were riding pretty well all day, but on the third day we came back to our quarters for lunch, and in the afternoon were treated to a very good display of *gekken*—the Japanese form of fencing. As *gekken* is as much practised in the Japanese army as boxing in our own—in fact more so—it will perhaps not be out of place to give a short description of it here.

The Japanese officer to this day carries a heavy two-handed sword when he goes into action, and in *gekken* this is represented by a kind of bamboo pole, shaped something like the army sword. The fencers wear lacquered body-armour, masks, and *hakama* (the Japanese substitute for trousers), and have their feet bare. The point of the "sword" is not used, the whole idea being to cut down your opponent, and, by way of lowering his *moral*, you let forth blood-curdling shrieks from time to time, including each time you slash at him. It is very interesting to watch, as the fencers attack each other with the greatest vigour, which leaves one in no doubts as to the necessity of the armour. It is excellent exercise and gives very good practice to the eye.

Though officers generally fight officers and men fight men, both very often practise with each other, and, though the men win at times, it in no way affects the discipline of a unit but, on the contrary, strengthens the good feeling between the officers and their men.

On this particular occasion, after the fencing had finished, we were given a concert by the band of the Guards Division, and, while this was in full swing, a procession of several hundred school children came along by way of celebrating the Armistice, each child waving a flag and "banzai-ing" the officers of the Allied nations who were present. As all the small girls were dressed in their gayest coloured *kimonos*, it was a very pretty sight.

A similar incident had taken place the previous evening, when several hundred school children, each holding a lighted paper lantern, had marched past the entrance to our "billets" with great shouts of "*banzai*" for the Allied officers and their respective countries. No doubt Armistice celebrations in London were of a somewhat different and more exuberant nature, but it was quite cheering to have some of our own in that little town in Central Japan. Those of us who belonged to the Allied nations went out to receive and return the "*banzai*," which, of course, pleased the children immensely.

On the evening of the third day of these manœuvres a party of four of us were taken out to inspect the outpost positions of the Blue Army, which had fallen back to a line of hills near by. Arriving back shortly after 11 p.m., we were up again at 4 a.m. next morning to watch the final stage of the operations, the manœuvres coming to an end about 7.30 a.m. after an attack at dawn by the Red Army followed by a counter-attack by the Blue.

It has already been mentioned that Japanese Grand Manœuvres are largely a test of endurance, and that such is the case will hardly be questioned when it is pointed out that, throughout the four days during which the operations were carried out, most of the higher commanders went without any sleep, while some of the units we saw on the third day had been on the move almost continuously, and had, when we passed them, been marching and fighting forty-eight hours without sleep. Even when sleep was obtainable it was carried out in battle positions, troops bivouacking in the open each night, though up in the Tochigi district there is hard frost most nights at that time of the year. One division we saw had done a march of thirty miles over the mountains in one day with nothing but muddy tracks to use.

Some of the reservists looked foot-sore, but all—both reservists and serving soldiers—were in excellent fettle. One interesting point in this connection was that about ten per cent. had discarded their boots and were marching in *tabi*, the Japanese "socks," some of them wearing *waraji*, the native straw sandal, as well.

After the "Cease-Fire" had sounded on the 16th the foreign attachés were taken by train to Ashikaga, a small town some twenty or thirty miles up the line, the rest of the day being spent in sight-seeing. At Ashikaga we found a young fleet of rickshaws waiting to take us to various places of interest, amongst these being a silk factory, a seven hundred year old temple, and a five hundred year old school. At each place crowds of school children were gathered to greet us and to cheer the Allied officers.

One thing that amused me very much was that I, personally, was taken for a Chinaman, the reason for this presumably being that I was wearing a Glengarry, the tails of which were apparently taken for a species of "pig-tail." During my subsequent attachment to the Japanese army, this same mistake was made times without number, chiefly by children, from whom I soon became quite accustomed to the cry of "*Shinajin*! *Shinajin*!" (Chinaman! Chinaman!) whenever I went about in uniform.

In Japan, especially in the country districts, a foreign officer in uniform is something of a *rara avis*, and, apart from the fact that I wore a Glengarry, Japanese country-folk are unable to distinguish one kind of foreigner from another. Presumably, therefore, the fact that "tails" were attached to my head-gear completed the delusion that I must be a Chinaman.

While we were at Ashikaga we were taken to see the memorial which had been erected there in memory of those from that district who had fallen during the Russo-Japanese War. Included in our party was Colonel Aivasoglou, the Russian Military Attaché, and in this connection the action of Colonel Terauchi, our chief "bear-leader," is worth mentioning. On the photographer asking us to group ourselves in front of the memorial, Colonel Terauchi walked up to the Russian colonel and taking him by the arm said, "Come along and be taken with the rest of us. This memorial was raised to the memory of those who died fighting your countrymen, but we are all friends now, so I know you will not take offence." One could not but be impressed by this action, exemplifying, as it did, that the Japanese officer is, above all else, a gentleman and a sportsman where matters of war are concerned, and never bears a grudge against a brave enemy.

On returning to Tochigi in the afternoon we were presented

to Prince Yi of Korea and to some of the Japanese Princes, after which we attended a banquet given by Prince Kanin to the principal military officers who took part in the manœuvres and to the foreign attachés.

The following day (November 18th) we set off about 7 a.m. and took train to Oyama, where our horses had been sent to meet us. Riding out of the town to a place a mile or so away, we waited for the arrival of the Emperor, to whom we were each presented in turn. This being done, the Emperor set off to review the troops which had taken part in the manœuvres, the rest of us following on horseback in rear.

There being no large open space available, the troops were drawn up by regiments and battalions in the paddy-fields to the left of the road the whole way back to Tochigi, each regiment presenting colours and sounding the royal salute as the Emperor went past. They looked a fine sturdy lot of men, though short in stature compared with European troops; and in spite of the great exertions of the past few days, they looked fresh and fit and stood well to attention, though many of them were more than ankle deep in the soft mud of the paddy-fields.

In the afternoon the Emperor gave a banquet to all the officers who had taken part in the manœuvres—about seven thousand guests in all. The Emperor himself sat at a table on a raised dais, this dais forming, as it were, the centre of a huge marquee shaped like the half of the imperial sixteen-petalled chrysanthemum, the eight petals of which were represented by eight very long tables radiating from the centre.

Towards the end of the banquet the foreign attachés and chief military officers, who had tables close to the dais, were called up, ten at a time, to drink the Emperor's health from the top step of the dais, each one being presented with a *sake* cup for the purpose, which cups we were allowed to keep as souvenirs.

The following morning those of the foreign attachés who elected to do so went by train to Sukegawa, where we and our "bear-leaders" were made the guests of the Kuhara Mining Company, one of the principal mining concerns in Japan. In the evening we were given a *geisha* dinner, and the whole of the following day was spent in seeing over the Hitachi Mine, the largest mine owned by the company and, I believe, about the largest in the Far East. It is beautifully situated up in the hills looking out over the sea, and is very well run. Whilst there we were taken down one of the coal mines and afterwards were shown the smelteries, foundries, and chief workshops.

Getting back to the quarters which had been provided for us, we were given another *geisha* show, and then set off back to Tokyo about 6.30 p.m., arriving there about midnight. This ended the manœuvres so far as we were concerned, and anyone who has read as far as this will no doubt agree with what was said earlier in the chapter, namely, that, from the military point of view, the foreign attaché who attends Japanese Grand Manœuvres can learn but little. Much of his time is, in fact, spent in sight-seeing, which is certainly interesting, but does not teach him very much about the Japanese army. It is only when he has the good fortune of getting an actual attachment to a military unit that he is able to make a proper study of it, and in this respect the British officer has a pull over officers of other nationalities on account of that clause of the erstwhile Anglo-Japanese Alliance which allowed for reciprocal attachments—British officers to Japanese units and Japanese officers to units of the British army. In the following pages will be found some personal experiences of attachments to Japanese units, but before giving them there is just one more point to be mentioned in regard to Japanese Grand Manœuvres.

A very noticeable thing about them is the great interest shown by the local inhabitants, who turn out in thousands in order to see them; moreover, though, as can well be imagined, they often get very much in the way and not infrequently give away gun positions by crowding round guns in order to see them being fired, they are encouraged to look on, children of local schools being given special holidays so that they can see as much of the manœuvres as possible. The reason for this is, that the military authorities are always alive to the necessity for popularising the army, and they are not slow to realise the advantages to be gained by using Grand Manœuvres for that purpose. Every opportunity and encouragement is therefore given to the civil population to see as much as they can in order that their martial ardour and loyalty may be roused and that they may be shown on what their money is being spent.

CHAPTER IV

REGIMENTAL ATTACHMENT

On November 21st, the day following that on which we returned to Tokyo, the official celebrations for the Armistice were held, these including flag processions of students, labourers, and other bodies of men, who marched to the embassies and legations of the various Allied powers and went through their grounds cheering and shouting. On the afternoon of the same day the Mayor of Tokyo gave an entertainment in Hibiya Park. But as these celebrations are not concerned with the main object of this book, they are only just mentioned *en passant*.

A few days later I left Tokyo for Shizuoka, where I had been ordered to go for six months' attachment to the 34th Infantry Regiment, and the following morning I set off to report myself at the barracks.

In England, when we talk about a regiment, we sometimes mean a single battalion, while at other times the term may be used collectively to imply all the battalions—Regular, Special Reserve, and Territorial, and, during the War, the Service battalions as well—of some particular regiment. In Japan, on the other hand, the term " regiment " is not used loosely in this way, but represents a definite organisation consisting, in the case of infantry, of three battalions. Moreover, all three battalions of a regiment are always kept together in the same barracks, and the whole regiment is always stationed at the same place in peace time, only leaving its station for short periods at a time for carrying out manœuvres and training. Thus the 34th Regiment, the one with which I did my first attachment, always has its three battalions together, the barracks of the regiment being in Shizuoka, a town about a hundred and twenty miles south-west of Tokyo on the main line to Kobe—a great tea-growing district.[1]

Some weeks before I began my attachment to the 34th Regiment I had received a letter from its Commander, who, though I had never met him previously, wrote to me in a very friendly vein on hearing that I was to be attached to his regiment. On reporting myself at regimental headquarters on the 26th, I found that there was a holiday that day, but the Adjutant was in barracks, as also was a subaltern whom I found spoke English and had been detailed to look after me in consequence. As Colonel Kimura, the C.O., was out of barracks, Lieut. Sakata, the subaltern, took me round to his house to introduce me to him. He received me in the most friendly manner, and told me to consider myself *persona grata* with him and with his officers, and, in fact, did his best to make me feel at home. This attitude he maintained towards me during the whole period of my attachment, and I not infrequently hear from him even now, his letters always being full of interest. Should a copy of this book ever fall into his hands, I hope he will forgive me for mentioning this in print, and that he will take it in the spirit in which it is meant.

The following morning I was taken round to make my bows to the chief civil officials of the place, and at noon was introduced to the officers of the regiment, or, to be more exact, had to introduce myself, as is always the custom in a Japanese regiment when a new officer joins it.

What happens is that the newly-joined officer waits till all the other officers of the regiment are seated in the mess-room. He then enters the room and stands at attention in

[1] This statement requires certain modifications. Every other year one division from the home country is sent to Manchuria for two years; on completion of its tour of duty abroad, however, it returns to its former home station. At the present time (1923), for instance, the 15th Division, of which the Shizuoka Regiment is a unit, is stationed in Manchuria.

the doorway, looking into the room. All the officers thereupon stand up facing him and bow towards him very ceremoniously. Having bowed, they all remain standing while he delivers a short sort of address saying who he is and for what reason he has come to that particular regiment. He ends up by asking them to honour him with their friendship and overlook his shortcomings. Having finished this little oration he bows to them, and they all bow to him once more ; whereupon the ceremony comes to an end.

This then was the ceremony through which I found I had to go, and, needless to say, I was very glad to get it off my chest, as it was a somewhat trying ordeal to one whose knowledge of the Japanese language was still somewhat limited.

To a British officer, this form of introducing oneself seems very stiff and formal, but during an attachment to a Japanese regiment one soon becomes accustomed to bowing to one's brother officers instead of shaking them by the hand. A great deal of bowing goes on, even the rank and file bowing to each other in some cases. In fact this custom of bowing is carried to such an extreme that in camp officers even bow to one another when entering and leaving the bath-house. Needless to say it is somewhat disconcerting for a British officer when he experiences this for the first time, and I remember being greatly amused, on entering an officer's bath-house in camp for the first time, to find a somewhat portly but smiling major, on seeing me come in, solemnly bow to me, though he himself was clad in nothing but a smile

A Japanese Officers' Mess is a very different thing from its British counterpart. It is, in most cases, a great barn-like room with bare whitewashed walls, and bare wooden tables with wooden benches on which to sit—no table-linen or decoration of any sort.

For food, each officer has a large bowl of rice and a plate of boiled fish or vegetables of the poorest quality. A piece of *daikon* (a kind of radish), a cup of green tea, and a small box containing his chop-sticks, completes his luncheon paraphernalia.

Normally the midday meal is the only one taken by officers in barracks, as they live in houses of their own outside—that is to say all except those on duty and those with less than a year's service.[1] Breakfast and supper, when taken in barracks, do not differ much from the midday meal. When it is said that the midday meal in the 34th Regiment during my attachment to it averaged only sixteen sen per day (about 4½d.), it can be imagined that the repast was not a very sumptuous one, though it was certainly economical.[2]

This simplicity of living is all part of the military training in Japan, both officers and men being taught that frugality is a soldierly virtue and one to be encouraged. Taken all in all the Japanese soldier leads a very Spartan-like existence, be he commissioned officer or one of the rank and file, and, as a result, he is as tough as you could wish and capable of withstanding the greatest hardships.

As mentioned earlier in this chapter, all three battalions of a Japanese infantry regiment always live together. As a result there are generally from ninety to a hundred members in an infantry regimental Officers' Mess. In the case of the 34th Regiment, and in most other messes which I saw while in Japan, there are three long tables in the mess-room —one per battalion—parallel to one another, while a fourth, but shorter one, is at right angles at the head of the three. The senior officers sit at the last, and, being a foreign attaché, I generally did likewise.

Thinking that I would not be able to manage the ordinary officers' food, the Colonel had given orders that I was to have special food prepared for me. It was very good of him, but as I did not wish to give more trouble than necessary, or to take special privileges of any kind, I persuaded him

[1] This refers to the home country. In Korea, Formosa, and Manchuria—and also in Hokkaido—special officers' quarters are provided.

[2] The Colonel and other officers of the regimental headquarters at Shizuoka used to lunch in the N.C.O.'s mess once per month, and it was noticeable that the food was the same as that eaten by the officers.

to let me always, in the future, have the same as the other officers. Though I cannot truthfully say I liked this food, I never regretted having made this request, as I found that it was greatly appreciated by the officers of the regiment. Other British officers who have had the same sort of experience will probably agree with this. It pays to try and live the same as the Japanese officers when attached to a unit, for, even though they may not show it, they nevertheless are apt to look down on you if you get special privileges in regard to food and quarters, as they immediately jump to the conclusion that you are unable to put up with the hardships and discomforts which they can. On the other hand, if they find that you are content to live in the same way as themselves, they are very appreciative, and you will find that they will become very much more friendly and will do anything they can to help you. Incidentally, judging from various remarks made to one at different times by Japanese officers, there is little doubt but that you go up in their estimation if they find that you are able and willing to live the same as themselves. In fact it is undoubtedly true that a certain type of Japanese dislikes foreigners for two reasons : firstly, that he has an idea that the foreigner looks upon him as an inferior owing to his being an Asiatic, and secondly,because he himself looks down on the foreigner, whom he considers as being incapable of enduring great hardships. As often as not he is wrong in both respects, though he certainly has a certain amount of justification in regard to the first-named idea, and it is a great pity that foreigners do not realise this. The Japanese are a proud race and rightly so, and one cannot blame them for objecting to being looked on as an inferior race. Rather should one admire them for it. Yet there is no doubt that the Japanese is seen at his worst when he thinks that he is being slighted or looked down on, as, for instance, in China and other parts of the Far East, where he comes into contact with large numbers of foreigners.

In China and elsewhere he is often accused of being arrogant, overbearing, and deceitful. But if you take the trouble to look into the matter, you will generally find that this is largely an assumed attitude—an attitude put on in an endeavour to show that he considers himself as good as anyone else, and that he does not intend to be regarded as an inferior. In ninety-nine cases out of a hundred, however, this attitude will vanish if you approach him in the right way and show him that you are prepared to treat him as an equal; in place of arrogance and rudeness you will be received with the greatest kindness and courtesy.

This slight homily on Japanese psychology has led away somewhat from the main story, but as it deals with a very important characteristic of a large proportion of Japanese, it will not perhaps be considered amiss.

Having been duly introduced to the officers of the regiment, I was told that I was to be attached to No. 6 Company, and was given a special introduction to the officers of that company and also to the C.O. of the 2nd Battalion, to which battalion it belonged. The Company Commander, Captain Kubo, was a capital fellow whom I came to know particularly well later on, as he was sent on a six months' course to the Infantry School in 1920, and I was sent there at the same time and was put into the same class. Like Colonel Kimura, the Regimental Commander, he always did everything he could to help, and nothing could have exceeded his kindness to me during the period of my attachment to his company and again, later on, during my attachment to the Infantry School.

The day following that on which I was introduced to the officers of the regiment, the ceremony of the "time-expired" men leaving barracks took place, and on December 1st a new batch of conscripts arrived.[1] Both of these ceremonies were of great interest, bearing, as they do, on the *Seishin-Kyōiku* or "morale training" of the Japanese soldier, a branch of his education which is considered to be of the greatest importance in Japan.

[1] Under the disarmament scheme formulated in 1922 as a result of the Washington Conference, the term of conscript service has been reduced forty days. Recruits, therefore, starting from this year (1923), join the "Colours" on January 10th each year instead of, as hitherto, December 1st of the previous year.

In the former case the "time-expired" men line up on parade, dressed in new khaki uniform of special cut, and wearing *tabi*—the native pattern of sock—on their feet. Each man wears on his tunic a silver discharge badge, with which he has been presented prior to leaving, and carries a cloth bag containing his personal possessions. The uniforms worn on these occasions are supplied by the villages to which the men belong, and are for use at any military function which the men may be called on to attend after leaving the Colours.

The Regimental Commander delivers a farewell address, in which he exhorts the men to become good citizens and to continue their loyalty to the Emperor and country. After this they are dismissed, whereupon they say good-bye to their late officers and leave the barracks, outside which they are received by their relations, village guilds, etc., who come to the entrance to meet them, and are marched off in triumph with purple banners flying, each village guild having its own particular banner.

The joining-up of the new conscripts is also carried out with great ceremony. In this case the relatives of the new recruits and members of their village guilds actually accompany them into the barracks. The recruits are then told off to their respective companies and are lectured by their company commanders, who also address their friends and relations, pointing out the honour conferred on them by having their sons and brothers selected to serve the Emperor. They are, moreover, told not to feel anxious about their welfare, as, during their period of Colour service, the regimental commander will be as a father to them, while their company officers and N.C.O's will treat them as younger brothers.

To a European this may sound a rather exaggerated promise, but though the Japanese soldier has to lead a pretty Spartan existence, he is certainly well treated by his officers, and the feeling between them is very good as a rule. Moreover, though the soldier has to undergo great hardships, the officer shares them with him.

As an example, however, of what the soldier has to undergo, it may be mentioned, in passing, that he is forbidden, even in the depths of winter, to wear an under-vest, and only a cotton shirt is allowed. He is never permitted to wear gloves, and one cannot but wonder how the unfortunate sentries on hard frosty nights in mid-winter are able to grip their rifles.

The Japanese soldier—and officer too for that matter—is taught that simplicity and frugality, and ability to withstand hardships, are among the principal military virtues, and throughout his whole period of military service he is made to practise these precepts. His quarters and food are of the simplest ; he is kept hard at work from morning to night ; and he is taught to disregard the elements. Just as he is made to bear the cold, so he is taught to disregard the heat. In mid-winter he is sent off on manœuvres lasting two or three days and entailing bivouacking at night-time in the snow on wind-swept hills ; and in mid-summer he has to carry out manœuvres in the heat of the day. He wears the same head-gear under the blazing mid-summer sun as he does all the rest of the year, namely, the ordinary service cap of a pattern similar to our own, with no kind of neck protection whatever.

But what recruits suffer from most on first joining is sore feet, as the majority of them, before they become soldiers, have never worn boots or shoes of any kind, the Japanese in civil life being accustomed to wear *geta*—a form of loose wooden clog—or *waraji*—a kind of straw sandal. The Japanese infantry are, as already mentioned, great marchers, and the unfortunate recruit on joining is taken frequent marches to accustom his feet to the wearing of boots, the marches being of short duration at the start, but becoming longer as the men's feet grow hardened. But from all accounts it is a painful process for the newly-joined soldier fresh from the country.

Up to a certain point this applies also to reservists when called up for training, as the Japanese soldier, on completing his Colour service, generally returns to his former mode of living, with the result that, on being called up for his periodical reservist training, he has once more to go through the somewhat painful process of re-accustoming himself to the wearing of boots. In the event of mobilisation for war the Japanese must needs take this fact into consideration.

One rather humorous point in connection with the joining-up of the men is that the majority of them have never worn European clothing and, in the case of those from the more distant country districts, have seldom even seen such things. As a result of this, so I am told by Japanese officers, it is not an uncommon thing for a recruit, on receiving his uniform, to put on the trousers back to front. When, however, one comes to think of it, this is really no more funny than it is for a Scotsman to see an Englishman putting on a kilt back to front—a not altogether unheard-of mistake.

CHAPTER V

REGIMENTAL ATTACHMENT (*Continued*)

THE day following that on which the recruits entered barracks the *Nyueishiki* [1] took place. The regiment was formed into a hollow square, the Commander standing on a platform erected in the centre. Colours were paraded and the regimental Adjutant marched on to parade carrying with him a copy of the Imperial Edicts covered with a purple cloth. These he handed to the Commander, who bowed solemnly to the books, and, opening them, read their contents to the regiment, who stood to attention while they were being read. Having finished, he once more covered the books with the cloth, bowed, and handed them back to the Adjutant, who then marched off parade. This having been done, the Regimental Commander delivered a speech impressing on the men their duties as loyal soldiers, the men being allowed to stand at ease during this address, but coming to attention every time the Emperor's name was mentioned.

Somewhat full accounts of these three ceremonies have been given—the leaving of the time-expired men, the entry of the new recruits, and the subsequent ceremony in connection with this entry—as they form an important part of that portion of the Japanese soldiers' training known as "*Seishin Kyōiku,*" which can perhaps be best termed " training of the martial spirit " or " training in *moral.*" In the Japanese army this forms a very important part of

[1] Literally, " entering barracks ceremony."

the soldier's education, every possible precaution being taken to inculcate what are known as the "seven duties of a soldier," namely, Loyalty, Valour, Patriotism, Obedience, Humility, Morality, and Honour. Ceremonial parades, such as those already mentioned, are one of the ways used to inculcate these duties. Special lectures are also given frequently with this end in view, other methods employed being the taking of the men to see places of historical interest, the personal influences of the officers and N.C.O's, the putting up of texts in the barrack-rooms on the subject of a soldier's duties to his Emperor and country, and so on. By these and a dozen other methods the Japanese soldier has this "training of *moral*" drummed into him from the very day he enters the barracks, various methods also being employed to guard against what in Japan is known as "dangerous thoughts," by which is meant anti-dynastic or anarchistic ideas. For this reason political controversy of any kind is forbidden, and no book or literature of a political nature is allowed to be brought into barracks.

A curious ceremony which takes place shortly after the entry of the new batch of recruits, and one which is really part of the *seishin kyōiku* portion of their training, is the handing over of rifles to them. Each company brings a long wooden trestle table out on to the parade ground, the rifles being laid on these tables. The recruits fall in on parade and are then lectured by their respective company commanders, who impress on them that it is the sacred duty of a soldier to keep his rifle and equipment clean and in good order, and that he must look on his rifle as though it were his own soul—a thing to be kept clean and unsullied. Each man is then called out in turn and is presented with a rifle by his company commander. On receiving it the man solemnly bows and then returns with it to the ranks.

The company commander's speech certainly seems to have the desired effect, for although the Japanese soldier is not as a rule much of a marksman, he takes infinite pains to keep his rifle clean and in good order, and a noticeable point on all training and manœuvres is the care taken by the men to keep their rifles from touching muddy or sandy ground.

This is not simply due to fear of punishment, as punishment of any kind is seldom meted out. In this respect the Japanese army is very different from our own, and lack of punishment is largely due to certain characteristics of the nation as a whole, namely, that a Japanese, instead of being improved by being punished, is generally made worse and, moreover, becomes morose and sulky. For this reason punishments are never inflicted if they can possibly be avoided, and there are no such things in the Japanese army as what are known in our own as "minor crimes." It is not, for instance, considered a "crime" to go for a week without shaving, and in the case of drunkenness no action is taken if the man is merely convivial; he has to be properly drunk before any notice is taken.

Even allowing for this, however, crime of any description is extraordinarily rare in the Japanese army, and the only case of which I heard in the 34th Regiment during the six months I was attached to it, was of a man who received six months' imprisonment for stealing three yen (about 6s.) from another soldier. Incidentally, the commander of the company to which I was attached told me that, in his fourteen years of service, this was the first case of stealing he had known.

One advantage of this lack of crime and of there being no "minor crimes" such as there are in our own army, is that there is no such thing as a daily company and battalion "Orderly Room" for the trial of offenders; officers are, therefore, spared a lot of petty annoyance.

Mention has already been made of the cordial reception accorded to me by the Regimental Commander on my arrival for attachment to his regiment. This was partly due to Major-General (now Lieut.-General) Sugano, who was at that time Commander of the 29th Infantry Brigade, to which the 34th Regiment belonged. I had met the General several times before, while in Tokyo, and it was partly owing to this that I had been sent to a regiment in his brigade, he being an old friend of the British Military Attaché.

General Sugano had, in former days, spent three years in England as a Language Officer, part of his time being spent in an attachment to the Grenadier Guards. As a result he always seemed ready to befriend British officers, and, on hearing that I was to be attached to a regiment under his command, he apparently issued special instructions to the Regimental Commander to look after me well and to see that I was well treated. Colonel Kimura certainly carried out these instructions to the letter and always showed me the greatest kindness and consideration.

During the first few weeks of attachment, nothing of special military interest happened, but I had an opportunity of getting to know my brother officers, most of whom, like their Regimental Commander, showed me the greatest kindness both in barracks and out, some of them making a habit of dropping in to see me at odd times of an evening.

On December 17th I had my first experience of a Japanese route march, the battalion to which I was attached starting off shortly before 6 a.m. and getting back about 3.30 p.m. after carrying out a march of some twenty-five miles. One interesting thing about this particular march was that advantage was taken of it to carry out instruction in *seishin kyōiku*, the " training in *moral* " to which reference has already been made, the particular form which it took on this occasion being a visit to Kunōsan, a famous hill some six or seven miles from Shizuoka. The route we followed went past the foot of this hill, and on reaching it the battalion was halted, and those who wished to do so were taken up to see over the shrine on the top.

The historical interest of this shrine lies in the fact that it contains the tomb of the great Japanese warrior, Iyeyasu, the founder of the Tokugawa line of Shoguns, who ruled Japan for some two hundred and fifty years up to the time of the Restoration in 1868. When Iyeyasu died early in the seventeenth century he was buried in this tomb, the shrine being raised there to his memory ; but his body was subsequently removed to Nikko, where the famous shrines were put up to his memory—shrines which are visited yearly by thousands of tourists from every corner of the world. Visitors to Japan, almost without exception, go to Nikko to see these shrines, even if they have only a week or two to spend in that country, though probably but few of them know that these shrines are but replicas of those on Kunōsan, and that the tomb of Iyeyasu which they are shown at Nikko is not the original resting-place of that great warrior —in fact the local inhabitants of Kunōsan maintain that his body was never removed, and that there is nothing but a piece of his hair at Nikko. Whether this is so or not I make no pretence to know; but the fact remains that Iyeyasu was originally buried at Kunōsan and that his tomb is there to this day; and for this reason the troops from the neighbourhood are always taken there one or more times during their period of Colour service, and are lectured on the deeds of the great warrior whose tomb is on this hill.

The hill itself rises about seven hundred feet from the sea at its foot, and is ascended by stone steps from base to summit. Being military, we were received with great respect by one of the priests, who showed us all round, including parts kept closed to the ordinary public. The shrines are beautifully lacquered and very picturesque, but are kept covered with some sort of straw matting in order to protect the lacquer.

Inside the temple grounds is a building containing a very fine collection of old Tokugawa armour, swords, and other weapons. An interesting point in regard to this collection is the way in which the armour of the earlier Shoguns differs from that of their successors. In the early days the armour was obviously a thing of utility, but it gradually changed to a thing of beauty with little or no value from a military point of view, thus showing how the Tokugawas gradually declined from the fine fighting men they were at the beginning and, as a result of long years of ease and comfort, lost all their military qualities, becoming weak and effeminate —truly a good example in the "teaching of *moral*," as showing the soldier one of the things against which he must guard.[1]

The Japanese soldier of the present day has little or no chance of becoming either weak or effeminate owing to too much ease and comfort, as he gets little enough of either; nevertheless, it is perhaps just as well to put him on his guard.

This route march, including the visit to Kunōsan, has been mentioned as a further example of how education in *seishin kyōiku* is constantly brought into even the everyday routine duties of the Japanese soldier, and is introduced in such a way that he does not realise that it is all part and parcel of his training.

Visits to places of historical interest are frequently carried out with this end in view, lectures being given at the same time, in order to bring out some particular lesson to be learnt from the events connected with the place.

The soldier is taught that loyalty is one of the most important of his seven duties, and, as an example of this particular virtue, the story of the forty-seven Loyal Retainers, which every Japanese child knows, is specially taught to him on the anniversary of their death.

This story is too well known to anyone who knows anything about Japan to be repeated here, as it has been very cleverly told by Mitford (Lord Redesdale) in his *Tales of Old Japan*, as well as by numerous other writers; but, for the benefit of those who do not know it, it may be mentioned that the story deals with the self-inflicted death of forty-seven retainers of Asano Takumi no Kami, a *daimyo*, whose death had been brought about by another noble. After years of waiting, they eventually avenged the death of their master and then, each in turn, committed *hara-kiri*, it being the law of those days that this should be done by anyone guilty of killing a nobleman. All forty-seven were

[1] This is not meant as a reflection on the Tokugawas, for although they ceased their military activities, they developed great powers of statesmanship, as exemplified at the present time in Prince Tokugawa, who headed the Japanese delegation at the Washington Conference.

buried in the grounds of Sengakuji, a temple on the outskirts of Tokyo, where their lord and master had already been buried and where their graves are to be seen to this day.

Every year on the anniversary of their deaths, men of the regiments stationed in Tokyo are taken to see the graves and have the whole story told to them as an example of loyalty and devotion. Some regiments have the "alarm" sounded at dead of night, and, all the men having fallen in on parade, the story is read to them by their respective company commanders by way of impressing it on them. This did not actually happen at Shizuoka while I was there, but is, so I am told, a not altogether uncommon occurrence in some regiments.

On December 24th I went off on a few days' leave, during which time, amongst other places, I visited Kamakura in order to see the famous *Daibutsu*, the great bronze Buddha. I had motored through Kamakura several times previously, but, up to that time, had never seen the *Daibutsu*, and as it had a special interest for me, I had been wanting to see it for some time past. So far as I myself was concerned, the main point of interest lay in the fact that a grand-uncle of mine had been murdered there some fifty or sixty years previously. In those days Japan was still unsafe for foreigners, and a British regiment was kept stationed at Yokohama at what is now known as Camp Hill.

This uncle (Lieut. Bird) was at that time a subaltern in the old 20th Regiment of Foot, better known in these days as the Lancashire Fusiliers. On the day of his murder he had ridden out with a party of friends to see the famous *Daibutsu*. It seems that they had been warned of the danger they ran if they ventured outside the foreign settlement, so they took certain precautions, one of these being that young Bird and another officer, Capt. Baldwin, should form a sort of rear-guard to the rest of the party. All went well till shortly after the return to barracks had started, when Bird and Baldwin were attacked from the rear without warning by two *ronin*, who had been lying in wait. Baldwin was killed outright, while Bird succumbed to his wounds a few hours later, both of them having been cut down by heavy two-handed Japanese swords.

They both lie buried in Yokohama Cemetery, though but few of the present-day Yokohama foreign community know of the existence of their graves. The inscription on each grave reads : " Cruelly assassinated by Japanese on the 21st November, 1864, at Kamakura, when returning from a visit to the Diebootsoo." [1]

This was the work of two fanatics with a distorted idea of patriotism, considering it their duty to kill any " hairy barbarian " (the term applied to foreigners in general in those days) who dared to defile the " Land of the Gods " by forcing his way into it. The two murderers were subsequently caught by the Japanese themselves and put to death for the crime, after being dragged through the streets of Yokohama in chains, according to one account.

The reader may consider the mention of the murder of Baldwin and Bird as being somewhat out of place in a book which professes to have as its main object the recounting of a British officer's experiences with the Japanese army. There is, however, this connection. Both the murdered officers belonged to the 20th Regiment of Foot, and the Lancashire Fusiliers claim that the Japanese army was born on its parade ground on Camp Hill in Yokohama. This must not, of course, be taken too literally, but the fact remains that the 20th Regiment of Foot was the first unit of a modern army ever seen by the Japanese, and there is probably a certain amount of truth in saying that the Japanese, as a result of seeing this regiment drilled and equipped in, what was then, the most modern methods, first got the idea of raising an army similarly trained. [2]

[1] A curious thing about the inscription is the spelling of *Daibutsu* —a very phonetic method having been adopted.

[2] It is of interest to note that the Crown Prince of Japan, during his visit to England in 1921, inspected a guard of honour formed by this regiment, and the connection between the regiment and the Japanese army was referred to in a speech of congratulation made to H.I.H. by the Secretary of State for War on the Prince's appointment as a Colonel in the British army.

CHAPTER VI

REGIMENTAL ATTACHMENT (*Continued*)

DURING January nothing of special interest occurred, most of the time being taken up with the training of the new recruits. On the last day of that month, however, the "second-year soldiers" of the regiment, organised as a battalion, set off about 4 a.m. on a two days' *setchū kōgun*—manœuvres held in the snow, reference to which has already been made.

On this particular occasion they started by marching some ten or twelve miles with a climb of four thousand feet or so to the top of Ryusosan, a bare and, at that time, snow-capped hill overlooking Shizuoka. Exercises in mountain warfare were then carried out until about 4 p.m., when bivouac-tents were set up for the night, snow falling all the time.

At 5 a.m. next morning they set off once more over the hills, which, owing to the lack of paths and to the fact that snow and ice were plentiful, made very rough and slippery marching. During the day they covered some twenty-five to thirty miles, getting back to barracks about 7.30 p.m. that evening, tired but sticking it gamely. It must have been a pretty strenuous two days, and it says a lot for their powers of endurance that not a single man fell out.

I should have liked to go with them, but owing to a game leg, it was useless to try. It was very amusing, however, to read an account of the march which appeared a day or two later in the *Yamato Shimbun*, a paper of the *Daily Mail* type. It must have been written before the march took place, as it mentioned that "Capt. Kennedy, a British officer attached to the regiment, accompanied the regiment throughout and came back in perfect condition "! My thanks are due to the paper for taking it for granted that I would not fall out on the line of march, but the fact nevertheless remains that, for the reason stated above, I did not take part in it.

While on the subject of *setchū kōgun,* it may not be out of place to refer to one of these " snow-marches," which took place some twenty years ago and ended in a ghastly tragedy. A party of the 5th Infantry Regiment from Aomori (in the north of Japan) set off to carry out manœuvres on Hakodo-yama, a snow-clad mountain some miles from the town. On the way the detachment, about four hundred strong, was caught in a very severe snowstorm and lost its way on the hills, weather conditions being so bad and the snow so heavy that the men began losing touch with each other. To cut a long story short, nearly three hundred officers and men died from exposure, frozen to death, and the battalion commander, Major Yamaguchi, who was one of the few survivors, felt the responsibility so deeply that he killed himself.

Committing suicide in this way in order to wipe out disgrace, or what is considered to be a disgrace, is, of course, not an uncommon event amongst Japanese officers, the usual *modus operandi* being for the man to write a farewell letter stating his reasons for ending his life and then quietly to perform *hara-kiri.*[1]

Several cases of this kind occurred during the three years of my stay in Japan, the first one being that of an infantry officer who fell out on a route-march. It was a case of sheer fatigue and nothing else, but after he had recovered, he went to his commanding officer and apologised and asked him to punish him. The C.O., however, knowing the facts of the case, refused to do so, and merely told him to get himself into better training for long-distance marching. Not content with this, the officer again asked to be punished,

[1] Literally " stomach-cutting," the deed being done by slashing at the stomach with a sword and disembowelling oneself.

and, as his C.O. still refused his request, he wrote a letter saying that he considered it a disgrace to his regiment to have an officer who had fallen out on the line of march, and that he had, therefore, decided to retrieve the good name of the regiment by relieving it of himself; and, having done this, he proceeded to take his life.

A somewhat similar case occurred during the 1920 Grand Manœuvres, when an artillery officer did away with himself by way of wiping out a disgrace, which consisted of nothing more serious than a failure to get through certain important orders to the attacking troops—a matter to be regarded as serious, of course, in actual warfare, but hardly an irreparable disgrace in ordinary peace-time training. The tragedy of the whole affair was increased by the fact that it was subsequently discovered that the failure to pass on these orders was due to the fact that the telephone wire connecting the headquarters, to which the orders should have been sent, had been purposely cut by some small children who had noticed it lying by the side of a road on which they were playing.

These two cases are quoted at random from amongst half a dozen or so which took place between 1917 and 1920, and should serve to show how deeply the Japanese officer takes his profession to heart; for suicides of this kind are not, as a rule, as some people imagine, carried out from fear of punishment, but are done from, to our minds, a mistaken sense of duty—a point in the psychology of the Japanese which it is difficult for a European to understand.

Other cases of this kind will be found elsewhere in these pages, but enough of them for the present.

On February 11th, the annual ceremony of unveiling the Emperor's photograph took place. February 11th, known in Japan as *Kigensetsu*, is, according to tradition, the anniversary of the founding of the Japanese Empire by Jimmu Tenno some thousands of years back. It is one of the principal annual holidays in Japan, and on that day every regiment and every school in the Empire holds the ceremony of making obeisance to the Emperor's portrait, a framed copy of which is kept in every barrack and school under lock and key, the picture only being taken out of its seclusion on this day every year. By this and other similar means the Japanese child is taught to revere its Emperor, while, in the case of the ceremony held by military units on this occasion, the object is, in addition, yet another method of helping on the *seishin kyōiku*—the teaching of *moral*, to which reference has already been made. It may, therefore, be of interest to give a brief outline of the proceedings as carried out by the 34th Regiment on this occasion.

The whole regiment lined up on the parade ground with the regimental colours unfurled, while in the front centre was a table on which were the unveiled photographs of the Emperor, Empress, and Crown Prince. The regiment having been called to attention and dressed, the regimental commander advanced by himself towards the table, and, having bowed to each photograph in turn, bowed himself away backwards. The battalion commanders then did likewise, followed by the headquarter officers, including myself. After that came each company in turn, and finally the regimental commander once more repeated the performance and the ceremony was ended. The rest of the day was a regimental holiday.

The following day the new brigade commander, Major-General Kozu, arrived to take over the command of the brigade, General Sugano, the former commander, having left some weeks previously to take up a new appointment in Tokyo. The regiment lined the streets while a guard of honour, together with the regimental headquarter officers, went to the station to meet him. On returning to the barracks all the officers in turn were formally introduced to him.

A few days after the arrival of the new brigadier, the divisional commander, Lieut.-General Ono, came with a number of his staff to carry out an inspection of the regiment, a three days' affair lasting from the 17th to 19th inclusive. It was a very thorough sort of business, and the regiment was kept hard at it from first thing in the morning to late in the afternoon. One interesting point in this inspection was a test for discipline, though the object of this test was not mentioned till after it had taken place, which made it all the better.

One company was told to advance against a certain specified position. Twenty yards or so in front of this was a ditch about thirty feet in width containing three or four feet of mud and water. On reaching the near side of the ditch the company lay down for half a minute or so and opened fire. The officer in command then gave the order to charge, and the whole line leapt into the water, holding their rifles above their heads so as to keep them out of the water, and waded or floundered across.

One could not help being struck by the unhesitating way in which the men obeyed the order to advance, especially considering the fact that it was a bitterly cold day, with driving sleet, and the men were without their great-coats. The test was to see whether the men's discipline was sufficiently good to get them to take the plunge without any signs of hesitation. The test was certainly successful, and was a decided, though somewhat drastic, proof of good discipline. One has to expect that sort of thing on active service; but to have to jump into icy water on a bitterly cold day in mid-winter, wearing full equipment, is a pretty severe test for an inspection. One can but feel glad that they are not so thorough in our own army on such occasions.

Instances of the kind mentioned above are not by any means uncommon in the Japanese army, and I saw a very similar case at the Infantry School in March, 1920—just one year later. On that occasion we had been out from about 7.30 a.m. to about 1.30 p.m. carrying out field exercises on the open moors. A bitterly cold wind had been driving rain and sleet into our faces, so that we were soaked through and just about frozen stiff. The men carrying out the exercises were without their great-coats and, as always with the Japanese soldier, without gloves. At the end of the exercises they were made to carry out an attack across flooded paddy-fields with freezing mud and water up to their knees, "in order to show that their *moral* was unimpaired," as the chief instructor, who ordered it, explained.

The Japanese are very keen on making sure that their *moral* is always up to standard, and for this reason unit commanders make a point of ending off a specially strenuous march, or operations of any kind, with five or ten minutes' steady rifle exercises or ceremonial drill, "just to show the men that they are not really so 'done' as they imagined." One could not help feeling sorry for the men and, of course, for the officers too, on seeing them being made to carry out such evolutions when they were obviously pretty well exhausted already; but there seems little doubt that an army trained to such things in peace time will find it less difficult when called upon in time of war to "exert just one more effort."

As has already been mentioned, the Japanese soldier—and officer too—is taught to disregard the cold. One of the methods adopted with this object in view, is for a unit commander to cause all his officers to attend barracks daily from 5 to 6 a.m. for a month during the coldest time of the year—generally from about the middle of January. During this hour they have to fence one another. In the case of the 34th Regiment, the commander himself, Colonel Kimura, was a great fencer and very keen on turning his officers into good swordsmen. He himself was rather taller than the average Japanese and very powerfully built, and he would often take on half a dozen or more of his officers one after the other and beat them all.

Though football, both rugger and soccer, is played in Japan, as also are baseball and tennis, they are mostly confined to the civil population, none of these games being played by regiments. Instead, the main pastimes in the army are fencing (with the Japanese two-handed sword), and bayonet fighting—*jujutsu* and wrestling also being practised. Though the two former are included in the regular training of both officers and men, they are also greatly carried out in much the same way as British regiments play footer, hockey, or cricket—that is to say, during off hours—and great enthusiasm is displayed. As a result the Japanese are excellent fencers and bayonet fighters, though the bayonet fighting is more after the style of our own in pre-War days than of that taught now, neither the butt nor trips of any kind being allowed.

As already described in the case of fencing, bloodcurdling yells are also emitted in bayonet fighting every time a parry or thrust is made, the idea being to demoralise the enemy, and throughout the fight the men are taught to mutter and growl at each other.

Twice a year inter-company bayonet competitions are held, and twice a year inter-battalion competitions take place. Inter-regimental competitions are occasionally carried out, but they are not as a rule encouraged, the military authorities being very averse to kindling inter-regimental rivalry, which they consider likely to arise under such circumstances. They also discourage the giving of prizes and do their best to inculcate the idea that the honour of winning should be sufficient reward in itself—a very sound principle in many ways.

In the case of the inter-company and battalion bayonet competitions, which I witnessed while attached to the 34th Regiment, no prizes were given to the winning teams, but, instead, the men who gained the most points each received a cake of soap, a pencil, or some writing paper to the value of 15 or 20 *sen* (about 3½d. or 5d.) by way of encouragement.

The inculcation of the idea that the honour of winning a competition should be regarded as a sufficient incentive to do one's best without any more concrete reward is, incidentally, shown in other ways as well, one of these being that an officer who passes through the Staff College and gets a staff appointment draws no extra pay, but, like his regimental *confrère*, merely gets the pay of his rank. The honour of being given a staff appointment is regarded as sufficient reward without being given any increase in pay. Here again one cannot help admiring the high sense of duty of the man who is willing to work his best without any other inducement than that of the honour attached to it, but it is doubtful whether it would appeal to the average officer in our own army. This, however, is not meant to cast any reflections on the British officer, who, it will be admitted, is ready to do his best when called upon to do so; and if a similar scheme were brought into force in England, there is no doubt that there would still be plenty aspirants for the Staff College and for staff appointments; there would, however, without doubt, be a considerable amount of "grousing."

Considering that honour in itself is regarded as the highest form of reward, it seems something of an anomaly to find that medals and decorations are earned so cheaply in Japan. It is not uncommon, for instance, to find a Japanese officer with a whole row of medals and to learn that he has never had any war service. This is due to the fact that decorations are bestowed for length of service as well as for skill or bravery in the field, and any officer who likes to give ten yen or more to the Japanese Red Cross Society is entitled to wear the Red Cross medal on his breast. Two other peace-time medals commonly seen are the Coronation and the Korean Annexation medals, whilst the Sacred Treasure and Rising Sun are amongst the commonest of the peace-time decorations, though both the latter have several "classes" which are granted according to the rank of the recipient. As the officer's or man's rank rises, so is the class of his decoration raised.

Apart from war medals, the only actual decoration which is never given except for service in the field is the Golden Kite, and for this reason it is the most highly prized. But although it is the best war decoration it can hardly be classed with our V.C., as it is given very much more easily. Rather might it be regarded as a combination of the V.C., the D.S.O., the M.C., the M.M., and the D.C.M., as it is open to all ranks and is given in such cases as might be covered by the award of any of the above decorations in our own army. Like the Sacred Treasure and the Rising Sun, it has several classes, and the class given depends, not on the degree of brilliancy of the exploit for which it is bestowed, but on the rank of the recipient. Unlike these other two decorations, however, it carries with it an annual monetary reward.

As shown above, the Sacred Treasure and the Rising Sun can both be obtained without war service, though the former is granted automatically, according to length of service, whilst the latter is generally given to those who have actually seen war service without necessarily having carried out any particular exploit.

Every officer, after a nominal, or actual, eleven years of service receives the Sacred Treasure. The modification " nominal " is used advisedly, because every year or portion of a year spent on foreign service outside Japanese home territory counts double, and every year or portion of a year spent on active service is trebled in computing the number of years of service towards entitling him to the award of the Sacred Treasure. Service counting towards a pension on retirement is similarly computed, but no wound pensions are given to officers or men until they have left the service.

From what has been said above it will be seen that decorations are granted more freely in the Japanese army than in our own, and in many ways it seems a weak point in their military system, as it tends to lower the value of their decorations.

The Duke of Wellington was often regarded as very stingy in bestowing honours of any kind, but his invariable retort was to the effect that it was the duty of the soldier to be brave and that there was no reason for rewarding him for merely carrying out his duty. Possibly it might have been better if he had been a bit more liberal with his awards, but there is no doubt that he was right in principle, and that the fewer the rewards given, the more highly will they be valued when received. It is probably largely due to him that the British officer to this day has the reputation of " pot-hunting " for foreign decorations less than his military *confrères* of any other nation. He may like a foreign decoration or two as a "souvenir," but he does not break his heart if he does not get one.

Most foreign officers who carry out an attachment with a unit of the Japanese army receive Japanese decorations before leaving the country. The Japanese military authorities have several times broached the subject of bestowing similar decorations on British language officers attached to Japanese units. The suggestion is always turned down, however, as our own military authorities are averse to encouraging the granting of foreign decorations to British officers in peace-time, and there is little doubt that they are right.

Before closing this chapter, there is one other decoration which may be mentioned as being distinctively Japanese. This is the Staff College badge which is granted to every officer who would, in our own army, be entitled to the mystic letters "*p.s.c.*" after his name in the Army List. It is hardly correct, perhaps, to call it a decoration, but it is mentioned here as being a mark of reward. This badge is made of white metal, oval in shape, and is worn on the right-hand side of the tunic on the waist-line.

CHAPTER VII

REGIMENTAL ATTACHMENT (*Continued*)

AMONGST the noticeable features of a Japanese regiment is the interest taken by the officers in the study of foreign languages and the great encouragement given in this respect. All cadets at the Officers' School [1] have to take up at least one language—English, French, German, Russian or Chinese—and the officers of a regiment are divided up into five sets, each corresponding to one of these languages, the best linguist of each being appointed instructor of his particular set, though occasionally outside teachers are employed, each officer of the set in such a case paying a small subscription by way of a fee.

Before being attached to the 34th Regiment I had always understood that English-speaking Japanese army officers were few and far between, but that the majority of officers spoke German. I was surprised, therefore, to find that a very considerable proportion of the officers in the regiment had a smattering of English and, moreover, showed considerable keenness to learn it better, two or three of the officers being quite good. I had not been many days with the regiment before I was asked to act as language instructor to the English-speaking set, so from that time on I gave them lessons from time to time.

Some of those who were specially keen on learning English used to come to my house in their off hours and carry out

[1] The *Shikwan Gakkō* (literally " Officers' School ") is equivalent to our Royal Military College and Royal Military Academy combined, future officers of all arms of the service being educated there.

an exchange in languages, they helping me to study Japanese whilst I helped them with their English.

Some of these officers used to send me letters in English during week-ends and get me to correct their mistakes, the grammar and spelling of the letters being very amusing at times.

On my leaving Shizuoka, the members of the English-speaking class presented me with a very fine old Japanese sword [1]—a beautiful bit of steel, as keen as a razor and, though about seven hundred years old, in as good condition now as it was when first forged by Uda Kunimune, a famous swordsmith of those days.

To a Japanese, of course, the presentation of a sword means a great deal more than it would to an Englishman, and is quite unlike the giving of an ordinary present, as it implies that the donor wishes to do special honour to the receiver. Thus, when I received this particular sword, it was brought to my house by one of the officers, who, with great solemnity, begged that I would treat it as a Japanese sword should be treated, remembering that the ancient *Samurai* regarded his sword as though it were his own soul, and took the greatest care of it so as to keep it clean and bright and free from dishonour of any kind. He then went on to say that some of the other officers had at first suggested giving me some lacquer-work as a parting gift, thinking that, as I was a foreigner, I would prefer something of that sort ; but he himself had thereupon pointed out that, as I was a *gunjin* (literally " military-man ") and had been wounded in battle, I ought to be treated as a *Samurai*, and, therefore, should be given a sword. It was extraordinarily good of them to give a parting gift of this kind, and certainly the one received from them was more acceptable than anything else they could have thought of.

Unfortunately I was in my bath when the officer arrived

[1] The steel of the Japanese sword is amongst the finest in the world, and it is an interesting fact that the Japanese swordsmiths of mediaeval days used the same processes for hardening the steel of their blades as are being used now in the most modern methods of making armour plating.

to make the presentation. Being a bachelor in those days and living by myself, I was accustomed to strolling through the house from the bathroom with nothing on but a towel. Not knowing that he was waiting to see me, I wandered into the room in which he was sitting, whereupon, though I was clad in nothing but the said towel, he at once started the presentation ceremony. I did my best to look dignified while he delivered his speech, but it is not by any means an easy matter to go through a formal ceremony when you yourself are thus attired.

To return, however, to the main narrative.

March 10th, kncwn as *Rikugun Kinenbi* (literally " Army Remembrance Day "), is the anniversary of the battle of Mukden and is one of the chief military festivals of the year in Japan. In the case of the 34th Regiment, on this particular occasion, proceedings started in the morning by the company commanders lecturing to their respective companies on the subject of this battle and the lessons to be learned from it.

Shortly after this the Brigade Commander and all the chief local officials and retired officers began to arrive, an exhibition of bayonet fighting and a sham fight being given for their benefit, after which a " banquet " was held in the Officers' Mess. This consisted mainly of oranges, nuts, *sashimi* (raw fish cut into slices), and *sake*—the latter being particularly plentiful. Everything was very formal at first, but once the wine had begun to flow, proceedings warmed up.

My opposite neighbours were the Brigade Commander, the Governor of the Prefecture, and a retired admiral. The admiral was a charming old fellow, and I found that he had, some thirty-five years previously, been to England to study ship construction at Newcastle and had spent three years there, going on later to France, so we found plenty to talk about.

It is the Japanese custom on these occasions for each officer to give a cup of *sake* to each of his friends and to receive one in exchange.[1] Towards the end of the banquet,

[1] A *sake* cup is very small and does not hold much more than a liqueur glass.

when the chief guests had left, one officer after another came to me to carry out this exchange, and, as it is considered an insult to refuse, I had to make a pretence of drinking it. As luck would have it there was a large flower-pot conveniently close by, so I managed to get rid of a good bit of the *sake* by "accidentally" upsetting the cup into it, and I noticed that several of them emptied theirs on the sly likewise.

When at last I thought it was about time to make a move, there being no one but the regimental officers left, I was promptly seized by half a dozen or so of the subalterns and carried into the next room, to the accompaniment of shouts of "*Banzai*" and singing of songs—in fact St. Andrew's Night in a Scottish Regimental Mess was not in it. However, it was all done in good fun and everyone was in great form.

Mention has already been made of the great reverence paid by the Japanese, especially the military, to their Emperor. An incident which took place a few days after the *Rikugun Kinenbi* celebrations showed that this reverence is also, to a certain respect, shown to foreign royalty as well. Two of the officers who came to dinner with me one evening about this time were looking at a book of war photos belonging to me, and, in doing so, came across the 1914 Christmas card from the King and Queen, a copy of which, it will be remembered, was sent to every officer and man at the "Front" that first Christmas of the War. This card, as everyone who received a copy will recollect, had a photo of the King and Queen on one side. Thinking that this might interest them, I took it out of the envelope and handed it to one of the two Japanese officers. Seeing what the photo was, he very reverently held it out in front of him, bowed to it, and then, with equal reverence, put it back in its envelope. One knew that the Japanese always made obeisance to their own Emperor in this way, but it was interesting to find that they were prepared to do the same to a foreign Sovereign.

From the 26th to the 29th of March the annual inspection held at the end of the First Term—the first four months of the soldiers' conscript service—took place. Though primarily carried out by the Regimental Commander, the Brigade Commander was also present throughout, and the Divisional Commander was present on one day, the 27th. Roughly speaking, the inspection was divided into three parts, the first day's inspection being in individual training of companies in drilling and handling of arms ; the second and third days in individual training in sentry work and skirmishing ; and the fourth day in the inspection of the machine gunners, communication troops, and stretcher-bearers.

The next event of importance so far as the regiment was concerned took place on April 4th, the anniversary of the raising of the regiment. This event, known as *Gunkisai*—literally " Colours' Celebration "—is made a great occasion for festivities each year, and, for the two or three days prior to it, great preparations are made and decorations of all kinds are rigged up on the parade ground, each company putting up its own. These decorations include dummy figures made by the men themselves, the figures being arranged in the form of *tableaux* representing topical events. Some of these on this particular occasion were extraordinarily good. The main one, erected by No. 6 Company—the one to which I was attached—consisted of two figures of the Kaiser : in the first he was standing holding a large globe above his head, the map of the world being painted on it ; in the second he was sprawling on the ground with the globe on top of him.

Another company had a very amusing representation of the Peace Conference (which was in full swing at the time), whilst another had a very good " zoo." Each company had something different, all the figures being very cleverly made by the men themselves out of odd bits of clothes and material of all sorts.

The ceremonies of the day started off with a march past and saluting of the Colours, after which we were taken round to see the decorations, etc.

On this occasion the saluting of the Colours was carried out with a semi-religious form of ceremony. A small shrine had been erected in the centre of the parade ground, offerings of food being placed upon it with paper prayers attached. The Colours rested on the right of this shrine, the colour party standing on guard close by.

The regiment, having been drawn up in hollow-square formation, was called to attention, whereupon the Colonel and Adjutant advanced to the centre of the square, where the former proceeded to read out an Imperial Proclamation. This having been done, both faced the shrine and stood to attention for some ten minutes in silence, while prayers were offered up for the souls of former officers and men of the regiment who had been killed in battle. Both then advanced to the shrine and saluted, after which more prayers were offered up in silence. After this, the whole regiment marched past in quarter-column, headed by the Colonel, and saluted the shrine and Colours.

All the chief civil officials and ex-officers in the district were invited to this ceremony, and, after it was all over, a banquet was held in the Officers' Mess on much the same lines as that of March 10th.

After the banquet we were given an exhibition of wrestling by men in the regiment, a temporary "ring" having been erected on the parade ground specially for the occasion.

In the afternoon the barracks were thrown open to the general public, anyone who cared to do so being allowed in to see the decorations, wrestling, etc.—a privilege of which large crowds from the surrounding district availed themselves.

CHAPTER VIII

REGIMENTAL ATTACHMENT (*Continued*).

It so happens that in the case of the 34th Regiment, the *Gunkisai*—the ceremony mentioned in the previous chapter—falls during the five days devoted to the annual festival of the Sengen shrine—a large Shinto shrine on the outskirts of Shizuoka. During this period—April 1st to 5th—practically the whole city, including the military, goes on holiday, and the inhabitants of the various towns and villages throughout the prefecture come tramping in to pay their respects to the shrine. It was interesting to see the number of old men and women trudging in on foot or on pack-ponies from places many miles off, wearing the quaint old-fashioned pilgrim's garb.

The city was beautifully decorated the whole week, and, with its strings of paper lanterns all lit up and gaily-coloured bunting and flags draped about everywhere, looked specially pretty at night time. In addition to all this, on each side of the main street was a row of cherry trees in full bloom, a very picturesque sight with the coloured lanterns swinging and twinkling among the blossom.

The main ceremony in connection with this festival took place on the 5th. Count Soyeshima, one of the Foreign Office officials whom I had met once or twice before while in Tokyo, happened to be in Shizuoka at the time, and, having heard that I was attached to the 34th Regiment, very kindly sent me an invitation to lunch with him at the local hotel, the other guests being Mr. Akaike (the

Governor of the Prefecture), General Kozu, and Colonel Kimura. The former had to attend this ceremony in his official capacity, and invited us all to go with him.

Being with the Governor, we were taken to the place specially reserved for him inside the shrine itself, thereby getting an excellent view of the proceedings and being enabled to see it all in comfort instead of having to stand in the seething mob of pilgrims and sightseers outside.

The main ceremony in connection with this festival was a religious dance, in which the principal "actors" were two men dressed as devils and two boys dressed in very fine ancient native costumes. The two devils performed various antics, the object of which was to make the two boys laugh. This went on for one and a half hours or more, the "audience" paying the greatest attention the whole time owing to the local superstition that, if neither boy smiles at all during the whole performance, the prefecture will have a lucky harvest year. The country people are said to put great faith in this "test," and certainly, judging by the rapt expressions on the faces of most of the on-lookers, one can well believe that they do so, for all seemed to be craning forward to see if they could detect the faintest trace of a smile on either boy's face.

Two boys are chosen from the prefecture each year and are trained for the part, and it is supposed to be a great honour for the families from whom they are selected.

When the great day comes they are carried in beautifully lacquered palanquins borne along by Shinto priests dressed in flowing white garments. The clothes worn by the two boys are used year after year for this ceremony and are, in the case of some shrines, hundreds of years old, though only brought out on this one day in the year.

It must have been a pretty severe trial for the two boys, as they were quite young, probably not more than eleven or twelve, but not the trace of a smile did one see from either on this particular occasion.

. . . . .

For the rest of the month nothing much out of the ordinary happened—just the normal "daily round and common task" of drill and training.

The next event of interest was the divisional competition meeting which took place at Toyohashi, the headquarters of the 15th Division, from May 3rd to 6th. About fifty men from each company, and all the officers who could be spared, were sent to take part in the shooting, bayonet, and *gekken* (Japanese fencing) competitions, each unit of the division supplying a similar proportion of officers and men.

Leaving barracks about 6 a.m. we went by special train to Toyohashi, arriving there about 11.30 a.m. During our stay at that place we were quartered in the barracks of the 18th Infantry Regiment, where we spent three days "living the simple life."

As Japanese officers do not normally live in barracks, there is no special sleeping accommodation for them, so, during our stay at Toyohashi the company offices were lent to the officers of the 34th Regiment as sleeping quarters.

As the living was of the simplest, especially in regard to food, Colonel Kimura wanted to put me up at an inn where I might live and eat in comfort, and it was only after great persuasion that I eventually induced him to let me be treated the same as his own officers. I was very glad I did, as, apart from the experience, I got to know and understand the officers better in those three days than I had done in all the previous time during which I had been attached to the regiment.

The barracks in which we lived were, like those at Shizuoka, built in amongst the remains of an ancient castle, the old original walls and moat being still in good condition. The outlook was very pretty—a river flowing along below, while in the distance were ranges of well-wooded hills.

My complete "luggage" for three days consisted of soap, towel, tooth-brush, shaving-brush, razor, and hair-brush; and that was exactly twice as much as that of any of my "brother-officers." They all dispensed with the three last, and were much surprised that I did not do likewise.

The Japanese officer always has his hair close-cropped, so he has never any need for a brush ; and as for shaving, they consider it a waste of time and rather effeminate to do so more than once or, at the most, twice a week.[1] The men are, of course, the same, and if a British drill-sergeant came on to a Japanese parade ground, he would have a fit. Three or four days' growth of beard, boots much patched and quite unpolished, clothes badly fitting and badly patched, and dirty buttons. To one accustomed to British standards of smartness, the Japanese soldier is the very antithesis of tidiness, so far as his turnout is concerned, but he is nevertheless a first-rate fighting man, with plenty of "go" in him and excellently disciplined. Appearances are certainly deceptive in his case.

In the afternoon of the day we arrived, as there was nothing special to do, I went off with two of our officers and a captain of the 18th Regiment, the four of us taking train to Toyokawa, a place some twelve or fifteen miles away, where there was a famous temple. Having got there, one of the officers with me bought some slips of paper on which were written prayers blessed by the priests, while one of the other two bought special sweets blessed by the priests. Both the sweets and the paper prayers were handed out that same evening to the men of the company, one per man, the men being told that, if they ate the sweets and put the paper prayers in their pockets, they were bound to do well in the forthcoming competitions. Personally I very much doubt whether either of these officers had much faith in the efficacy of these "charms," but they probably did this, knowing that a certain number of their men would be ready to believe that the sweets and prayers were possessed of special powers by reason of their having been blessed, for the Japanese are a canny race. Thus, most Japanese are both Buddhists and Shintoists, and it is not by any means

[1] Although, owing to his habit of going unshaven for several days on end, the Japanese officer seems untidy and slovenly to us, it must be remembered that the British, or other foreign officer, with his hair long enough to require parting, seems just as strange to his close-cropped Japanese brother-in-arms.

an unknown thing to find one who professes both these faiths and Christianity into the bargain, apparently on the assumption that, as he is not certain which religion is the true one, he can always be on the safe side by adopting all three. Similarly these two officers probably had but little faith in either the paper prayers or the sweets, but they no doubt considered that they could certainly do no harm to the men and they might on the other hand do some good.

Whilst at Toyohashi, I shared a room—one of the company offices already mentioned—with five other officers, our beds, very narrow and very hard, with a thing like a wooden block for a pillow, being ranged in a row touching one another.

Our programme each day was roughly as follows: Got up at 4 a.m. and had a wash down in the open with a bucket of cold water; 4.30 a.m., breakfast; set off for the day at 5 a.m., getting back about 4 or 4.30 p.m. and having a tub; evening meal 6 p.m., turning in for the night about 8.30 p.m.

Except for the food, the three days at Toyohashi were most enjoyable. We were out in the open pretty well twelve hours each day, and the weather was perfect, though the first one and a half days were very cold compared to the heat we had been having at Shizuoka. Breakfast at 4.30 a.m., or, for that matter, at any time, is not the most appetising thing when it consists simply of boiled rice and *miso* soup, which is the usual Japanese army breakfast. Nor were the midday or evening meals much better—just boiled rice and a piece of raw or pickled fish, generally mixed with seaweed, *daikon* (an evil-smelling species of radish), or other similar "delicacy." The Japanese army certainly does not believe in pampering. Still I had only myself to blame, as I knew what to expect when I refused the colonel's kind offer.

Sunday, May 4th, was the day of the divisional shooting competition in which the four infantry regiments (twelve battalions), the cavalry, engineers, and A.S.C. of the division, took part. We (the 34th Regiment) came out third of the whole lot, and No. 6 Company, the one to which I was attached, was second of all the companies in the division, possibly the result of the blessed sweets and paper prayers. The competition was won by the 63rd (Hamamatsu) Regiment.

That evening at 5.30 a "banquet" was given to all the officers in the division, the main thing being, as always on such occasions, a plentiful supply of *sake*—in fact the food merely consisted of *sushi* (rice and raw fish), lotus root, and pea-nuts.

The fencing and bayonet fighting competition took place next day, and the following morning we left for Shizuoka once more.

The day following that on which we returned, the ceremony of the Crown Prince's coming of age was held, the actual date having been postponed owing to the death of Prince Takeda.[1] The main celebrations were, of course, held in Tokyo, but each regiment also held a ceremony of its own. In the case of the 34th Regiment, this started at 8 a.m., when each company commander addressed his own company on the subject of the Imperial Family in general and the Crown Prince in particular, ending up by calling for "*banzai*." This was followed at 9 a.m. by all the officers filing into a room at the back of the Mess in groups of five or six at a time. In this room were the portraits of the Emperor, Empress, and Crown Prince, specially unveiled for the occasion. Each officer gave three short bows and one long one to these pictures and then backed out of the room.

After the officers had made their bows, each company lined up in turn outside the room (the entrance to which was guarded by two sentries) and presented arms while the bugles sounded the royal salute. Each company having done this, the ceremony came to an end, and the rest of the day was spent as a holiday.

A day or two later, by way of celebrating the thirtieth anniversary of Shizuoka City, the regiment was given a species of "Sunday School Treat" on the beach at

[1] Major-General Prince Takeda was a brother-in-law of the Emperor, and died on April 23rd, 1919.

Mochimune, a fishing village some five or six miles out of Shizuoka. The regiment itself marched there, though I followed later with some of the mounted officers, the whole lot of us arriving about 9 a.m.

Some boats and fishing nets having been hired for the occasion, some of the men were sent out to trawl, the rest of the regiment helping to drag in the nets and retrieve the fishes caught—mostly little ones of the sprat variety. Enough fish having been caught, they were served up to us to eat raw—beer, *sake*, and bananas being added to the repast, and the head-men of the village being invited to partake of the banquet with us. Everyone was in very good form and appeared to thoroughly enjoy the meal, except myself, although I perjured myself right nobly and tried my best to look as though I were enjoying it. Still, it was great fun in its way, and, though at that time I could not truthfully say that raw fish appealed to me very much, I subsequently became very fond of it, which is, perhaps, just as well, as *sashimi*—raw fish cut into slices—is always an important item of a Japanese *menu* and is really very good when you get used to it.

A week or so later, May 19th, the Crown Prince came to stay at Shizuoka for the night on his way to visit the Imperial shrines at Ise. All the officers of the regiment and the local civil officials went to the station to meet him, after which we proceeded to the palace in order to be presented to him.

The following day the wife of my battalion commander died, the funeral taking place the day after. Most of the officers of the regiment attended, the four company commanders and the adjutant of the battalion walking beside the coffin in full dress, the funeral being held under Buddhist rites at Hodoji, a temple in Shizuoka.

The procession was led by coolies, carrying large banners, and others with wreaths and decorations of all kinds. Following this came four more coolies bearing aloft a large sort of cage containing half a dozen or so doves, these doves being subsequently let loose to symbolise the freedom of the soul from the body.

Having reached the temple, most of the officers sat on benches on one side, while the relatives and others squatted in Japanese fashion on the other, the coffin being placed on a kind of raised dais in the centre.

The three priests who officiated wore richly embroidered vestments, not unlike those worn by Roman Catholic priests.

The service commenced with a sort of wailing by professional mourners, after which prayers were read, accompanied by the beating of drums and brass clappers and the burning of incense before the altar. Each priest, one at a time, then solemnly bowed to the altar, then to the congregation, and then to the coffin, after which each in turn recited prayers and burnt incense before the coffin. This being done, each of the three small children of the dead woman prayed and burnt incense before her coffin, followed by all the chief mourners in their turn.

The whole service lasted about forty minutes and, in its way, was very impressive, and when it was over the funeral *cortège* set off on its way to the crematorium, it being the custom in Japan to cremate the dead.

Ten days later my first period of six months' attachment to the Japanese army came to an end, those last ten days being taken up by numerous farewell dinners, including one by the regiment itself, one by the regimental commander, and one by the officers of the company to which I was attached. The two latter took place at *geisha* restaurants in true Japanese style, while the former was held in the Officers' Mess, the brigade commander also being present.

It was, in many ways, with great regret that the period of attachment came to an end, as I had received nothing but kindness from the regiment during the six months I served with it. Being attached to a unit, you get to know and understand the Japanese in a way which it is difficult, if not impossible, to do by any other means. The " brotherhood of arms " is a very real fact, and there is probably no other profession in the world which brings men of all nationalities together, in such a way as to win the mutual respect of each other, as that of the army or navy. A period of attachment to a foreign army cannot but be an aid to a good understanding and to the forming of friendly relationships.

One of the chief causes of misunderstandings between nations is the fact that the people of the respective countries do not know each other, and those of the one are content to believe any "cock-and-bull" story told against those of the other. In the case of Japan, one of the greatest difficulties in the way of most foreigners is the language. In addition to that, the Japanese are by nature reticent, and the average foreigner has but little chance of getting to know them well, and is, therefore, apt to misjudge them and to take offence at some of their habits and customs. My own short experience of them is, that if you can once gain their confidence and are prepared to meet them half way—remembering that many of one's own habits and customs are equally objectionable to the Japanese—one will find them as kind, friendly, and courteous as you could wish. A six months' attachment to a Japanese regiment is as good a way of proving this as anything else that could be imagined.

In a letter written on the conclusion of my attachment to the 34th Regiment, I made the following remarks, and have had no reason for altering my opinion since then:

"Many of the other officers of the regiment, especially those in my own company, have been very good to me and have done their best to make me feel at home amongst them. Some certainly appeared to be very 'standoffish' at the outset; but that is rather a characteristic of a large number of Japanese towards foreigners in general. Many of those, however, who seemed the worst in this respect at first, have turned out to be the most friendly since I have come to know them.

"Taking the officers of this regiment, therefore, as typical of the Japanese regimental officer, I would say that he is difficult to get to know, but once you have gained his confidence and have got to know him properly, he is a first-rate man.

"From my own observations I would say that the best way to gain this confidence is to adapt oneself, as far as is practicable, to his ways—in fact, try to make him forget that you are a foreigner; try to understand his point of view; mix with him as much as possible both in and out of work hours; accustom yourself to his food and even wear his—*i.e.* Japanese—clothing when you have him to your house in the evening or at any other such time. If you do all these things he will be very appreciative and you will find that you get to know him very much better.

"The main reason, so it seems, for the apparent 'standoffish' attitude of Japanese towards foreigners, is that the average foreigner is too apt to deride the Japanese manners and customs, quite forgetting that many of his own manners and customs appear equally unpleasant to the Japanese."

Before going on to the next chapter, one final anecdote in regard to the termination of these six months with the 34th Regiment is perhaps worth quoting from my diary of that period:

"I had a number of parting gifts from them (the officers), and have collected a regular young picture-gallery of photos. Even Nakamura (my soldier servant) had his photo taken in order to give me one, which is really very good of him, considering that the Japanese soldier's pay is only *yen* 3.30 (about 7s.) per month.[1] When I wanted to give him a parting present he was quite hurt about it, as he said he was not a servant for profit but for honour!"

The Japanese soldier-servant receives no extra pay, yet he has to do all his ordinary routine work in addition to his duties as batman. But it is considered a great honour to be selected as an officer's servant, as only the best men are chosen as such. Hence the remark that he was "not a servant for profit but for honour."

[1] The pay has been raised since then, but is still very poor.

CHAPTER IX

IN CAMP AT BASE OF FUJI

THE proper period of my attachment to the 34th Regiment ended on May 31st, but, as the regiment was to go into camp a short time later for three weeks' training, I obtained permission to rejoin and go with them.

Leaving barracks about 5 a.m. on June 17th, the regiment marched to its camping ground at Itazuma, a hut encampment lying at the base of Mount Fuji, which we reached about 10.30 a.m. on the morning of June 19th.

It was an interesting march in its way, some fifty or sixty miles in all—especially the experience of being billeted on the local inhabitants on the nights of the 17th-18th and 18th-19th.

A noticeable feature of the whole march was the way in which we were treated by the people of the towns and villages through which we passed. Nearly every house had flags flying, and numbers of men, women, and children, even of those places through which we passed in the very early hours of the morning, turned out to see the regiment march through ; and in all the larger townships and villages the local head-men, reservists, boy-scouts, and school-children lined up to greet us, the latter chirping out the regimental song of the 34th Regiment. The amount of interest shown by everyone was really rather extraordinary, and, had one not known otherwise, it might have been imagined that we were part of a victorious army returning from the fray.

At every place at which we halted we were given tea and,

generally, fruits and cakes as well by the local inhabitants, whilst the people on whom we were billeted gave us terrific "spreads" each night, and did everything they could to make us comfortable. Of course, a soldier is somewhat of a *rara avis* in parts of the districts through which we passed, and the whole route of the march was through Shizuoka Prefecture, the main recruiting area of the 34th Regiment, which no doubt helps to explain matters. But even so, one could not help being impressed by the treatment accorded to the troops—both officers and men—as many of the people who gave us food and drinks so liberally looked as though they had hardly a penny to their names—just the common coolie class. On my commenting on this fact to one of the officers, he replied that by giving food and drink to the soldiers they were merely serving their Emperor and their country. Be that as it may, the fact remains that, in the country districts of Japan, you will almost invariably meet with the greatest hospitality and courtesy whether you are a soldier or a civilian.

Though it was the beginning of the rainy season, we were lucky in having but little rain during the march, and, though it was swelteringly hot, we did not suffer much from the sun, though four men collapsed from heat-stroke on the second day out. Considering that no protection from the sun, save that afforded by the ordinary service cap, was worn, the wonder is that there were not more cases of sun-stroke and heat-stroke.

On the evening of the second day out I was billeted with one of the subalterns of my company in the house of Dr. Ohashi, a very good fellow with a charming wife. Nothing could have exceeded their kindness, and though we sat up talking till close on midnight, when we got up at 3.15 a.m. next morning, as we had to do, we found that Mrs. Ohashi was already up and about, and had made some tea for us, and had even gone to the trouble of making some ham sandwiches for me, as she said she felt sure I would like some European food for a change. As we had been living on ordinary Japanese army rations—mainly rice and cold fish—the sandwiches were certainly most acceptable, and it goes without saying that her kind thought was warmly appreciated.

When we finally arrived in camp on the morning of the 19th, rain was beginning to fall, and for the first three or four days we had more than enough of it, and it was just as well that we were in huts instead of under canvas, as it developed into a typhoon on the 22nd with torrents of rain and a howling gale. But, in spite of the weather, it was good to be in camp again, and the air up there at the base of Fuji was like a tonic after the sultry heat of Shizuoka.

Though the rain hindered training a certain amount, we were kept pretty hard at it throughout the period in camp, the day's work starting at 5 a.m. and generally ending with night operations.

On the morning of the 24th I was just falling in for parade when Colonel Kimura sent for me and invited me to join him and a party of officers who were setting off to climb Mount Fuji. There is a Japanese proverb to the effect that: "A man who has never climbed Fuji once is a fool, while he who climbs it more than once is likewise a fool!" As I was at that time in the former category, I decided to try the climb, though owing to my "game" leg I was doubtful about being able to manage it.

Setting off about 8 a.m., we reached the second "station" (a rest-house on the way up) some three hours later, four of us riding while the remainder went on foot. From that point onwards it was impossible to continue on horseback, so we dismounted, and, after partaking of the cold rice and pickled onions which served as our day's rations—a somewhat unappetising meal—we started to climb the remaining 8000 feet or so on foot.

Mount Fuji rises to a height of 12,365 feet, whilst Itazuma, where we were camped, is only about 1000 feet above sea level. From there to the second "station" is a distance of some nine or ten miles, the ground rising gradually all the time, but from that point onwards the gradient becomes very much steeper, and the remaining 8000 feet or so have to be covered by zig-zagging.

The actual climb is very uninteresting—simply a steady grind upwards and sideways along the bare sides of the hill. There is not a sign of life or vegetation of any kind from about the 3000 feet level upwards—just bare lava like a huge mass of cinders. In fact there is certainly a great deal of truth in the aforementioned Japanese proverb. The view from the top, provided the weather is clear, is wonderful, and the Japanese are well entitled to say that a man is a fool if he misses the chance of seeing it once, but the monotony of the climb before you get there is such that anyone that does it a second time must be on the verge of mental deficiency. The old saying that " distance lends enchantment to the view " is very true in the case of this wonderfully symmetrical mountain. Seen from a distance, with other hills in between you and it, Fuji is a magnificent sight with its snow-capped peak towering up into the clouds or outlined against a clear blue sky, but when you meet it at close quarters, as you do when you essay to climb it, the bare cinder slopes denude it of all its former beauty.

It was shortly after 11 a.m. when we set off from the "second station," and, though the meal we had just taken consisted of nothing but cold boiled rice and pickled onions, we had nothing more to eat till 6 a.m. breakfast next morning in camp, except chunks of frozen snow mixed with brown sugar, which we ate from time to time on the way up, the former being obtained from the hill-side while the latter was served out by the orderlies who accompanied us. This may sound rather like starvation diet, but it was quite sufficient, for the rarefied atmosphere at the higher altitudes seemed to take away one's appetite completely, and made one feel sick and headachey, so that the very thought of food was revolting.

From time to time we passed small stone and wooden rest-huts built into the sides of the hill like dug-outs. During the climbing season (July and August), one can stop at these huts and get tea, or, if a storm comes up, as very often happens, you can go inside for shelter—in fact people are sometimes forced to stay cooped up inside for three or four days at a time owing to the severity of the storms which frequent those parts, and which are apt to come on suddenly and without warning.

Luckily, however, we had a fine day for the climb, though we struck one or two patches of heavy mist on the way up, and could, at times, only see a few yards ahead of us. It was just as well that we did not get caught in a storm, as we went up before the climbing season had begun, so the rest-huts were all shut and empty and no one else was up the mountain at that time. These rest-huts are dug into the face of the hill, owing to the heavy gales which would otherwise blow them away.

We began to strike small patches of snow as low down as 5000 feet or so, while up at the top there were some fine large stretches of it, certain patches being known as *mannen yuki* (literally " 10,000 year snow "), as it is supposed never to melt.

The temperature at, and near, the summit must have been many degrees below freezing-point, and, as we were clad in our thin summer uniforms owing to the heat in our camping ground 11,000 feet or so below, one felt just about chilled to the bone. Add to this a splitting headache due to the rarefied atmosphere, and a feeling of sickness brought on from the same cause, and also the sensation of being " all in " as a result of climbing that height with a paralysed left foot two to three inches shorter than its fellow, and the reader will perhaps have a slight idea of what I, personally, felt like as we neared the summit of Mount Fuji on that 24th day of June, 1919. Apart from anything else, the fact of feeling sick when your last meal was made off cold rice and pickled onions is anything but pleasant. I had intended to take some photos when we got there, but felt so deuced sorry for myself, while at the same time trying to appear as though nothing was wrong, that I found it a sheer impossibility.

The one redeeming feature of the whole thing, apart from the wonderful view, was that I could see by the colour of the faces of my " brother officers " that they were apparently in the same condition themselves. We were all pretty well burnt black as a result of the march from Shizuoka to Itazuma and our life in camp, but, by the time we reached the top of Fuji, everyone was a ghastly pea-green colour. It did not strike one as so humorous at the time, any more than such things strike you that way when you are being tossed about on a cross-Channel mail boat. But on thinking it over later, after the effects of the atmosphere had worn off, one saw the funny side of it.

Apart from the fine view to be had from the top of Fuji, we were lucky enough to get a large mass of fleecy white clouds below us in one part, these clouds having the appearance of a huge snow-field—pure white—and, when the sun was sinking, they acted as a mirror in which Fuji could be seen clearly reflected.

The top of the mountain is the lip of a large volcanic crater. Unfortunately, however, we had no time to go round it or down into it, but, after a few minutes' rest, we had to start back again in order to reach the base before dark set in, in case we lost our way.

It had taken from six to seven hours to climb from base to summit, but we got down in about an hour and a half, one reason for this being that, whereas you go up by a very zig-zag path, you come down pretty well straight, and, moreover, as it is all loose cinders in that part, you can take long strides with the help of a kind of boy-scout's pole (bought for a few *sen* at the base before starting) and slide through the ash.

We reached the base about 7.30 p.m., just as it was growing dark, and eventually arrived in camp about 11 p.m., the colonel and myself completing the last eight or nine miles on horseback, our horses having been sent to meet us.

It had been an interesting experience in its way, and I was glad that I was no longer, according to the Japanese proverb, a fool. But if ever I decide to return to the " fool " category by doing the climb a second time, I shall certainly not attempt it out of the climbing season when there are no rest-houses open and when the whole climb has to be completed in the hours of daylight, nor shall I try it on a meal of cold rice and pickled onions. In fact, taken all round, it will probably be best to abide by the advice tendered between the lines of the proverb and rest content with the one single ascent of the Sacred Mountain.

Before leaving the subject of Fuji, one final word might be added. Those who climb it generally invest in one of the boy-scout poles mentioned above, in order to help them in their climb. During the five or six weeks of the year which are regarded as the climbing season, the pilgrims, and others who go up, generally have these poles stamped at the top station or rest-house, in order to prove to their friends that they have actually reached the summit. As, however, the climbing season had not opened when we went up, there was no one to stamp ours. By way, therefore, of providing me with a souvenir of the occasion, my battalion commander, a very cheery but somewhat rotund gentleman, got me to give my pole to him the following day, and, on receiving it back, I found that he had written on it in Japanese to certify that I had been to the summit of Mount Fuji with it. Owing, as he put it, to the fact that he was no longer as young nor as slim as he had once been, he had not accompanied us on the climb, but I have cut off the end on which he wrote, and now keep it, together with other mementoes of the very pleasant six months spent with the 34th Infantry Regiment.

For the next few days we were kept hard at it "from early morn to dewy eve," carrying out company training. *Réveillé* generally sounded at 5.30 a.m., and at 6 a.m. we had the usual army breakfast, consisting of a large bowl of *mugi-meshi* (rice mixed with barley) and *miso* soup, washed down with green tea—an unappetising species of repast, but in the bracing air of the camp one felt ready to eat anything.

In camp and on manœuvres in Japan, barley is always mixed with the rice as a precaution against *beri-beri*, which is likely to be brought on by a constant diet of rice. The men are given this *mugi-meshi* always instead of plain rice, even in barracks, but as officers generally only have the midday meal in barracks, and can eat anything they like in their own homes, where they have their other meals, they are always allowed plain rice, except when in camp or on manœuvres. With that one exception, the food of both officers and men is the same. This somewhat Spartan-like form of diet is not by any means liked by the officers, who, in their own homes, are accustomed to more appetising food ; but one never hears them complain of it, as they are brought up to look on comfort and good feeding as a sign of weakness—a thing to be avoided at all costs by those who choose the profession of arms.

In the camp at Itazuma, companies generally paraded each day at 7 a.m., and carried out training until 3 or 4 p.m., each officer and man taking his so-called " midday " meal with him—a ration of cold rice and barley with a little fish or pickles of sorts to help it down.

On returning to the camp in the afternoon everyone had a " tub," each company having its own bath-house, whilst a separate one was provided for the officers.

About 5.30 or 6 p.m. the evening meal, similar to the midday one, was eaten, though on this occasion one could help out the somewhat monotonous diet of rice with omelettes, *soba* (a kind of spaghetti), or fried fish, obtainable at the local canteen, and the officers generally got in bottles of *sake* to wash it down.

After this, if there were no night operations to be carried out, the officers were generally kept busy working out tactical schemes or preparing programmes of training until 8 or 9 p.m., when they turned in for the night.

Apart from the food, the camp life at Itazuma was a thoroughly enjoyable one, and, living constantly with the officers and sharing the same comforts and discomforts with them as one did, it afforded the best possible chance of getting to know them intimately. The Japanese are by nature reticent, and it is largely due to this characteristic that the average foreigner gets the impression that they are arrogant and unfriendly. It is perhaps unfortunate, therefore, that more Europeans in Japan have not the same chances of breaking through this reticence as are afforded by a few months' attachment to a regiment with periods of camp life thrown in. Personally I shall always look on my own experiences of this kind as some of the most enjoyable of my life, for, almost without exception, the officers did their best to make me feel thoroughly at home with them, as though I were one of themselves, and nothing could have exceeded their kindness and consideration on my behalf.

It was while we were in camp that the Treaty of Versailles was signed, and, on receipt of the news, a special ceremonial parade was held by way of celebrating the occasion. Actually the Treaty was signed on Saturday, June 28th, and though the news confirming its signing was not received till a day or two later, a special service of thanksgiving was arranged by the British and American communities of Tokyo to be held on Sunday, June 29th. Seeing the announcement of this service in a paper on the afternoon of the 28th, I asked for, and obtained, permission from the regimental commander to go up to Tokyo to attend it. It meant a start at 2 a.m., and I had to be back in camp the same night, but as I had missed the Thanksgiving Service at the time of the Armistice, owing to manœuvres being on at that time also, I specially wanted to be present at the one for the signing of peace. Apart from that, and looking at it from a more mundane point of view, I was beginning to grow a bit tired of a diet of rice and green tea, and felt that a meal or two of European food would make a welcome break in the monotony.

A few days later the period in camp came to an end. The regiment was to begin the return march on July 4th, completing the sixty odd miles in two days and bivouacking one night on the way. As, however, I was not returning to Shizuoka, I left them on the 3rd and went back to Tokyo.

On the morning of the 3rd, the company to which I had been attached all the time fell in on parade, and I was asked to say a few words to them by way of farewell. I had been warned of this beforehand, and so had prepared a short speech in Japanese, and in due course delivered it. One of the subalterns, who spoke a little English, then stepped forward and made me a short speech in English on behalf of the company. As he had written it out previously, I asked him to let me have a copy of it as a memento. That copy lies before me as I write, and it reads as follows :

" Now I shall just say you good-bye in the name of all our company soldiers.

" We are all indeed gratifying for your kind and polite speech just you given us.

" Please excuse us our impolite manners in many cases and our having giving you little assistance during you attachment to our company which in some case they we expect, occured on account of the difference between our country manner and your own.

" We wish to restrain you longer here as an honourable British officer attached to this company, but as we hear that you are now going up to Tokyo by order to investigate more great many things so we shall see you off with our hearty thanks.

" It is a short distance from Shizuoka to Tokyo or Hakone, therefore if you have spare time please visit our company.

" Finnaly ; it is getting hart (hot) day be day please be more careful for your health.

" And we hope you good luck."

The ceremony ended with a farewell speech in Japanese by the company-sergeant-major on behalf of the men.

The Japanese military year is divided into four " terms " of training, and at the end of each an inspection is held by the divisional commander. The first term—recruit training—ends in March and, in the case of the 34th Regiment, has already been mentioned.[1] The inspection at the end of the second term—company training—took place from July 1st to 3rd—the last three days in camp at Itazuma—and was pretty strenuous. Major-General Kozu, the Brigade Commander, had carried out the first two days' inspection,

[1] *Vide* p. 75.

and was joined by Lieut-General Ono, the divisional commander, on the last day—the day I left.

Having said good-bye to them and to the regimental officers I set off on foot for the station at Gotemba, the railway being some three or four miles from the camp. Though it was pouring with rain, my company commander and two other officers insisted on accompanying me, while a number of others were profuse in their apologies for not coming to see me off also, as, owing to the final inspection, which was still being carried out, they were not able to do so.

The Japanese form of farewell, like that of meeting, is to bow deeply and draw in the breath with a hissing sound through the teeth. I had grown quite accustomed to this during my attachment to the regiment, though both the divisional and brigade commanders had always greeted me with the European method of hand-shaking. But as the train steamed into the station each of the three officers who had accompanied me came up to me in turn and, instead of bowing in the usual Japanese fashion, shook me warmly by the hand. Two of these officers are now in Manchuria on garrison duty, whilst the third is, or at any rate was until recently, in Siberia. May they all have the best of luck, for they were excellent fellows and always the best of company.

CHAPTER X

1919 GRAND MANŒUVRES

As the main purpose of this book is to give some idea of the everyday life of the Japanese army as seen by a British officer, little or nothing but passing reference need be said of the six or seven months immediately following the termination of my attachment to the 34th Regiment.

After a few days in Tokyo, in which were included a *soirée* at the Foreign Office and a garden party at the Embassy in honour of the signing of peace, I went up to the cooler air of Hakone, and spent a couple of months there at a native inn on the lakeside. Leaving Hakone I went down to the Inland Sea, and spent five most interesting weeks wandering round the islands of Shikoku and Kyushu as well as paying visits to the sacred island of Miyajima and other "beauty spots" down that way—on the move most of the time and putting up at Japanese inns. One could write a whole volume on the impressions gained on a trip of this kind, living *à la Japonaise* and steering clear, for the most part, of the "beaten track" of the tourist. This book, however, is not meant to be one on travel in Japan, so no more need here be said of this particular trip, though one or two points of military interest noted on it will be found mentioned later on in these pages.

For want of a better place in which to settle down before the beginning of my next period of attachment, I returned to Shizuoka early in October. The old man and his wife whom I had had as servants ever since I arrived in Japan, had left me in the summer for a more lucrative post elsewhere, but I was lucky enough to get hold of an old fellow of sixty-five and his wife in their place, though the two letters of reference with which they supplied me were dated June, 1890, and January, 1903, respectively. However, they turned out to be an excellent old couple, and I was very sorry to have to part with them when I left for England a year or so later.

The old gentleman professed to be a Christian, having, in days gone by, been servant to one of the first missionaries to come to Japan on the opening up of the country to foreign intercourse. His knowledge of that religion, however, appeared to be a bit rusty and had, no doubt, not been renewed since the death of the worthy missionary who had been his master in the "seventies," or possibly he might be described as a "broad-minded" Christian, for, hung on the wall of his kitchen, side by side, were a crucifix and a small shrine to the spirits of his forebears.

Nothing special in regard to military duties took place during the first month or so after my return to Shizuoka, though, at the request of some of the officers of the regiment, I used to go to the barracks twice a week to take classes in English. One way and another, therefore, I saw a fair amount of my former "brother-officers," many of whom would drop in to see me at odd times or would invite me to their houses or to one of the local *geisha* restaurants.

It was towards the end of October that a certain amount of interest was aroused by the "death" and subsequent "return to life" of the veteran soldier and statesman, Marshal Count Terauchi, whose eldest son, Colonel Terauchi, had been our chief "bear-leader" on the 1918 Grand Manœuvres.

On his "death" the aged Marshal was promptly raised to a higher court rank, in accordance with Japanese custom; hundreds of telegrams of condolence were received by his family, and great preparations were made for a big public funeral. Then he suddenly came to life again, although, according to the papers, *rigor mortis* had actually set in. Great commotion was caused thereby, as obituary notices had appeared in all the papers, and his court rank had to be promptly cancelled.

Colonel Terauchi, on hearing of his father's dying condition, had hurriedly left his regiment while on manœuvres in order to say a last farewell, and it is said that the old Count, on "coming back to life" and finding him by his side, sat up and scolded him severely for having left his military duties, and gave him peremptory orders to return at once. It was not till two or three weeks later that Marshal Terauchi breathed his last. By his death Japan lost one of those who had worked so well to raise her to the level of one of the "Great Powers" of the present day.

Shortly after the death of the aged *Genro*, one of my teachers, a master at the local "Middle School," took me to see the annual "sports" held at his school. In many respects the sports were similar to those held at our own public schools, but two of the events were particularly interesting and perhaps worth recording, as they are not altogether unconnected with military training in Japan.

The first of these was a pitched battle between two sides with *gekken*, the Japanese two-handed sword (bamboo ones used in practice). Each side was commanded by a "general" with his four "strong men" and about a dozen "soldiers" under him. Each man was clothed in the "armour" used in this kind of fencing (mask, gauntlets, body-protector, etc.), and on the point of each man's mask was a sort of rosette, the side which knocked off the most rosettes in about ten minutes being declared the winner. On the word being given, both sides advanced with "swords" raised above their heads, and then, with blood-curdling yells, ran forward and "fell upon" their opponents, each "soldier" selecting, or being selected by, one or more opponents, while the four "strong men" of each side dashed about, laying out right and left wherever help was most required, the "generals" giving directions from the rear and attending to any one of the opposing side who managed to break through his front line. It was a first-rate show and gave one a rough idea of what Japanese warfare must have been like in ancient times when the two-handed sword was the principal weapon used.

Another good show combining wrestling and *jujutsu,* and somewhat reminiscent of a rugger-scrum, was a fight between two sides (some twenty or so a side) for the possession of the enemy's standard. Each side had a long pole representing a standard, and, on the word being given, half of each side rushed across to the enemy standard while the remainder stayed to guard their own. They went for each other with a will, grappling with one another and wrestling or throwing one another with *jujutsu* throws. The fight lasted about ten minutes, but neither side won, and the majority of the combatants were sorry-looking sights by the end, and somewhat deficient of even the scanty clothing worn at the start.

A few days after this, I had to go up to Tokyo to take the examination held at the end of the second year of each Language Officer's stay in Japan. Having successfully defeated the examiners, I stayed on there till the evening of the 9th, when I left, together with a number of the foreign attachés, for Kobe to take part in the annual Grand Manœuvres, which were being held in that neighbourhood shortly.

At Kobe the foreign attachés were divided into two sets, one, consisting of the Military Attachés and British Language Officers (three of the latter, including myself), being quartered in the Tor Hotel, whilst the other was composed of officers of various military missions who were in Japan at the time, and was housed at the Oriental Hotel. In all, thirteen different nationalities were represented, those in our party consisting of four British, two Americans, two French, and one from each of the following countries, viz. Italy, Russia, China, Holland, Peru, Bolivia, Chile, and Czecho-Slovakia. Lieut.-Colonel Ninomiya was the chief "bear-leader" of those staying at the Tor Hotel, and a very excellent one he made.

Amongst those at the Oriental Hotel were Colonel Faure of the French aviation mission to Japan and three other

French flying officers under him. This mission had arrived in Japan in January of that year, and consisted of some fifty or sixty officers, mechanics, and others, though some of them had already returned to France before the Grand Manœuvres began. The good work which they had put in since their arrival was very evident, for the aerial work carried out by the Japanese aviators during the 1919 manœuvres, as compared with the almost pitiful exhibition given just a year previously, was by far the most noticeable point of the "fighting" which took place from November 11th to 15th, 1919.

With Colonel Faure and his three flying officers at the Oriental Hotel were some Chinese generals, two Siamese officers, an Italian cavalry officer, two other French officers, and a Russian and an American colonel—quite a good mixture, but nothing to touch our party, for we had officers of most of these nationalities and a number of others as well.

Our quarters and feeding were excellent, the only trouble with the latter (including wines and spirits of all kinds) being that there was too much of it; in fact we seemed to spend half our time in eating and drinking.

But though everything was done very well for us and we were given the best of everything, we had a pretty strenuous time of it with every minute of the day filled up. We seldom got to bed till 11 p.m. or later, and most mornings had to be up again at 3.30 or shortly after, and one morning at 3 o'clock, so there was not much sleep to be had.

In the afternoon of our arrival at Kobe, we were motored over to Suma (half an hour or so west of Kobe by car), where the Emperor took up his headquarters for the manœuvres. After going to the station to meet him on his arrival, we motored round to pay our respects to the Crown Prince, Prince Kanin, General Uehara (Chief of the General Staff and now Marshal), and a number of other military officers who had also taken up their headquarters at Suma, the houses used as such being lent for the occasion by rich Kobe merchants.

The morning had been spent, partly in settling in and partly in having the plans for the forthcoming operations explained to us by our " bear-leaders," and in the evening, after returning from Suma, further details were given out in connection with the manœuvres which began that night.

The divisions taking part in these manœuvres were : the 4th (Osaka), 10th (Himeji), 11th (Shikoku), and 17th (Okayama), the two former, under Lieut.-Generals Machida and Kanakubo respectively, being in the Eastern army, which was on the defence, while the two latter, under Lieut.-Generals Saito and Furumi, were in the Western army, the attacking force. General Shiba Goro, with Major-General Isomura as his chief of staff, commanded the former army, whilst General Akiyama, with Major-General Kikuchi as chief of staff, commanded the latter. Both General Shiba and General Akiyama have had brilliant careers, and each has held several important appointments at different times ; but to students of the 1904-5 operations in Manchuria, the latter, now an oldish man but still as keen as ever, will probably be best remembered owing to his fine work as an independent cavalry commander.

In addition to the divisions mentioned, each side had a regiment of heavy artillery, two cavalry regiments and an air battalion of eighteen machines, together with cable and wireless units, whilst the Western army also had a battery of mountain artillery (7.5 cm.). The heavy artillery batteries of this army consisted of 12.0 cm. guns, those of the Eastern army being of 15.0 cm. calibre.

On the morning of the 11th we took train to a place some twenty miles or so to the west of Kobe, and spent the rest of the day riding round seeing various phases of the fighting, horses having been sent to meet us on our arrival at the station. Major-General Inouye, Chief of the Air Force, dined with us that evening after our return to the hotel, and, it being the anniversary of the signing of the Armistice, special toasts were drunk.

The following morning we were called at 3.30 and, after an early breakfast, set off in a heavy drizzle and took train to Akashi, arriving there about an hour and a half later, being met once more by the grooms with our horses.

After riding round for some hours, we returned to Akashi and were taken for a cruise in the Inland Sea in a couple of motor launches, provided by the Suzuki Shoten, who also gave us an excellent lunch on board. Unfortunately the weather continued dull and drizzling, but the scenery itself was very fine, the coast line being hilly and well wooded.

That evening the same commercial firm gave us a big *geisha* dinner, and the following evening we were taken to another one, given by the Mayor of Kobe. Suffice it to say that both entertainments were very cheery shows and that everyone was in great form.

The 13th was spent in much the same way as the 12th, and on the 14th the actual manœuvres came to an end. Getting up at 3 a.m. we went by train to a place some ten or twelve miles from Osaka, where, as on previous occasions, our horses were waiting for us. Mounting them we set off to see the final stage of the manœuvres.

From a spectacular point of view, the fighting on this last day was certainly the best show of the lot ; but, as far as the infantry tactics were concerned, it showed that the lessons learned in the War had not been taken to heart.

The "Eastern Army" had been retiring for the last couple of days, but on the final day turned round and assumed the offensive, delivering the assault in huge masses, the men marching shoulder to shoulder in massed formation, in much the same way as the Germans did in the early days of the War. One would have thought that the Japanese would have learned the impossibility of such tactics, just as the Germans did, but apparently they had not done so at that time. Under modern conditions they would not have had a chance, but would simply have been mown down in thousands. However, since the 1919 Grand Manœuvres, numerous experiments have been carried out in new formations, new weapons, etc., and a great deal of research work on the lessons to be learned from the War has been done by the special branch of the General Staff formed for that purpose. It is doubtful, therefore, whether massed tactics, such as those of 1919, will ever again be employed by the Japanese in the event of a war in the future with a modern military Power.

From the point of view of modern warfare, the 1919 Grand Manœuvres showed that the Japanese army was still, at that time, far behind the times both in regard to weapons and tactics, though both officers and men were, as usual, up to the highest standard in discipline and fitness. In fact the remarks made earlier in this book regarding the 1918 Grand Manœuvres would apply equally well to those of 1919, with one exception. In 1918 aircraft was chiefly conspicuous by its absence, and one never saw more than two machines in the air at the same time; moreover, it was only on comparatively rare occasions that any were visible at all. No fighting in mid-air was seen and machines seldom, if ever, flew over the enemy's lines at altitudes of less than 2000 ft. or 3000 ft. But a year later, in these manœuvres of 1919, it was very different. The sky was seldom free from aircraft, half a dozen or more being often visible at one time, while on the final day there were twenty or more machines in the air at the same time, chasing and scrapping with each other, bombing and "ground-strafing" enemy infantry, swooping down at times to within 100 feet or so of the ground and carrying out "stunts" of various kinds. Moreover, though thirty-six machines took part in these manœuvres, there were no serious accidents or mishaps of any kind—a point well worthy of note by way of comparison with what had happened in the Grand Manœuvres of the two previous years. The chief credit for this improvement must be given to Colonel Faure and his officers of the French aviation mission to which reference has already been made.

A nation which sets itself out to teach the Japanese anything of value is always looked up to by those instructed, and the latter will always have a soft spot for them in their hearts—a friendly feeling born of gratitude. If anyone questions this, he need only turn to the history of the Japanese fighting forces. The army, notoriously pro-German up to quite recently and inclined that way even now; the navy, for the most part, pro-British. And why? The reason is not far to seek; for is not the Japanese army of to-day copied from that of Germany, which for several years prior to the war of 1894, supplied Japan with some of her smartest officers and N.C.O's as instructors. Similarly, the navy selected Great Britain as a model, and owes much to this country for its present high state of efficiency. A number of other cases could be quoted, if required, in order to show this tendency on the part of the Japanese to give their friendship as gratitude to those who have instructed them, but the two instances just given should be sufficient to convince any thinking man or woman on this point. Having once acknowledged the truth of this statement, it is probably not too much to say that the Japanese aviators will, for many years to come, manifest their gratitude to France in much the same way as the army has done to Germany in the past and the navy to our own country. The Japanese Aviation Corps is not yet, as it is in England, a separate organisation under its own minister, like the army and the navy, but the authorities concerned are fully alive to the vital importance of a strong air force, and plans exist for a great expansion both in *personnel* and *materiel* as well as for the creation of new units; and, as numbers increase, the opinions of the Japanese flying officers are likely to bear more and more weight, so that friendship for France is likely to increase rather than to decrease.

No doubt the French counted on this being the case at the time they offered their services as instructors of aviation to Japan, and they thereby showed themselves to be fully awake to the advantages to be gained by such a friendship. As a result one will always hear Japanese army officers, when talking about aviation, referring to French methods, but one seldom hears any reference to British flying. This was most noticeable in the lectures on aviation and matters relating to flying, which were given at the Infantry School at Chiba to which I was attached for six months in 1920.

One reason for the French having risen so greatly to

favour in Japanese military circles of late years, is that their War Department, from the earliest days of the War, offered facilities to Japanese military observers which were not given by any of the other belligerent armies. Following on this, and quite apart from the prestige gained for her by her great feats in the War, France brought herself into still greater favour by coming to Japan's help in regard to aviation. In addition to this aviation mission, the French also sent over instructors to teach the use of the carrier-pigeon, a service which has greatly developed in Japan since 1919 in consequence, and in 1920 they supplied the Japanese with a number of light tanks of the Rénault type, besides giving assistance in numerous other ways. With all these things to their credit, is it to be wondered that the French are rapidly usurping the high place which Germany once held in the eyes of the Japanese army? It is hardly necessary to add that he who holds the respect of the army in Japan at once gains high favour in the councils of the nation, for the Military Party, voiced by the General Staff, has, in many respects, more power in matters of foreign policy than has the Foreign Office itself. There are those who say that the power of the Military Party is on the wane. Possibly this may be so, but even should this be the case, its voice is likely to bear very great weight for many years to come; for a nation, such as Japan, which has, from time immemorial, looked up to its fighting class, and which owes its present position as a world Power to its military leaders, is not likely to reject their counsels easily.[1]

However, all this talk about Japanese aviation has led us away somewhat from the 1919 Grand Manœuvres, so let us get back to the point where we branched off.

The "Cease Fire" was sounded about 8.30 a.m. shortly after the somewhat spectacular attack by a brigade of

[1] It is perhaps incorrect to say that Japan has looked up to her fighting class "from time immemorial," because actually this fighting class did not start coming to the fore until about the end of the eighth century in the reign of the Emperor Kwammu (*vide* Murdoch's *History of Japan*). The fact, however, remains that, for many centuries past, the *Samurai* or military class have held almost undisputed sway in Japan.

massed infantry. In commenting on this form of tactics to one of the Japanese officers attached to our party—an officer who had himself been in France as a military observer during part of the War—he admitted the impossibility of such methods of attack under modern conditions, and intimated that massed tactics of this kind would probably be abolished in the near future together with other relics of the past, such as the carrying of regimental colours into action and the constant use of the drawn sword by officers leading their men to the fray. Admittedly both of these last-named customs have their uses as stimulants for raising the *moral* of the men, and, in the days of the smooth bore gun, were invaluable assets to a fighting force. Under modern conditions, however, they merely serve as targets for the machine-gunner and the sniper, let alone the artillery man and the aviator, and are bound to involve carnage, especially amongst the officer ranks, out of all proportion to the *élan* and *moral* which their presence inspires in the men.

As already mentioned, the officer to whom I spoke about this hinted that the time was not far distant when an end would be put to all these survivals of the more spectacular and picturesque side of warfare. On being questioned further, he said that they would have been abolished long ago had it not been for certain high commanders who still held to the old conservative idea of war, chief amongst them being that fine old warrior and statesman, the late Marshal Prince Yamagata, whose death took place early in February of last year (1922). For many years prior to his death, Prince Yamagata, as chief of the *Genro*, or "Elder Statesmen" of Japan, had been regarded, both in politics and in military affairs, as the power behind the throne, the maker or breaker of Cabinets, and the man whose word was law. Whether or no he really had the extraordinary influence commonly accredited to him in his latter days, he was undoubtedly a great power in the land.

From what was said by the Japanese officer with whom I spoke about the continued use of massed tactics and other matters akin to them on that last day of the 1919 Manœuvres, the impression obtained from him was, that the more advanced type of military officer considered it essential that the Japanese army should adopt more modern methods; but knowing how averse Prince Yamagata, and others of his type, were to departing from the old-time custom of carrying swords and colours into action and other similar practices, they did not wish to do anything likely to injure the feelings of those to whom they owed such a deep debt of gratitude for all they had done for their country as a whole and for their army in particular. Prince Yamagata himself was then a man of over eighty and could not be expected to live very much longer, so they felt that the least they could do was to wait patiently for his death and not embitter his last days by any radical changes. That veteran warrior is now dead and there are but few of his contemporaries left. It will be interesting to see whether their removal from the scenes will have the effect forecasted.

Having digressed somewhat from the main narrative, we nust return once more to November 14th, 1919.

Shortly after the "Cease Fire" sounded, the foreign attachés rode to Minomo, a place some miles out of Osaka, famous for its maple trees, which at that time of the year were at their best—a mass of scarlet and gold, additional beauty being added to the scene by the presence of a waterfall and a rapidly flowing stream tumbling and splashing down the narrow valley over a rocky bed. Lunch and a very cheery *geisha* show were provided by a wealthy Japanese merchant at his country residence close by—a beautiful place commanding an excellent view, perched, as it was, on the hillside. In the afternoon we went by light railway to Osaka, where we were met by a regular fleet of cars, in which we were taken to see the sights of Osaka, including the castle, a wonderful old place built by the great Hideyoshi some three centuries ago.

Having done the sights we went to the Osaka Officers' Club, where General Uehara, Chief of the General Staff, gave a banquet to the foreign attachés and chief naval and military officers who had taken part in the manœuvres.

The following morning the Emperor held a review at Osaka of all the troops that had taken part in the manœuvres. The troops were drawn up all round the parade ground belonging to the city and His Imperial Majesty drove round in an open carriage, followed by a number of the principal Japanese military officers and the foreign attachés on horse-back, each in turn having been presented to the Emperor previously.

Having completed the tour of inspection, His Imperial Majesty proceeded to the saluting base and each division marched past, all the infantry first, then the artillery, then the sappers, and last of all the cavalry. They looked none the worse for their somewhat strenuous manœuvres, most of them having been hard at it for the past month, starting off with regimental manœuvres, followed in rapid succession by brigade, then divisional, and, finally, Grand Manœuvres. An officer of the 21st Infantry Regiment, to whom I had spoken the previous day, told me that his own regiment had been constantly on the move in this way since October the 19th, averaging some ten *ri* (about twenty-five miles) a day, and that not one man in his company had fallen out. Not a bad record !

The review having ended, the foreign attachés were given a formal lunch at the Town Hall by the Mayor of Osaka. The hall was a fine large building which had only recently been completed ; and the main part alone (so we were informed) cost a million *yen* (over £100,000) and was presented to the city by a very rich merchant who, however, lost all his money a short time later and committed suicide.

As soon as the lunch was over we had to hurry off to the banquet given by the Emperor to all the officers and high civil authorities who had taken part or helped in the manœuvres. As, however, the proceedings were similar to those at the one given on the conclusion of the 1918 Grand Manœuvres, mention of which has been made in an earlier chapter, no more need be said.

The Emperor and the Crown Prince left Osaka *en route* for Tokyo later in the afternoon, and, having seen them off, we ourselves returned by train to our quarters at Kobe, where we had a very cheery farewell dinner that evening with a few short speeches. Some of the foreign attachés left for Tokyo late that same evening, but most of us stayed on till the next day. So ended the manœuvres. They had served as a most enjoyable break in the daily round, though one could well have done with a little more sleep; and, as in the case of the 1918 manœuvres, there had been rather too much dining and too little real work so far as we ourselves were concerned, though, no doubt, the troops would have liked a bit more of the former and rather less of the latter for themselves.

CHAPTER XI

ATTACHMENT TO INFANTRY SCHOOL

ON returning to my house at Shizuoka at the end of November I found that several of the men belonging to the company of the 34th Regiment, to which I had been attached, had been round during my absence to say good-bye to me, their period of service with the colours having come to an end. I was sorry to have missed them, as they were all men whose homes were in out-of-the-way country districts, so that I was not likely to see them again.

For the next two months my military duties were few and far between, most of the time being taken up with further study of the language and a couple of hours outdoor exercise per day, by way of keeping fit. Twice a week I went off to the barracks to take the class of officers in English, most of them showing more enthusiasm than skill in mastering the language. But they were always very cheery about it all, and, though some of their attempts at English were most amusing, I have no doubt that my efforts at Japanese were often just as comical to them.

It is characteristic of the Japanese race as a whole, that, on first acquaintance, they generally appear rather stiff and formal ; and owing to his strict views on etiquette, combined with his fixed ideas on the subject of courtesy, the Japanese officer will seldom, if ever, laugh at mistakes made by foreigners—at any rate not in their presence—however incongruous they may appear. This applies not only to grammatical errors in the language, but also to unintentional blunders of other kinds. A case in point is a bad " break "

I myself made the second day of my attachment to the 34th Regiment—a " break " of which I was quite unconscious until several months later, when better acquaintance with the officers had brought about a less stiff and formal attitude on their part towards me and some of them reminded me of the incident and admitted to me the amusement which it had caused them at the time.

On my attachment to the regiment, the colonel had, as already mentioned, wanted to give me better food than they themselves had. On my request, however, to receive no special privileges in this respect, the necessary orders had been given to the Mess orderlies to provide me with the same food as the other officers. Now it is the custom in a military Mess in Japan for a large bowl full of rice and a smaller bowl for tea to be placed in front of each officer. When, however, I sat down in my place I found that, instead of this, they had set before me two small bowls for tea (the Japanese tea-cup has no handle), and a kind of wooden tub half full of rice. Thinking that this tub was provided in place of the big bowl of rice set before each of the other officers, and being rather hungry at the time, I sat down to polish off as much of it as I could, eating direct from the tub in the same way that the other officers were eating direct from their big bowls. It was not till several months later that I discovered that the tub from which I had eaten was really the " unexpended portion of the day's ration " for the whole table—the source of supply from which officers could help themselves if they wanted a second helping of rice. The commanding officer, thinking that, as I was a foreigner, I should not be able to eat a whole big bowl of rice like his other officers, had very thoughtfully had this tub placed near me so that I might help myself, the second tea-bowl mentioned being given me to eat from. One can well imagine the amusement caused by this " break " on my part, and it says a lot for their powers of control that not a single officer had even smiled at the time. A somewhat parallel case in a British Mess would be if a strange foreigner, unaccustoned to European customs, began to drink out of the port bottle when it was passed round. One hates to think of the scene that would follow.

To return, however, to the main narrative. December and January passed comparatively uneventfully. The last five days of January were spent in packing and farewells, as I had received orders to report myself on February 1st at the Infantry School at Chiba for a six months' course there.

On January 31st, therefore, I left Shizuoka, a number of officers from the regiment turning up at the station to see me off. It was the third time that I had taken leave of the regiment and, incidentally, my final one, for I did not again return to Shizuoka, much as I should have liked to do so. Though I had left the regiment for good, I did not lose touch with it entirely, for, apart from letters received from officers in it from time to time, amongst others who attended the same six months' course at the Infantry School as myself was my old friend and erstwhile company commander, Captain Kubo, and a better fellow than he it would be hard to find. Small, even for a Japanese, he was an excellent company commander, an indefatigable worker, and very popular with his men, by whom he was greatly esteemed, owing to his having won the most coveted decoration in the Japanese army—the Golden Kite—a decoration given only for personal bravery in action. Always ready to help, he showed me the greatest kindness from first to last, both in his own regiment and at Chiba, and when at last we parted at the close of the course at the Infantry School, he gave me an old Japanese sword as a token of friendship, a form of present which, as previously stated, means more to a Japanese than a mere gift.

As the course did not open till February 2nd, I stayed in Tokyo till the afternoon of the 1st, though I went over to Chiba—some twenty or thirty miles away—on January 31st, to look for some sort of accommodation. Captain Kubo had already gone there with his wife and child, and had made inquiries about rooms for me, so, after giving me lunch, he took me round to see some of which he had heard.

On arriving at the station to catch the train back to Tokyo,

I found a number of officer instructors from the school there and was very much impressed by the friendly way in which they greeted me when they heard who I was. Amongst them were the two school adjutants and the musketry instructor, all three of whom I came to know very well during the next six months, and an excellent trio they were. Possibly their friendly welcome was due to the fact that two of them knew Colonel Kimura, and he had previously written to them about me, for which I felt truly grateful, as an adjutant is always a useful " friend at court."

On the afternoon of February 1st—a Sunday—I set off for a six months' stay at Chiba, and the following morning reported myself at the school, which lies a mile or more outside the town. Before giving an account of my experiences there, a few words of explanation about the school will be necessary.

Without going into any minute details as to the history, organisation, administration, or curriculum of the school, all of which have undergone considerable changes of late years, it should be sufficient to say that, during the period that I was attached, the system was roughly as follows:

Three courses were held each year, a senior course of six months for captains, from February to July inclusive, and two junior courses of four months each for subalterns, the first being held from December to March and the second from April to July—all inclusive. The curriculum for the senior course consisted mainly of tactics, machine-gun training, musketry, and communications—all of them both practical and theoretical—and training in the latest forms of warfare, new weapons, camouflage, carrier-pigeons, trench fighting, etc. The junior courses were split up into two sets each, one specialising in machine-gun training and the other in the service of communications—mainly the field telephone.

Each course consisted of between seventy and eighty officer students, the idea being for each infantry regiment (other than those on service in Siberia) to send one captain per year to the senior course and one subaltern to each of the junior courses, one being sent to the machine-gun set and the other to the communications set. By this means every infantry regiment in Japan obtains one officer per year who has specialised in the latest form of infantry warfare, one who has just been through the latest course in machine-gun work, and one who has specialised in field communications. As every infantry regiment has its own machine-gun company and communications section, the two latter take charge of the training of these two units respectively as soon as they return to their regiments on the completion of the course, and they hold appointments as such until another two subalterns have been through a similar course a year later, when they, in their turn, take over the duties of machine-gun and communications specialists. In the same way, the officer who has completed his six months' senior course generally, on returning to his regiment, becomes a kind of instructor to it, and is expected to impart the knowledge gained at Chiba to the regiment in general and to the junior officers in particular. This position of "guide, philosopher, and friend" he retains until a year later, when he, in turn, is relieved by another captain who has been through a more recent course. The system is a good one, for the courses at the school are very thorough and well run and are well suited to fit officers to act as regimental specialists on returning to their units.

Another point about the Infantry School which should be mentioned here is that, in addition to the actual staff of the school, there is a training regiment attached for the purpose of practising officer students in the handling of troops, and for helping the research section to carry out experiments in new weapons, new formations, etc., and, when practised sufficiently, to demonstrate these experiments to the officer students.

The research section mentioned above consists of a number of officers whose duty it is to investigate the lessons learned from the War, to keep in touch with the latest methods of warfare, to carry out experiments in new forms of tactics, new organisations, new weapons and so on, and to impart the knowledge thus gained to the officer students at the school, who, in their turn, impart it to their regiments on their return on the completion of the course. In time, no doubt, most of the military educational establishments in Japan will have similar research sections in addition to their educational and administrative staffs, but, owing to financial considerations, plans for their formation have not so far been carried into effect.

Owing to the existence of its research section, the Infantry School, in 1920, was certainly the best equipped military educational establishment in Japan, and more advanced in the imparting of knowledge learned from the War than any of the others. The great value placed on infantry by the Japanese is clearly shown thereby. Their cavalry never has been very good, the Japanese, taken as a whole, being very indifferent horsemen, while their artillery tactics, even as taught at the various educational centres, are very much out of date. Their infantry, however, is by far the best branch of their service and the arm in which the Japanese most place their faith. No doubt, therefore, it is due to this fact that the infantry is receiving the chief and first attention in regard to the issue of the most modern arms and equipment, as well as to new methods of training and the modifying of tactics to meet modern conditions of warfare.

The above rough outline of the workings of the Infantry School as it was in 1920 having been given, it should help to explain many of the points to be brought out in the following pages, and we can now, therefore, carry on with the main narrative.[1]

The first day of the course was spent in introductions and in receiving instructions of various kinds. Shortly after 10 a.m. I was taken to one of the lecture halls, where all the officers of the senior course were assembled, together with their instructors. The commandant (Lieut.-General Kawamura) gave an address of welcome, in which he referred to the presence of a British officer in the school, and said

[1] A certain amount of reorganisation has taken place since 1920, but, in the main, the courses have not undergone much alteration.

that, as Japan and Great Britain were allies, he hoped the other officers would do their best to help me. He then went on to explain the main objects of the school.

After the address I was taken to the room set apart for my use, and later on was taken in to see the commandant, who received me in the most friendly way and had a long talk with me.

For the first month or so at the school, nothing of special interest, apart from the work itself, took place. The weather was atrocious, either snow, sleet, or rain falling pretty well every day, turning the roads—poor at the best of times—into regular quagmires and making outdoor training most unpleasant.

Apart from anything else it was interesting running across officers from every part of the Japanese Empire—men from regiments in the extreme north, where the country is snow-bound for six months of the year; from the sub-tropical climate of Formosa; from the garrisons of Korea, Manchuria, and North China; and from all parts of Japan itself—for, as already stated, every infantry regiment, other than those which were on service in Siberia, was represented at the Infantry School. Many of the officers had but recently returned from Siberia, and were full of the state of affairs there, while a few of them had taken part in the Tsingtao campaign and a fair number in the 1904-5 war against Russia. It was interesting living amongst them and hearing the Japanese view in regard to such matters and also to hear their accounts of Japanese military life in the different parts of their empire.

Amongst the officer instructors were several who had studied in Europe, some of them having been out on the French and Italian fronts during the War. It was, therefore, of great interest hearing the impressions formed by them of the fighting powers of the various belligerents from their own observations, one thing in particular which seemed to have impressed most of them being, that the discipline of the British troops appeared to improve in direct ratio to proximity to the front line—a fact which they said was just the reverse in their own army. Another point which impressed them very much in regard to Britain was the way in which men from the upper classes—men from the public schools and universities—had hurried forward to join up the moment war was declared. In Japan, so they maintained, it is the peasantry and uneducated classes who have the most patriotism, while it is becoming more and more difficult to stimulate the nobility and better educated men with military ardour.

In regard to the fighting qualities of the Japanese army, a conversation I had about this time with a subaltern whom I met in the train is perhaps pertinent. I was travelling up to Tokyo and got into conversation with him, and though I was surprised to hear a Japanese officer speak so openly on the subject, and did not altogether agree with what he said, there may be some truth in it; and any way it tends to prove that many thinking Japanese are not quite so confident of themselves as one might imagine.

The subject itself cropped up while discussing the fighting qualities of the Germans. He asked me what I thought of them as fighters, and amongst other things I had replied to the effect that they were very good so long as they felt that they were winning, but that they had not sufficient stamina to pull themselves together again once they were on the run. Much to my surprise he said, " Yes, and that is just where we Japanese fail too. We are too cocksure of ourselves because we have never been defeated, and the result will be that a reaction will set in if we ever run up against a stronger nation than ourselves, and irretrievable disaster may result."

Personally I rather doubt this, for, as I pointed out to him at the time, an army with its discipline as good as that of the Japanese is not likely to " cave in " so easily, especially when both officers and men hold so fast to the idea that death is better than surrender—a precept which, one would imagine, would make them fight on to the bitter end, long after all hope of eventual victory had disappeared. However, he stuck to his point, and whilst admitting that that might be true of the old *Samurai* type—of whom there are still a number left[1]—commercialism, combined with socialistic and democratic teachings, had now such a hold on the people as a whole, especially those from the big towns and cities, that the fine old ideals of former days were rapidly dying out, with the result that, though the old shibboleth of "death rather than surrender" was still spread abroad, it was not to be counted on as anything more than an idle boast by most of those who uttered it, especially if ultimate defeat became a certainty.

By way of showing how seriously these defects were regarded by the military authorities in Japan, he mentioned that General Otani, a former War Minister and the G.O.C.-in-C. of the original Japanese expeditionary force to Siberia, had recently delivered a lecture to a large gathering of military officers and had, amongst other things, upbraided them and the Japanese in general for holding such good opinions of themselves. He pointed out that, although they had beaten both China and Russia, and had never themselves known defeat, it did not mean that they were invincible, and he warned them to guard against overrating their own abilities for fear of reaction setting in if ever they found themselves against an enemy stronger than themselves. Finally, he ended by telling them outright that he considered that the best thing that could happen to Japan would be for her to be defeated in battle, not badly, but just sufficiently to bring her to her senses.

For an officer of such high standing as General Otani to speak out so plainly, it would seem that the military authorities are really anxious as to the future—anxious, not only to combat the weakening effects of the "dangerous thoughts" mentioned earlier on in these pages, but also lest over-confidence should lead to disaster in the event of any future war.

[1] As a matter of fact, when conscription was first adopted in Japan it came as a great surprise to most people when it was proved that the trained conscript from what had hitherto been regarded as the non-fighting classes turned out to be better than most of his *Samurai* countrymen.

One point quoted by the subaltern in support of his argument that the Japanese army might collapse as suddenly as did the Germans, if ever they were got on the run, was, that cases frequently occur in which Japanese business men "cave in" suddenly when faced with misfortune. So long as they are making money, or can bluff their competitors into believing that they are doing well in business, they struggle on, but once they see that their position is hopeless, they throw up the sponge, sink into the depths of despair, and not infrequently commit suicide. Whether or not this is a typical characteristic of the Japanese race as a whole, or whether it can be taken as a parallel case, it is not for me to judge, but from what this particular officer said on this occasion and from what other Japanese officers have told me at different times, it seems true that there is a very considerable feeling of anxiety amongst the military in Japan that even the army may not be entirely free from such failings if ever they should be faced with certain defeat. It is largely owing to this fact that so much attention is paid to raising the *moral* of the army by constant application of *seishin kyōiku*—the "spiritual training" described elsewhere in these pages—in order to eradicate as much as possible any such failings in the character of the Japanese soldier.

CHAPTER XII

INFANTRY SCHOOL ATTACHMENT (*Continued*)

THE conversation narrated in the previous chapter took place on March 10th, 1920, when I was on my way to attend the *Rikugun Kinenbi* celebrations at the Military Club in Tokyo, March 10th being the anniversary of the battle of Mukden and one of the chief military festivals of the year. Before going on to describe it, it may not be out of place to quote from a letter I received a few days later from this same officer, whom I met that day for the first time, the somewhat quaint wording of the letter being typical of the Japanese officer's way of expressing himself on matters relating to his own profession. It so happened that March 10th was also the anniversary of Neuve Chapelle, and I had mentioned this fact to him and that it was the occasion on which I had been knocked out; hence his remarks about our first meeting having been brought about on that particular day "by the divine order," apparently meaning that it was not mere coincidence:

"It was a chance meeting and you are a chance companion if I say literally. But I don't think so, you are one of my good friends. For we first met on the 10th of March, by the divine order, which was the 15th memorial day of our victory at the battle of Mukden, and we have also just the same duty and office; moreover your brilliant deeds in the great conflict, which your limbs explain well, made me take off my hat, and in addition to them your kind heart attracted my love toward you.

But can I be a friend of yours?

Be kind enough to write me when you have spare time.

Hoping you to be my good friend,

Yours sincerely,

Lieut. . . . . .

P.S.—As I have few knowledge in English and English customs, I fear there may be many impolite things toward you. But pardon them all please."

To the British way of thinking, the wording of this letter may seem too flowery and effusive, but one must remember that the Japanese always express themselves in their own written language in a very high-flown and poetical style, and even those who speak good English generally lapse into somewhat literal translations of their own classical style when writing in a foreign language.

The Japanese officer is as keen as mustard on his own profession, and anyone who has been wounded in battle at once goes up in his estimation. But apart from whether one has been wounded or not, the mere fact of belonging to the same profession—" we have just the same duty and office," as he puts it in his letter—and, therefore, having much the same interests in common, is enough to serve as a bond of friendship for a Japanese officer. Any British officer sent to Japan for language study, provided he is keen on his profession, should, therefore, find plenty of opportunity for forming friendships with the Japanese officers he may meet, and it is no doubt largely due to this fact that British Language Officers, almost without exception, return to England, on completion of their tour of duty, with a real liking for their erstwhile brother officers in the Japanese army, in spite of the all too prevalent anti-Japanese feelings which one finds amongst the British and other foreign merchants who only come across Japanese of their own profession.

To return, however, to the military festival of March 10th.

The main event in Tokyo was a display of wrestling at the *Yasukuni Jinja*, the shrine erected to the memory of all those who have fallen in battle. I had received an invitation to attend, owing to the fact that I was attached to the

Infantry School at Chiba, and I found on arriving there that there were no other foreign officers present, though the enclosure was crowded with officers and men of the Tokyo garrison, whilst the central portion was reserved for the heads of the various military departments. Being a foreign guest I was given a seat amongst the latter, and was taken in "tow" by my former brigade commander, whom I found up there, and who was always very friendly to any British officer who came his way, he having, in days gone by, been attached to the Grenadier Guards at Aldershot for a time.

Most of the wrestlers were professional, but there were also some very good bouts between soldiers.

After the wrestling was over we went to the Kaikosha, the Officers' Club, for the special meal provided there annually on the anniversary of Mukden—a simple meal taken standing up round tables and consisting largely of *sake* and roasted pea-nuts, the *menu* on this occasion being the same each year and being, so it is said, symbolic of the simplicity of the rations served out before the great attack on March 10th, 1905.

Marshal Kawamura presided and called for three "*banzai*" for the Emperor, a toast to which response was made with great vigour and enthusiasm. The Marshal has always been a good friend of Great Britain and was a staunch supporter of the Alliance. His exploits during the war with Russia have made his name famous to students of military history. A first-rate fighting man, he has also a certain charm of manner combined with an open, friendly disposition which attracts you towards him from the first.

During the banquet he came across to where I was standing and exchanged a cup of *sake* with me—an act of friendliness which impressed me very much at the time.

That same evening I returned to Chiba, but apart from the ordinary school work nothing of interest took place during the next few days. The hours of work at the school itself were not very strenuous—about four hours in the morning and two in the afternoon—but this did not by any means represent the sum total of work done, as a great deal of home-work was entailed solving problems of various kinds. These problems were chiefly combined schemes, questions on the theory of rifle fire, preparing schemes for field firing, and so on, and it was on the solving of these problems that the officer student was judged. Marks were allotted but were not made known to the officers themselves, and, even at the graduation ceremony at the end of the term, the order in which they had passed was not made known, except that the first man on the list was presented with a gold watch from the Emperor.

This non-publication of graduation lists is universal in the various military educational establishments throughout the country, and is said to be due to the fact that many officers think that they have done better than they really have done and would become despondent were they to learn the truth—a well-known Japanese characteristic. Moreover, it is felt that, if the position of each officer were made known, inter-regimental rivalry and jealousy might be aroused, a thing greatly discouraged in the Japanese army, owing partly to another characteristic of the Japanese nation as a whole, namely, that competition tends to bring out the worst side in the people.[1]

The first-named characteristic—despondency on learning that they have done badly—is sometimes so acute amongst Japanese students that cases of suicide are not by any means unknown. Lafcadio Hearn mentions several instances of this in his books, he having had plenty of opportunities of observing Japanese psychology in this respect owing to his position as a professor in a Japanese university. Other foreign teachers bear out his statements.

This characteristic is closely akin to others already mentioned, such as despondency arising from being punished, or from having done something, the supposed disgrace of which can only be wiped out by death. The Japanese take

[1] This characteristic partly helps to explain the almost universal unpopularity of the Japanese in business, especially abroad. Competition arises and they are therefore seen at their worst.

things to heart very much more than the average European. This being so, it is not to be wondered at that care has to be taken even in such comparatively small matters as the publication of graduation lists.

The Japanese officer is, however, a very hard-working individual and, as a rule, takes his profession very much more seriously than his British counterpart; in fact, from personal observations—and most other erstwhile British Language Officers agree on this point—he is inclined to take it too seriously to the exclusion of all else. As a result it comes about that Japanese army officers are practically a caste of their own and normally mix but little with their civilian fellow nationals.

Possibly the British officer is inclined to spend too little time at his work, but at any rate he generally works his hardest when he is doing so and derives much benefit from it. The Japanese officer, on the other hand, works practically all day and, at military institutions such as the Infantry School, very often all night as well. Officer students at Chiba, for instance, were working in their houses at tactical and other problems till past midnight most evenings and sometimes till 3 or even 4 a.m. the following morning. As often as not they had to work on Sundays as well.

It is doubtful whether continuous work of this kind benefits a man more than if he worked fewer hours and had more time to digest what he has learned. Many Japanese officers, especially those who have been to Europe, admit this and agree that the system of cramming, in force both in the military and civil educational establishments throughout Japan, requires certain modifications.

The next event of interest, outside the ordinary routine work which took place at the Infantry School, was a *Shinto* ceremony held in honour of seventeen men of the training regiment who had died during a recent outbreak of influenza, a kind of thanksgiving service being held as a result of the epidemic having been stamped out.

The day selected for the *Shokonsha*—the feast of the dead —was Sunday, March 21st, the proceedings starting at

10 a.m. with a *Shinto* Mass for the souls of those who had died.

The ceremony took place in the open, a kind of altar having been erected inside a *marquee*, officers being lined up on the right and the regiment in front, whilst the relatives of the dead men were to the left.

The ceremony opened with Lieut.-General Kawamura (Commandant) and two or three staff officers advancing towards the altar. Two priests in ancient *Shinto* ceremonial costume then recited prayers before the altar, after which the elder of the two, a venerable old man with a long grey beard, blessed the Commandant by waving a branch over his head. He then did likewise to the officers and men in batches, after which he handed a twig of laurels to the Commandant, who advanced, hat in hand, and after bowing and reading out the names of the dead men, laid it upon the altar. This ceremony was repeated by the regimental commander, battalion commanders, and company commanders of the dead men, and also by their relatives in turn, each one receiving a branch of laurels and laying it on the altar. The whole ceremony lasted about thirty or forty minutes and was very impressive in its simplicity.

After the religious part of the ceremony was over, the Commandant gave an address to the officers and N.C.O.'s who formed up into three sides of a square. After thanking them for their help in getting the outbreak under control, he exhorted them always to think of others before themselves and to help them, and he warned them of the present tendency to think only of oneself and of how to get rich. He also pointed out that, as the men had died whilst serving their country, they must be considered as very fortunate, and it was therefore a time for rejoicing and not for mourning.

The narrow-minded, so-called Christian may look down on the Japanese and other non-Christian nations as, to quote Kipling's words, "pore benighted 'eathen," yet there was not a thing that took place in the religious ceremony that day, nor in the subsequent address given by the Commandant, which was not similar to Christianity in sentiment, and the simplicity of the whole proceedings struck one as extraordinarily impressive.

The Buddhist ceremony is certainly more spectacular than the Shinto, just as the Buddhist temple is very much finer in appearance than the Shinto shrine; but the keynote of Shintoism is simplicity, whilst Buddhism is rather the reverse, and the former appeals to one more than the latter.

After the Commandant's address, a very good imitation fight took place, two lines of infantry with machine-guns, starting about four hundred yards apart, advancing in extended order towards each other. When within fifty yards or so of each other, both lines ran forward to the assault, or rather men in bayonet-fighting kit, who had followed just in rear of each line, did so. Each of these men had a thick ration biscuit tied on over his heart, and after two or three minutes' hand-to-hand fighting, the side which had lost the most biscuits was declared the loser, each man of the winning side receiving an orange by way of a prize!

The rest of the day was given up to inter-company tugs-of-war and wrestling, followed by theatricals and a variety show, with conjuring, knock-about turns, and trick bicycling, which were all very good. The last was done by a reservist of the training regiment, the man performing extraordinary balancing feats both on a two-wheeled and on a one-wheeled machine.

The British "Tommy," at gymkhanas of this kind, generally likes to dress himself up in weird and wonderful attire, and to select a special name for himself when entering for a competition; his Japanese *confrère* likes to do the same. Those entering for the wrestling competition all had names for themselves, amongst them being *Doku Gasu* (Poison Gas), *Dai Tanku* (Big Tank), *Toyo Chapurin* (the Eastern Charlie Chaplin), *Wiruson Daitōryo* (President Wilson), and *Demokurashi* (Democracy).

It is probably unnecessary to add, in view of the last two *noms de plumes*, that President Wilson and his views on democracy were not at that time regarded very seriously by the Japanese *heitai san* ("Tommy"), who treated both him and his somewhat idealistic schemes as something of a joke. The League of Nations likewise came in for its fair share of ridicule, and at a former gymkhana, to which I had been, one of the competitions had been announced by its Japanese title of *Kokusai Remmei*.

A religious ceremony—especially a Mass for the dead—to be followed by wrestling, theatricals, etc., may sound rather a strange mixture, but the idea, as already stated, was that the men had died whilst serving their Emperor, so that their deaths were a matter for rejoicing rather than for sadness. No doubt the gymkhana was also carried out partly by way of cheering up the comrades of the dead men, in order to keep them from brooding over their loss, in much the same way as in the case of our own army, when lively tunes are played by the regimental band when returning from a military funeral.

The next event of importance at the Infantry School after the *Shokonsha* was the graduation ceremony held on March 30th in connection with the termination of the junior course which had begun the previous December.

On such occasions it is the custom for the officer who passes out first on the list to receive a gold watch from the Emperor. In the case of this particular junior course two gold watches were given, one to the subaltern who passed out top of the machine-gun set, and the other to the best officer of the communications set.

General Otani, Director of the Military Education Bureau, carried out the presentation on behalf of His Imperial Majesty, and, after the main ceremony was over, various displays of machine-gun and communication work were to have been given, but, owing to heavy rain, that part of the programme had to be cancelled. Proceedings, therefore, ended with a farewell lunch, at which, as usual on such occasions, the main item was the imbibing of much *sake*, everyone exchanging cups of it with the others in the Japanese manner. Meals of this kind are always very cheery affairs in Japan, but it is just as well to have a fairly strong head for alcohol if you wish to walk straight at the end of it.

The new junior course opened a day or two later and ended in July at the same time as the senior course, so that the next graduation ceremony was a combined affair—both captains and subalterns. Before, however, that took place, and my attachment to the Infantry School came to an end, several other things worth noting occurred.

CHAPTER XIII

INFANTRY SCHOOL ATTACHMENT (*Continued*)

SIX months' attachment to an infantry regiment had afforded an opportunity of learning something about the training of an infantry regimental officer, and an attachment to the Infantry School at Chiba helped still further in this direction.

There are, however, a dozen or more military educational establishments in Japan, and I asked the Military Attaché if he could arrange for me to carry out an inspection of the more important military schools and colleges during the period of my attachment at Chiba, a scheme with which he readily fell in, as he himself also wanted to see them. The Japanese military authorities having been requested to afford the necessary facilities, a programme of visits was fixed up for the end of April, the first on the list being the School of Heavy Artillery at Uraga, a suburb of Yokosuka. This visit was to take place on April 21st, but, as the annual Cherry Garden Party was to be held on the previous day, I came up to Tokyo on the 20th in order to attend it.

The Emperor himself was unable to be present, but the Empress and Crown Prince, together with most of the other members of the Imperial Family, were there, plus, of course, all the members of the *Corps Diplomatique* and the chief naval, military and civil officers—about three thousand in all. The garden party was held in the grounds of the Shinjuku Palace on the outskirts of Tokyo, numbers of cherry trees being in these grounds, all of them at that time in full bloom.

The visits to the military educational establishments were spread over a period of about a week, during which the

Military Attaché very kindly put me up at his house in Tokyo. The schools visited during that time were as follows: Heavy Artillery School at Uraga on the 21st, Cavalry School at Narashino on the 22nd, School of Artillery and Engineers and the School of Physical Training on the 23rd (both in Tokyo), Staff College and Officers' School on the 26th (both in Tokyo). At each of these institutions we were received with the greatest courtesy by the respective commandants, and were shown round and given explanations on the methods of instruction, the objects and organisation of the school, and other particulars of that nature, so that, by the end of it all, one had a fairly accurate working knowledge of the methods employed in the Japanese army for training officers.

Without going into details, it may be of interest to some who are reading these pages if a rough outline, in regard to the training of Japanese officers, is given at this point.

The two main sources from which officers are recruited are the so-called Middle Schools and the Military Preparatory Schools. Candidates from the former have to serve in the ranks for a year and those from the latter serve six months before entering the Officers' School—an institution similar to our Sandhurst and Woolwich combined—cadets of all arms of the service being trained there. After eighteen months at the Officers' School, where all the cadets rank as sergeants, they return to the units in which they have previously served in the ranks and, for the first six months, hold the rank of Special Sergeant-Major and perform the duties of Second-Lieutenants.[1] If, at the end of this period, he is approved of by the officers of the unit—a special meeting being held to decide this point—the young cadet is granted a commission as Second-Lieutenant. Subsequent rises in rank depend on his fitness for promotion and whether or not there is a vacancy. There are no such things as promotion examinations in the Japanese army.

[1] This system has recently (1921) been modified. Candidates from both sources now enter the Officers' School direct and do a two years' preparatory course before entering the ranks. After six months in the ranks they return for a further period of two years at the Officers' School for an advanced course and then pass out as Special Sergeant-Majors.

Those who have passed through the Staff College receive accelerated promotion, and, for this reason amongst others, there is great competition amongst junior officers to enter that institution, only officers under the rank of captain at the time of entry being admitted. A qualifying examination, followed by a competitive one, has to be passed in order to enter the Staff College, and after three years there, student officers, on graduating, return to their units for a short period and are then, as a rule, given staff appointments, or sent to Europe or America for special military study.

The Infantry School, the Cavalry School, the School of Artillery and Engineers, and other such institutions are, as their names imply, military establishments to which officers are sent in order to specialise in matters connected with their own particular branch of the service.

The above is only a very brief outline of the Japanese system of training commissioned officers, as these pages are not meant to be a military treatise but are merely written with the view of giving a rough idea of the daily life of the Japanese army as seen by an attached British officer. The subject has been lightly touched on here owing to its bearing on the visits to the military educational establishments mentioned in this chapter.

In regard to these visits, it may have been noticed that none took place on the 24th and 25th. As there was nothing arranged for those two days, and as the officer students of the senior course at the Infantry School had, in the meantime, gone off to Mishima [1] for a week or so to carry out certain tactical schemes in that neighbourhood, I left Tokyo shortly after 5 p.m. on the 23rd, and went off to join them there.

On arriving there some five hours later I found a room had been reserved for me at a local inn where the headquarter staff was also billeted.

The following morning a tactical reconnaissance scheme was carried out, but, as there was nothing special to be learned from it, I only attended it for two or three hours

[1] About eighty or ninety miles south-west of Tokyo at the head of the Izu Peninsula.

and then set off about 11 a.m. with two of the officer instructors by light railway for Nanjo, in the Izu Peninsula, and spent the rest of the day going round the various sights of the neighbourhood. Amongst these was a temple over a thousand years old in which were two wooden Buddhas, said to have been carved by the famous Buddhist saint, Kobo Daishi, about eight hundred years ago. They are generally kept locked away, but as a great favour the old priestess, who appeared to be in charge of the place, unlocked them for us to see. A curious thing about one of them was that it had its right eye made of what looked like solid gold, which gave out a curious glitter.

As there was no proper inn in the neighbourhood we had our midday meal in a small tea-house, the food consisting of a raw egg each, plain dry bread, and sugar, this apparently being the local idea of European food. Personally I would have preferred Japanese food, but as it was specially ordered to meet my foreign taste, I did not like to hurt the feelings of our hosts by commenting adversely on what they, in the kindness of their hearts, had served up for my benefit.

After this repast we went off to see the remains of an old arsenal built by a man named Egawa at the time of Commodore Perry's famous expedition to Japan, this arsenal being constructed in order to make guns with which to drive out the "hairy barbarians," who had dared to come in their black ships to defile " the land of the gods." It consisted of four large furnaces with tall chimney-stacks all made of brick. Some of the cannon turned out by the arsenal were there also—short, stumpy, brass muzzle-loaders—a strange contrast to the mighty guns turned out at Yokosuka, Muroran, and Osaka at the present time.

No doubt the products of Egawa's enterprise were looked on with awe and admiration at the time that they were made, but the Japanese soon learned from bitter experience at Shimonoseki, Kagoshima, and elsewhere, that ordnance of that type was no match for those death-dealing machines, which not only out-ranged them every time, but even spat out elongated cannon-balls which exploded on hitting anything.[1] It was something quite new to them and it appealed to their imagination, so much so that they lost but little time in sending men off to England and elsewhere to learn the secrets of their death-dealing properties. The success in mastering these secrets attending these men, who set forth into the—for them—unknown world beyond, but fifty or sixty years ago, is seen by the mighty weapons turned out by Japanese arsenals at the present day.

On getting back to our quarters at Mishima that evening I had something to eat, and then set off, shortly after 7 p.m., to join another party of officer students who were billeted at Yoshiwara, a village at the base of Mount Fuji (south side). The horse tramway connecting it with Suzukawa, the nearest railway station, was a very primitive affair. "The horse must have been one of the original lot landed from the Ark, while the tram looked as if Noah, or one of his fellow passengers, had constructed it in his spare time when not employed in navigating the vessel. An absolute relic of prehistoric days."

A sergeant, a Kyūshū man of the best type, had been sent to accompany me from Mishima. The native of Kyūshū has a great reputation as a fighting man and, from my own experience of him, he is certainly one of the best types of Japanese. Not, on first acquaintance, as friendly disposed as others of his countrymen, his friendship, once you have gained it, is generally more sincere, and, added to this, he seems to have more of the ancient *Samurai* spirit about him. This may be imagination on my part, but it is the impression gained as the result of two trips in Kyūshū and from meeting with numerous officers and others of Kyūshū families from time to time.

There is nothing special to mention about the trip to Yoshiwara, and the following day, after attending a ground

[1] An old Japanese gentleman whom I met in London after my return from Japan and who, as a young man, had been in Kagoshima at the time of the bombardment, told me that it was the ability of these "elongated cannon-balls" to burst that had impressed him and had gained his respect for the "hairy barbarian" so much that he had at once gone off to Yokohama—a long and arduous journey in those days—in order to try and learn from them.

reconnaissance and tactical scheme in the morning, I had to set off back to Tokyo. One amusing incident is, however, perhaps worth recording. The village of Yoshiwara was all decked out in gala attire, and, on inquiring the reason for this, it turned out to be that they were celebrating the anniversary of the removal of the police-court from one part of the town to another—a somewhat novel form of festivity.

The following day (26th) was spent, as already mentioned, in visits to the Staff College and the Officers' School, and on the 27th I returned to Chiba, after a most interesting week of inspecting military educational establishments.

The next three days were spent in carrying out ordinary routine work at the Infantry School. On the 30th, however, there was a whole holiday for the *Yasukuni-Jinja* festival —the festival to the souls of those killed in battle—so I went off for the day with Withers [1] to the southern end of the Boshu Peninsula, an interesting trip, but one which need not be described here. For the next fortnight the work at the Infantry School kept me fully occupied, one or two quite realistic exhibitions of trench-warfare being included in the programme.

On May 13th I went off for a few days' leave up to Karuizawa, a favourite summer resort for foreigners, though practically deserted at that time of year. Situated some 3300 feet above sea-level in Central Japan and lying in a hollow ringed all round by hills, it has few rivals for anyone keen on walking and hill climbing, and the scenery all round is magnificent. One's first impressions of it, however, on a dull day, such as it was when I arrived, cannot but be of a depressing nature if it happens to be the "off season," as most of the houses are empty all the year round, except

[1] Lieut. Arthur Withers, R.A., was a Language Officer who had recently come to Chiba to be attached to the Field Artillery School of Gunnery. Some two years later, in February 1922, he was taken ill with appendicitis whilst on his way back to England on completion of his period of service in Japan and had to be landed at Singapore, where he died in hospital—a great loss to his many friends in Japan and elsewhere.

during the summer. This feeling of depression is not exactly dispelled when you come across:

(*a*) The remnants of some houses which you learn were "washed away in last year's flood."

(*b*) Curious little pebbles dotted about which, on inquiry, turn out to be "lava which rained down on the village a few months ago when Asama[1] erupted."

(*c*) A particularly desolate-looking house standing in a patch of dark fir trees, and you are told, "Oh yes, a missionary and his wife were murdered there the summer before last by an armed robber."

(*d*) A house with a large crack down one side in regard to which you elicit the cheerful information that "That was done by the last earthquake or else one of the typhoons last summer. I forget which."

Having in the space of but five or ten minutes come across all these little examples of "what Karuizawa can do," one can hardly be blamed for recording the fact that the first impressions received on a dull day out of season are anything but cheerful. However, one soon finds that floods, volcanic eruptions, murders, earthquakes, typhoons and other pleasantries of a like nature are not quite the daily lot of this mountain resort, and it is with feelings of real regret that the last day of one's leave arrives and, with it, the necessity of leaving for work in lower altitudes.

Before closing this chapter, it may not be out of place to touch here on a subject which has hardly been mentioned hitherto. It will very possibly have been noticed that, although several up-country trips have been described, little or nothing has been said as to sport in Japan, a subject which, to the average British officer, is an all-absorbing topic.

Sport in its true sense is, unfortunately, somewhat limited in Japan. The Language Officer who goes to that country is apt to be disappointed if he expects to get polo, hunting, or shooting, for the two former are entirely unobtainable,

[1] Mt. Asama is an active volcano about 8000 ft. in height, a few miles to the north-west of Karuizawa.

whilst opportunities for the latter are rapidly diminishing, and one has to go far afield to obtain any.[1] In this respect the officer sent to China for language study certainly has the advantage. In Peking, for instance, ponies can be bought for a comparatively small sum and trained for polo or for " hacking," according to one's wishes. Everyone there keeps one or more ponies as a matter of course, and, though neither the polo nor the hunting is of a very high standard, both are obtainable, the latter in the form of a " drag " which meets from time to time during the winter months. Similarly, excellent shooting is to be had without much difficulty—a very different state of things from that existing in Japan.

In spite of the absence of this, however, the Language Officer in Japan need not lack means of exercise. Excellent ski-ing and skating are to be had in winter if he knows where to look for it, while good fly-fishing can be obtained in the summer months in the Hokkaido and elsewhere.[2] Football —both rugger and soccer—and cricket are played at Yokohama and Kobe, whilst tennis and golf are to be had in various parts of the country. The so-called Japanese Alps afford great scope for the keen mountaineer, whilst, failing all else, one can always fall back on walking as a means of exercise, a pastime to which Japan is eminently suited. In my own case, for instance, I was, owing to my lameness, debarred from entering into most of the forms of sports enumerated above, but I nevertheless made up for it as much as possible by " hiking it " on foot through the length and breadth of the country and thoroughly enjoyed every bit of it, and, much as I should have liked a game of rugger at times, or to have been able to join in other games of an equally active nature, I never grew tired of the excellent

[1] The Japanese have a form of polo of their own, but it is only played by members of the Imperial Household. Chamberlain describes it in his *Things Japanese*, pages 384-388. Though hunting is unobtainable, one can get riding in many places, though the mounts are not, as a rule, much good, and opportunities for a gallop or canter are few and far between.

[2] Ski-ing forms part of the training of the Japanese soldier in some of the regiments.

opportunities for seeing the country afforded by walking trips, even though unable to walk as many miles per day as I could have wished.

In an island country like Japan, a country, moreover, of mountains and lakes, it goes without saying that plenty of opportunities for both bathing and boating are afforded, both sea and lake, and the keen yachtsman need experience no difficulty in finding the necessary water on which to sail.

Whilst carrying out a period of attachment with a Japanese military unit, a Language Officer may find himself far removed from any possibility of golf, tennis, or any other form of European sport. Under such circumstances he might well do worse than take up Japanese fencing and *jujutsu*, both of which are excellent forms of exercise, and are, moreover, the normal forms of recreation amongst Japanese officers. Not only will he thereby obtain exercise and amusement for himself, but it will afford him the best possible opportunity for coming to know his brother officers and, through friendly competition with them, gaining their friendship and respect.

Another form of exercise in which many Japanese officers are interested is archery, butts for which are to be found in most, if not all, towns throughout Japan.

From what has been written above on the subject of games and sport in general, it will be seen that, even without his polo, hunting or shooting, a British officer, sent to Japan on the so-called Language Course, ought to find plenty of scope for good, healthy exercise and enjoyment, and if he leaves the country "grousing" at the lack thereof he can only have himself to blame.

CHAPTER XIV

INFANTRY SCHOOL ATTACHMENT (*Continued*)

A FEW days after my return to Chiba from Karuizawa, I went up to Tokyo to see the wrestling at the Kokugikan, General Tanaka, who was at that time Minister for War, having issued invitations to the foreign attachés and others to go there as his guests.

The Kokugikan is a fine large wrestling hall with accommodation for some ten thousand spectators, and it is there that the bi-annual wrestling championships for the whole of Japan are held in January and May of each year. The present building had only been opened in January of that year (1920), the original one having been burned down in the late autumn of 1917, whilst its successor had collapsed when nearing completion.

As a short account of Japanese wrestling has already been given, no more need be said about the performances on this particular occasion.

The following day (May 21st) the officers of the senior course at the Infantry School went into camp at Shimoshizuhara to carry out ten days' field-firing exercises, our quarters during that time consisting of a wooden hut encampment on the moors some five or six miles from Chiba. As usual on Japanese manœuvres, officers and men had the same kind of food—three large bowls of mixed rice and barley each per day, with boiled *daikon*, sea-weed, cuttle-fish or other similar " delicacies " to help it down. The midday meal of cold barley and rice with its trimmings we usually took with us and ate in the open in the interval provided for that purpose. *Reveillé* sounded at 5 a.m., and we were out on the moors most days till 5 or 6 p.m., carrying out field-firing schemes with ball ammunition, so that one always felt as fit as the proverbial flea and was ready to eat anything.

The school authorities had at first wanted me to put up at an inn close by, but after some persuasion they saw that I really preferred to live in camp along with the other officers, and, taken all round and apart from the food, one could not have asked for anything better.

The officer students were divided into two sets, one long hut being allotted to each set with five or six officers to a room. Another hut was reserved for the headquarters staff consisting of instructors, administrative staff, and headquarters of the battalion of the training regiment which was lent for the carrying out of the field-firing exercises. Each officer of the headquarters staff had a room to himself in which was a table and chair, whilst a straw mattress on the floor served for bedding.

Some of the officers formed a sort of Mess among themselves and for the evening meal got in extra things from the canteen. I was invited to join them, and for the first two nights they refused to let me pay anything towards these extras, and it was only when I insisted on paying my proper share or else having my meals by myself that they very reluctantly, even then, consented to let me do so.

The Shimoshizu-hara camp broke up on the evening of May 29th, when we returned to Chiba, and some three weeks later the officers of the senior course set off on a four days' tactical scheme. The weather, as is usual at that time of year, was atrocious, and half our time seemed to be spent in emulating the antics of a mountain goat by clambering about steep and slippery hills with only bare suspicions of paths, the rain having effectually blotted out nearly all trace of them.

The set to which I was attached, consisting of twelve other officers, was provided with quarters in the village of Tōgane at one of the local inns, where we were billeted in a sort of dormitory. Both evenings we were at Tōgane they called in *geisha*, and became very full of *joie de vivre* on the good wine of the country.

The Japanese officer is a curious mixture in that way. At ordinary times he is generally very reserved and serious, and thinks of nothing but his work, but give him a couple of *geisha* to sing to him, and a little *sake* with which to wet his throat, and it is hard to believe that he is the same man. He throws off all his reserve, appears to forget that he ever had such a thing as work, bursts forth into singing and dancing, and becomes as cheery a soul as you could meet anywhere. Probably none of the twelve officers in the set were less than thirty-five years of age, but, by the way in which they acted, they might well have been a set of young subalterns on a specially cheery guest-night; and it is always the same. It is, of course, characteristic of the Japanese in general to throw aside all their troubles when out to enjoy themselves, and to enter heart and soul into their pleasures.

On the third day we were out from about 7 a.m. to about 4 p.m. in pouring rain most of the time. Arrangements had been made for us to have our midday meal at the house of a local Japanese, and one was again struck by the extraordinary hospitality shown. Here we were, fourteen in all, wet and muddy, yet we had the whole house opened to us. In true Japanese style we sprawled about on the floor, the majority of us discarding the most of our clothing for coolness' sake. Whilst we lay stretched on the *tatami* with our maps spread out in front of us, working out plans, etc., the good people of the house looked on, squatting round their *hibachi* (no weather is too hot for that to a Japanese), and when we had finished, they supplied us with *sake*, raw fish, raw eggs (great delicacies from the Japanese point of view), and food of all kinds *ad lib.*, everything being free and *gratis*.

That evening we had another very cheery *geisha* dinner, and next day were up by 4.30 a.m. in order to work out plans before leaving by the 7.40 a.m. train for Hamano, where we arrived at about 10 a.m. Up to that time we had been working in sets of a dozen or so (tactical schemes without troops), each set being quartered in different villages; but on this, the final day, all the officers met at Hamano and carried out the same scheme, operations ending about 2 p.m., when we all—eighty or ninety of us—adjourned to the "Maruya," a local inn where food had been prepared for us, after which we left for Chiba by train about 4 p.m.

Some two or three days after our return to Chiba from Hamano, the Crown Prince of Roumania, who was at that time on an official visit to Japan, paid a visit to the school. He seemed greatly surprised to find a British officer there, and I personally was equally surprised when he sent for me and greeted me in the most friendly manner with the words, "What on earth are you, a British officer, doing here?" Throughout his inspection of the school, I had noticed that he was speaking in French and my knowledge of that language is somewhat weak. When, therefore, he sent for me, I at once tried to rack my brains for some suitable remarks in French and had just concocted one which seemed fitted to the occasion, when he came forward with a broad smile on his face and, shaking me warmly by the hand, made the remark just quoted.

A few days after Prince Carol's visit to the school, the officers of the senior course went into camp at Narashino in order to carry out regimental training for a week. The camp, as usual in Japan, where tents are but seldom used, consisted of a number of wooden huts and was originally erected at the time of the Russo-Japanese War for the internment of Russian prisoners. Subsequently it had served the same purpose for the German prisoners from Tsingtao, who had but recently left it.

The nearest railway station was at Tsudanuma, some four or five miles away. We had been told that it was possible to charter cars from there as far as Okubo, a village about a mile from camp. As, however, there were none to be had, we had to content ourselves with a couple of *garagara basha*,[1]

[1] *Garagara* really means "rumbling" or "clattering," and anyone who has ever been in a *garagara basha* ("clattering carriage") will not need to ask how it received this name!

eight of us per vehicle, wedged into a space which might possibly seat two with a moderate degree of comfort. The roads were awful and the *basha* boasted of no springs, and there was only one miserable, half-starved horse to each one. The road on from Okubo was impassable for wheeled traffic of any kind, so we had to walk the remaining mile or so.

It was a Sunday when we went into camp, and on the Monday, Tuesday, and Wednesday we were out all day on the moors from 7 a.m. to 4 or 5 p.m. carrying out field exercises. Several officers of the Guards Cavalry Regiment and the 1st Infantry Regiment were present each day as onlookers, both these regiments being in camp close by.

The training carried out included schemes in both attack and defence, but owing to a full regiment not being available, only one whole battalion was employed, the remaining two being represented by skeleton forces. Two schemes were carried out each day, the regimental commander, the battalion commander, and the company commanders all being officers of the senior course, while the platoons were commanded by subalterns of the training regiment, the N.C.O's and men also being supplied from the same source. Cavalry co-operated in most of the schemes, and a couple of dazzle-painted whippets were used once or twice ; but artillery co-operation was entirely imaginary, except that, in each scheme, an officer was detailed as artillery commander, and had to select artillery positions and shew them by means of flags. Shell bursts were always depicted by means of smoke puffs fired from rifles in positions selected by the umpires.

Each officer had to prepare a scheme, but no officer was allowed to carry out his own one. Instead, he acted as one of the umpires (the others being instructors) and had to give out his criticisms after the scheme had been carried out.

As usual in the Japanese army, these criticisms lasted very much longer than the actual operations themselves, a point which always strikes the foreign observer and, moreover, a point which it would seem advisable to rectify, as these criticisms are apt to defeat their end if they are too long, as most of the hearers lose their interest long before they are finished.

Officers not taking part in the schemes had to attend as onlookers and were required to write out and hand in notes on (1) How they thought the scheme should be carried out (done prior to the carrying out of the scheme), and (2) Their criticism on the way in which it was carried out (done after its completion). This method of instruction, known as *kengaku* ("learning by seeing"), is, it may be said, one that is much employed in the Japanese army and one from which great benefit is undoubtedly derived.

Though the rest of the senior course stayed on at Narashino for a week, I personally left after three days in order to travel up to Sendai to see the machine-gun class of the junior course carrying out machine-gun field-firing at Ojoji-hara, a camp near by.

Leaving Narashino on the afternoon of the 7th, I rode to Makuhari station, some three or four miles away, on one of the machine-gun pack-ponies which had been lent me for the purpose, while my orderly and one of the machine-gun men followed on foot, the former to carry such kit as I had with me, the latter to take the pony back after I had finished with it. While passing through a small village on the way, several of the villagers began jeering at me and calling out, "*Doitsu no horyo*" ("German prisoner"), apparently thinking that I was one of the former inmates of the camp, and that the two soldiers with me were my guard taking me for an airing. The opportunity was too good to be missed, so I turned round and let off a string of the best coolie Japanese of which I could think, telling them that I was British and giving them my opinions of Brother Bosche. My unexpected eloquence seemed to surprise them somewhat, and they apologised profusely for their error.

After a very hot night spent in the train, we reached

Kouda, some twenty or thirty miles north of Sendai, about 7.30 next morning, and from there went on by another train to Nakaniida, the nearest station to Ojoji-hara.

The country up there was very pretty, the camp itself being in a patch of fine large cryptomerias a hundred and twenty feet or so in height, bordering on wild open moors lying at the foot of the central mountain range which runs more or less through the whole length of Japan from north to south. This part of the country is more or less snow-bound for five to six months in the year, the snow on these moors during that time being six or seven feet deep. The hills all round are fine and rugged, with peaks rising eight thousand to nine thousand feet, many of them still having patches of snow on them even at the time I went there in July. The moors themselves were looking very pretty just then, with masses of wild flowers of every kind and shade in full bloom, the purple iris being especially fine.

I was met at the station by a sergeant sent down for that purpose, and we at once set off by *kuruma* for the camp, which lay some six or seven miles away.

It was the best hut encampment that I had seen in Japan and really belonged to the Sendai (2nd) Division, the regiments of which go out there for field firing, battalion training, etc. There was even a special house for the divisional commander, a very pretty little place standing in a garden of its own, and, as the general was not up there at the time, I was given the use of it.

The three or four days spent at this camp do not call for any special remarks. Most of the time was spent out on the moors watching various machine-gun field-firing tests of the usual type, while in the evening, groups of officers would foregather and talk over matters of general interest. As usual I was treated with the greatest kindness and consideration by everyone, both instructors and officer students doing their best to make me feel one with themselves.

On the morning of the 12th, I bade them farewell, and, after spending the day seeing the beauties of Matsushima, one of the three famous " beauty spots " of Japan,[1] returned to Tokyo from Sendai by the night express and from there back to Chiba.

The next week or so was spent in visits to places of military interest and a succession of farewell dinners prior to the ending of the course on July 21st. Included in the former were visits to the Tokyo Arsenal, the Ordnance Depôt at Otsuka, the Army Provision Depôt at Eitai-bashi, and the Clothing Depôt at Akabane. It was interesting seeing over all these places, at each of which short lectures describing their uses, their organization, the method of running them, and so on, were delivered. The only jarring note was the heat, which averaged 90 degrees or more in the shade, the main difficulty being to find the shade.

On July 21st the graduation ceremony for both the senior and the junior courses took place, gold watches from the Emperor being presented by one of his A.D.C's to the two best in the former and the best in the machine-gun course and communications course respectively in the latter. General Otani, who was then Chief of the Military Educational Department, and a number of other officers, in addition to those of the school itself, attended and a few short speeches were made.

On the completion of the ceremony, a farewell luncheon took place with the customary exchange of "liquor" amongst the various officers present, everyone consequently being in the best of form. Having said good-bye to all those at the school, I carried out a round of visits to the local officials and, on arriving back at my house, found two or three farewell presents awaiting me, one of these being a very fine old Japanese sword accompanied by a letter from its donor—one of the officers at the school—together with his photograph. The letter, which I have by me now and which is written in English, reads as follows : " Sir, I wish to present you this sword. This is made by Rai Kindo, famous sword maker, about three hundred years ago. The Japanese

[1] Itsukushima (Miyajima) and Amano Hashidate are the other two classed as such.

sword represents 'Bushido.' [1] Please receive this as memorial and honoured respects."

One could not help being struck by the extraordinary kindness of this officer and others at the school, for, in addition to being given a number of farewell dinners, I received a dozen or more farewell gifts during those last few days, including two other old Japanese swords, perfectly plain but beautiful bits of steel, meant for use rather than for ornament—truly representative, in fact, of the whole spirit of the Japanese army.

Though the majority of the officer students left to rejoin their units the same day as the graduation ceremony took place, the permanent members of the school staff stayed on. Accordingly, on the following day, General Kawamura, the Commandant, invited a dozen or so of the more senior of the instructors and myself to go with him for an outing, two Chinese officers who had been attached to the school being also included in the party.[2] Setting off shortly after breakfast, we went by train to Yawatajuku, a village on the coast some ten or twelve miles away, and going to one of the local inns, we were each provided with a *yukata* [3] into which we changed. This having been done, we set off to sea in a large *sampan* which had been provided for us and spent the rest of the day cruising about and fishing.

The method of fishing in these parts is rather curious, the sea all along that part of the coast being so shallow that you can wade out two or three miles with the water barely above the knees. On the outward journey the boat was propelled by means of punt-poles, but two or three times we ran on to sand-banks, on which occasions we all, including

[1] Literally "The Way of the Warrior," corresponding more or less to the old English rules of chivalry. By this expression he means to convey the fact that he has selected to send a sword as a gift, as it implies a special compliment to the recipient.

[2] Most, if not all, of the military educational establishments in Japan admit a certain number of Chinese officers as students. In the case of the *Shikwan Gakkō* or Officers' School there is one whole company of Chinese cadets.

[3] A *yukata* is one of the numerous forms of *kimono* and one which is always provided as a matter of course to each guest at an inn.

the general himself, had to get out and push her into deeper water.

Some two or three miles out were forms of mazes made of light bamboo sticks. The fish enter these mazes and then forget the way out, and the fishermen come down with a sort of shrimping net and scoop them out. On this occasion we acted as the fishermen, and it was really a splendid sight to see the general, together with normally rather dignified colonels and majors, clad in *yukata* tucked up round their waists, paddling about in the water, scooping up the fish with as much zest and enjoyment as a party of schoolboys at the seaside! Unfortunately I had forgotten to take my camera with me, so was unable to obtain a photographic record of what would have done justice to the Kodak "Happy Moment Competition" of former days.

We consumed some of the fish (raw), washed down with beer, on the way home, and, on reaching the inn at Yawata, had a *geisha* dinner at which everyone waxed merry.

As already mentioned in these pages, the Japanese officer does not believe in doing things by halves. When he works he concentrates his whole attention on the work in hand, and similarly, when he plays he gives himself up entirely to the enjoyment of the moment, saying to himself, metaphorically, "To blazes with work and worry. We had enough of that yesterday, and we shall have it again to-morrow; meantime let us enjoy ourselves whilst we may."

This day's outing with General Kawamura was a typical example of this principle and showed that it held good not only in the case of the junior ranks but also in that of the senior officer with high official standing, and I came in for a further example of it when, two days later, I took part in the annual end of term dinner given by the staff of the Infantry School at the chief *geisha* restaurant in Chiba.

Those who have read *The Yellow War*, by "O," may remember how he describes, in one of the chapters entitled "The Military Triumvirate," the *geisha* dinner attended by the late Marshal Prince Oyama, General Kodama, and General Fukushima, on the evening before leaving Japan for

Manchuria " to control the destinies of the army in the field." After giving a description of these three, whose brilliant exploits had made their names household words throughout the world at that time, " O " shows them at work on their war plans, and then leaving to attend " a farewell, complimentary dinner given by the heads of sister departments." To quote part of this account :

" They are entranced with the semi-barbaric dancing of the *première danseuse* of the house wherein they sup, and they partake of the merriment of the cup as if there were no such distraction in the wide world as war. Yet even as they sit, there has come to the men on duty at the War Department a detail of new ground which has been broken within two thousand metres of Port Arthur's outer works, of grim casualties to covering infantry entailed in this pushing forward of the parallel. Nevertheless, as the messenger who brought the news from the War Bureau stands outside in the passage, sipping the cup of green tea which some *mousme* has brought him, all he hears is the spirited rhythm of the *samisen* . . .

" On the morrow the ministers plenipotentiary and envoys extraordinary of all the great Western Powers, glittering in their bullion-charged dresses, will be present on the platform to wish the Triumvirate 'God-speed.' "

Whether or no this account by " O " is an actual matter of history it does not matter, though in all probability it is. The main point about it is that it shows in the most skilful manner this truly Japanese characteristic of being able to throw aside worry and care for the moment, and thereby bring to bear on the serious things of the morrow a mind refreshed—not unlike the famous example in our own history, the story of Drake and his game of bowls.

A day or two after the Yawata fishing trip, I left for Tokyo in the morning, a number of the officers from the school being at the station to see me off, and that ended my second, and last, proper period of attachment to the Japanese army.

Without wishing to cast any reproach on the Shizuoka

Regiment, the attachment to which I had thoroughly enjoyed, viewed, nevertheless, from the purely military standpoint, the six months spent at the Infantry School were certainly more profitable and, in many ways, even more enjoyable than the period spent at Shizuoka. As stated earlier in these pages, the training and equipment of a Japanese regiment is still somewhat behind the times as compared with all the changes which have occurred in our own and other European armies since the outbreak of the War in 1914. From the point of view therefore of tactics, of training, or of equipment, there was not much of a purely military nature to be learned from an attachment to any unit of the Japanese army, though, of course, one could not but admire the discipline and the *moral*, the marching powers and the hardiness of the men, and, last but not least, the obvious love of, and keenness on, their profession shown by the officers. On the other hand, a course of six months at a military institution, such as the Infantry School, is of invaluable use, as it gives one an insight into what the military authorities are aiming at—research work in regard to new weapons, new organisations, new methods of attack and defence, and the thrashing out of the hundred and one lessons learned from the recent World War. In addition, you get to hear the views of officers from every part of the Japanese Empire and, by so doing, you come to have an insight into the Japanese military mind such as is vouchsafed to but few other foreigners.

There are some who may say that close association of this sort tends to make a foreigner become pro-Japanese. If by this it is meant that you come to see the Japanese point of view on various matters of discussion, there is a certain amount of truth in the assertion.

Apart from this, however, it is possible, even if one has come to appreciate the Japanese view-point on any particular subject, to adopt an attitude of strict impartiality without necessarily being " pro-Japanese."

The fact of the matter is that the Japanese, being merely human, have their good and their bad points, just as we and other nations have. The difference is, that their good points are different from our good points, and their bad traits are found in different places from ours. The superficial observer is apt either to note all the good points or else all the bad points, because they happen to be more pronounced owing to their being found in qualities different from our own. The result is that Japan is often depicted in books either as an ideal country or else in the blackest colours, but seldom in a happy medium. The safest course, therefore, to take in summing up the Japanese nation as a whole, is to steer between the idealistic gush of the globe-trotter and the embittered asseverations of a certain type of foreign merchant, who judges the whole country by his own experiences with the worst class of treaty port Japanese merchant and petty official.

CHAPTER XV

1920 GRAND MANŒUVRES

RATHER less than four months after leaving Chiba I started off on my return to England, the intervening period being employed in seeing something of the Hokkaido and of the Japanese troops in Eastern Siberia, Manchuria, and Korea, accounts of which will be found in Part II. of this book.

The last few days in Japan as a Language Officer were spent on Grand Manœuvres, to which we set off on November 5th. The theatre of operations on this occasion was in Kyushu, the divisions employed being the three raised in that island, namely, the 6th, 12th, and 18th. These, together with one mixed brigade and various auxiliary troops, were split up into two armies as follows:

Southern Army, commanded by General Hongo (Fusataro), with Major-General Muraoka as his Chief of Staff.

6th Division, commanded by Lieut.-General Koike.

50th Mixed Brigade, commanded by Major-General Fukuhara.

Northern Army, commanded by General Matsukawa (Toshitane), with Major-General Hishikari as Chief of Staff.

12th Division, commanded by Lieut.-General Kinoshita.

18th Division, commanded by Lieut.-General Takayama.

Each army had a force of twelve aeroplanes attached.

In the absence of the Emperor, owing to illness, the Crown Prince took his place, while General (now Marshal) Baron Uehara (Chief of the General Staff) directed the operations.

As in the case of the 1918 and 1919 Grand Manœuvres, there was little or nothing to be learned by the foreign military observers from the point of view of tactics, and, as usual, the main object of the manœuvres seemed to be in the nature of an endurance test for the troops, combined with a chance of raising the loyalty and military ardour of the local inhabitants, by showing them on what their money was being spent.

The "general idea" of these operations was that a Southern force had landed at Beppu on the north-east coast of Kyushu, and was trying to force its way across to Moji, in order to obtain possession of the Shimonoseki Straits and the forts guarding the entrance on either side, whilst the Northern army was marching from Kokura (near Moji) in order to oppose them. On the second day of the manœuvres, the two armies met near Nakatsu, about half-way between these two points, and after an engagement lasting well into the third day, the Southern commander had to retire, owing to the Northern army being reinforced. Further reinforcements were received by both sides during the night that followed, and at day-break the next morning a pitched battle was fought, ending in a victory for the North.

Although, as already stated, there was little or nothing to be learned from the tactics employed (unless it were the fact that they still appeared to be too much based on pre-War principles), one of the outstanding features of the operations was the forced march of the 12th Division, which covered a distance of fifty-three kilometres in ten hours, the route followed being mainly through mountainous country with but few proper roads. An officer of the 14th Infantry Regiment told me that his own particular unit had covered seven and a half miles without a halt in under an hour and a half, the men doubling for five minutes and then reverting to quick time for ten minutes alternately.

Except when marching at attention, Japanese troops never attempt to keep in step, and their appearance is, therefore, not always as smart as it might be, but, nevertheless, they are excellent marchers and are capable of enduring the greatest hardships.

During the four days in which they carried out these manœuvres the troops bivouacked in the open each night without blankets and had but little sleep. Nevertheless, when the review was held on the completion of the operations, they looked none the worse for their exertions.

Like their predecessors of 1918 and 1919, the 1920 Grand Manœuvres, so far as the foreign attachés were concerned, were confined largely to sightseeing with an excessive amount of eating and drinking thrown in at odd intervals. There were twenty-five of us in all, representing eleven different nationalities, or, with the addition of our Japanese "bear-leaders," twelve. As we were led about more or less *en masse* we must have looked rather like members of a travelling circus, and certainly the mixture of uniforms seemed to leave that impression on the crowds of onlookers, who always appeared to regard us with a look of indulgent amusement on their faces.

Quarters had been prepared for us at Beppu, and the morning following our arrival was spent in being taken round in cars to see various "hells" (small volcanoes really), etc., which abound in that district—"Sea of Hell," "Bloody Hell," "Priests' Hell" (these are literal translations), and so on. The afternoon was spent in riding round some of the "battle" positions in the Nataksu area.

It would take too long to describe the whole of the next few days, so the diary will once more be brought into play to supply extracts.

On the second night of the manœuvres we slept under canvas, three per tent, instead of in our usual hotel quarters, and next morning were up at 5 a.m. "Quite like old times to wash and shave in cold water in the open in the dark and then, just as dawn was breaking, to hear the guns beginning to tune up."

All the morning was employed, like the previous afternoon, in riding round watching the various phases of the fighting.

In the afternoon we were taken off to be entertained by a Japanese merchant at Hiji, where he had a house up in the hills with an excellent view across Beppu Bay.

"Reached Hiji a bit before 2 p.m. and had to walk up an avenue lined with school children, each of whom carried a flag, which she waved with great vigour to the accompaniment of shouts of '*Banzai!*' as we came along.

"The Japanese certainly know the art of stage-managing things, and are really overwhelming in their hospitality. Throughout these manœuvres—and it was the same last year and the year before—we have simply been treated like princes. . . ."

At Hiji we were given a big luncheon, after which we were treated to a display of *geisha* dancing inside a large *marquee* which had been erected in the garden. After this was over, we had only just time to motor back to Beppu, have a tub, and change, before setting off by car to Oita to attend a dinner given in our honour by the Mayor in the town hall.

It was past eleven when we got back to our quarters that night, and four and a half hours later we were up again in order to take train for Yanagiura, where the closing stages of the fighting took place that evening.

The following entry in the diary on that day is significant of events which have taken place since then :

"On our way back to the station after witnessing the final assault, a Japanese staff officer rode up to the General [1] to say that the Crown Prince wished to speak with him."

The significance of this entry lies in the fact that such a thing had never been known before. All foreign officers attending Grand Manœuvres are presented to the Emperor, if he is present, or, as in the case of those in 1920, to the Crown Prince, but this presentation simply consists of filing past him one at a time and saluting. A precedent, therefore, was set in 1920 when the Crown Prince actually sent for, and conversed with, one of the foreign attachés personally. Although, so far as I know, there had been, up to that time,

[1] Brigadier-General C. R. Woodroffe, C.M.G., C.B.E., at that time British Military Attaché in Tokyo.

no serious mention made of the Crown Prince's intention to visit Europe, it is interesting to note that he arrived in England just six months later and that, throughout his stay there, he was accompanied, by his special request, by this very same officer for whom he had sent on the 1920 manœuvres. It is hardly necessary to add that, by this visit to Europe, the Crown Prince set a still greater precedent, for never before had an Emperor, or future Emperor, of Japan left the shores of his own country.

Those who read these pages may recall the forebodings which arose in the breasts of many of his more conservative future subjects at the very thought of such a break with tradition, some of them, with a mistaken idea of patriotism, even doing away with themselves by way of protest. Nevertheless there is no doubt that the Crown Prince and his advisers did well to break with tradition in this particular case.

. . . .

Having seen the last stage of the operations we were taken off for more sightseeing, the afternoon being spent in a visit to the famous Yabakei Valley. While there, we were taken to see the sixteen hundred year old temple of Rakanji, over which we were shown by one of the priests.

" Was very amused to find amongst the treasures of this ancient and somewhat remote temple, a British gas-mask of all things ! A bit of a contrast to everything else there and quite one of the last things one would expect to find in such a place."

That evening General (now Marshal) Uehara gave a dinner at Nakatsu, and it was late at night before we got back to our quarters at Beppu.

The next morning we were up once more at an early hour in order to reach Bizenkoji in time for the review which was to be held by the Crown Prince there. As in former years, each of the foreign attachés was presented in turn, and the Imperial party then set off to review the troops, the foreign attachés following in rear.

" As the *cortège* set off, the band struck up the National

Anthem while the bugles sounded the Imperial Salute—very impressive in its way.

" The troops were drawn up in the paddy-fields on the left of the road while bodies of reservists, school children, etc., were lined up in the fields on the right. . . . These Kyushu troops are a fine sturdy-looking lot. Look fit for anything and have the reputation of being the finest fighting men in Japan. . . . The more one sees of the Japanese troops and their tattered colours, the more one comes to admire them."

After the review was over we had lunch and were then taken off to attend the annual end-of-manœuvres banquet given by the Crown Prince, a simple meal consisting of red beans and rice with *sake*, but more than enough in view of the fact that we had only just finished our proper lunch.

This banquet was held in the enormous *marquee* erected annually for the purpose, the ceremony likewise being the same as in former years, except that the Crown Prince took the place of the Emperor, who was too ill to attend the manœuvres.

After the banquet we were taken over the Hachiman Shrine by the Shinto priests in charge of it. It is a fine old place and was specially interesting on this occasion as, Hachiman being the god of war, the place was crowded with Japanese officers of all ranks who were taking this opportunity to offer up prayers to their patron deity. Headed by General Prince Kuni, Prince Kanin, Marshal Kawamura, and other high officers, each in turn stood for a few moments in silence bareheaded before the shrine, and then moved away to make room for those who were waiting their turn. It was an impressive sight to see these grizzled old warriors, many of them veterans of the war with Russia and not a few who had also taken part in the war of 1894-5 against China, standing thus in silence with their heads uncovered, invoking the god of war to help them in their military careers and giving thanks to him for what he had done for them in the past. One may scoff at this sort of thing as idol worship, but is it just merely the worship of a graven image ? Is it not, in fact, similar to the practice carried out by Catholics of all times, whereby they invoke their patron saints to help them ?

That evening we had to attend another large *geisha* dinner at the Beppu Club, and the following day the party of foreign attachés broke up and set off to return to their normal routine work.

As I was due to leave Japan in a couple of days, I only went as far as Shimonoseki and there bade farewell to the others, most of whom set off for Tokyo that night. One of those to whom I said good-bye was Lieut. Withers, another British Language Officer. Little did I think that the next time I was to see him would be a few hours before his death at Singapore, just eighteen months later. On that occasion I was returning to Japan to take up a civil job after being invalided out of the Service. It was by the merest chance that, on reaching Singapore where the ship had put in to coal, I heard that Withers had been landed there more than a month previously, having contracted appendicitis while on his way back to England on the completion of his three years in Japan. He was unconscious when I reached him and died that night. *Requiescat in pace.*

The manœuvres mentioned in this chapter were the last which I attended, and, after a wait of some three days at Shimonoseki, I left Japan on the first stage of the journey back to England.

After three years of more or less close connection with the Japanese army it was but natural that, though glad to be returning home, one was sorry to part from those whom one had come to know so intimately and who had, moreover, shown such a friendly spirit at all times.

Apart from anything else, this last occasion of seeing Japanese troops on manœuvres was of added interest in that I was able once more to see many of my old friends from Chiba. Not only did one find them in the various regiments taking part, but it was noteworthy that a very considerable number of the umpires were drawn from the staff of the Infantry School. No doubt, being a foreign officer,

I must at times have been a confounded nuisance to them at Chiba, but they never gave any signs to show that such was the case, and when meeting them again on the Kyushu manœuvres, one was struck by the obvious sincerity of their welcome. Little wonder, therefore, that one left Japan with mixed feelings, knowing that the chances of meeting them again were not very great. Fate, however, though harsh in its decision to induce the Medical Board to declare me "permanently unfit G.S.," has been kind in that it has brought me back to Japan, though only in a civil capacity.

I have met a number of these officers again since my return, and it does one good to find that, in spite of eighteen months' or more absence, they are as friendly as ever, and seem genuinely pleased to welcome one back in spite of my being no longer a soldier.

CHAPTER XVI

FURTHER POINTS NOTED WHILE ATTACHED

BEFORE leaving the subject of military life in Japan as seen during actual periods of attachment to the Japanese army, a few final experiences and impressions may be worth mentioning.

Nothing has so far been said about military music or marching songs, yet both exist up to a point. The former consists, for the most part, of bugle tunes, every unit having a fixed establishment of buglers. Except for the buglers, no such things as regimental bands—brass, drum and fife, or pipe—exist, though the Guards' Division is the proud possessor of a brass band, as was the 4th (Osaka) Division until a few months ago.

On the march, however, the buglers are frequently employed, and the troops are taught certain military songs into which they occasionally burst when out marching. Unlike our men, however, Japanese troops do not sing spontaneously, and, even when they do sing, they do not indulge in the latest music-hall ditties or their Japanese equivalent. Most of their marching songs are, in fact, of a stereotyped nature, and are to do with military matters, extolling deeds of courage and loyalty, or telling of those killed in action. Similarly the songs sung by either officers or men at *geisha* entertainments are generally of a semi-military nature and, as a rule, deal with the love affairs of a soldier. Military *geisha* songs and marching songs in the Japanese army are alike in that they are few in number, and the same ones are to be heard year in and year out, and are sung each time with as much gusto as though they were the latest "hits."

As an example of the former type, a verse of the *Rappa Bushi* or "Bugle Song" may be quoted:

"Ima naru rappa hachiji han
Kore ni okurerya jūeiso
Kondo no nichi-yō wa nai ja nashi
Hanase guntō ni sabi ga tsuku"

A somewhat literal rendering would be:

"The bugle is sounding! It's half-past eight!
If I am late for it (*i.e.* returning to barracks) I shall be severely punished and
Next Sunday I shall not (be able to get leave)
Let me go or you will rust my bayonet."

The idea is, of course, that a soldier has been visiting his lady love and has overstayed his leave out of barracks. He only realizes the fact when the 8.30 p.m. bugle sounds. The lady tries to induce him to stay and therefore catches hold of his bayonet; hence the fear of the gentleman that the steel of his bayonet will be rusted by the moisture of her hands.

An alternative rendering of the last line is:

"Hanase gunsō ni shikarareru,"

which may be translated:

"Let me go or I shall be 'strafed' by the sergeant."

There are, of course, innumerable verses to this song, but the one just quoted should be sufficient to serve as an example.

As an instance of a Japanese marching song, the *Manshū Bushi*, or "Manchurian Song," is typical, the first few lines being:

"Koko wa o kuni wo nambyaku ri
Hanarete tōki Manshū no
Akai yūhi ni terasarete."

This may be rendered:

"Here he lies buried many hundred miles
From his home
The red wintry sun of Manchuria shining on (his grave)."

The song then goes on to tell how the soldier in question had been full of strength and vigour only the day before, and had advanced fearlessly in the leading ranks of the attacking force—and so on.

Most of the Japanese marching songs have some such theme, and are seldom, if ever, of the humorous persuasion such as are the songs in which our own " Tommy " indulges when on the march.

While on the subject of songs as sung in the Japanese army, it may be mentioned that quite a number of English tunes have been pirated and have had Japanese words put to them. In addition to this there are certain English songs which are partly known. Such a one is " Tipperary," and, on several occasions during attachment to the Japanese army, officers have asked me to sing it and even to teach it to them. *Geisha* dinners have generally been the occasions for such requests, but once, while in camp at Shimoshizu-hara, I had to act as instructor, as the following extract from the diary will show :

" The officer students of the set to which I was attached asked me to look them up in their quarters after the evening meal. On going along to see them, they ordered several bottles of *sake* from the canteen, and then started a 'sing-song,' each officer in turn being made to add his quota to the performance. While this was going on, one of them suggested that I should teach them some English songs, one of those selected being our old friend 'Tipperary,' whilst another was 'Auld Lang Syne.' At first I tried singing them over and getting them to sing after me, but, not content with this, they sent for a blackboard and got me to write out the words on it. It was very amusing to see how serious they became in their endeavours to master these two songs, especially the former, which they practised for half an hour or more and copied down in their note-books. Most of them knew the tune of the latter, as there is a Japanese song called *Hotaru* (' The Fire-fly ') which goes to it, though some of them were surprised to learn that it was a Scottish composition and not a Japanese one ! "

In regard to " Tipperary," it seemed curious to see those fifteen or twenty Japanese officers gathered round the black-board under the flickering light of half-a-dozen candles stuck in the necks of empty *sake* bottles, each man scanning the words with a solemn, set expression on his face, and repeating them after me as though it were a matter of life and death. Little did the writer of that now world-famous song think, when he composed it, how it would be carried to the far corners of the earth.

The sight of those Japanese officers striving to master that song took one back to a certain night in France in the winter of 1914, when a little French merchant, in whose house they were billeted at the time, insisted on playing a flute to three weary officers of a certain famous British regiment. Starting with the " Marseillaise," he ran through the whole gamut of national anthems of the various Allied Powers and at last ended up with " Tipperary," which he apparently considered to be in the same category as " La Brabançon " and " God Save the King."

Although " Tipperary " can hardly be called classical music, the fact remains that the number of Japanese interested in foreign music is rapidly increasing, and a curious thing about it is that, if the buying of gramophone records is any criterion, it would seem that they have but little use for jazz and other music of a low standard, but almost invariably, it is said, go in for the highly classical operas and oratorios. A more extreme change from their own national music than this it would be hard to conceive.

The subject of music leads more or less naturally to that of poetry, and it may be said, in passing, that some of Japan's most famous soldiers have been noted for their writing of poems and couplets, the late General Nogi being a typical example. These couplets, however, can hardly be termed poetry in the true sense, but are rather a set of half-a-dozen or so hieroglyphics expressing certain sentiments.

As an example of these epigrammatic poems an amusing instance is told of one written by the late Empress for the wife of the late Sir Harry Parkes, the first and one of the most famous British Ministers to Japan. Lady Parkes was about to return to England and, as a mark of esteem, the Empress composed and wrote out for her a farewell poem. To a Japanese the sentiments expressed were truly beautiful, but when rendered into English they sounded anything but flattering, for they read :

"The old grey goose flapping lazily homewards."

It certainly does not do to try translating too literally from a foreign language, as the sentiments (as in the case just quoted) are apt to become distorted and cause offence.

Leaving aside, however, the composition of poems or epigrams as frequently practised by both military and civilian Japanese, it may be mentioned in passing that, just as in the British army we have such expressions as "A Penniless 'Sub.'" and "The Gilded Staff," so in the army of our erstwhile Far Eastern ally you find similar expressions in common use. Amongst Japanese officers, for instance, you find the equivalent of "The Penniless 'Sub.'" in the saying, "*Bimbō Shōi* ; *Yarikuri Chūi* ; *Yattoko Taii*," which may be rendered, "Penniless 2nd Lieutenant ; Make-shift Lieutenant ; At length (able to live) Captain."

In regard to "The Gilded Staff" and the so-called "Badge of Shame," as the staff officer's red tabs were sometimes jokingly termed by regimental officers during the War, it may be said that the slang term for a staff officer in the Japanese army is *Tempo*, *i.e.* "Heaven Appointed." It is really a play on the word, as a *tempo* is also the name of an ancient Japanese coin, oval in shape, and the *p.s.c.* badge in Japan is a metal disc worn on the tunic and shaped like the coin in question!

While on the subject of expressions, another amusing instance may be quoted to show how a too literal translation of a word may give quite a wrong impression of its meaning.

The story goes that, when General Shiba was Military Attaché in London, he received a report on two of his officers from the C.O. of a British regiment to which they had been attached. The report was highly complimentary, and ended up with the statement that both officers had been most popular with the regiment, and had shown themselves to be "thoroughly good sportsmen."

To an Englishman this last statement would be as great a compliment as one could wish, but the General, unfortunately, misunderstood the sentiment implied and took it to mean that his two officers had been wasting their time on sports instead of attending to their military duties. Instead, therefore, of congratulating them for good work, he proceeded to give them a thorough "strafing" for being lazy. It was not until the two officers had appealed to the British C.O. to explain that no reproach but a compliment was meant by the expression "sportsmen," that the General realised that a too literal translation had been made, and that his "strafe" had been quite unmerited. In fairness to General Shiba, who is a Japanese officer of the best type, it must be added that no one enjoys the story of his mistake more than he himself, and he is never tired of telling it against himself.

In regard to mistranslations and semi-understood ones, a certain number of instances of somewhat curious English in letters received from Japanese officers have already been given.

At the risk of boring the reader, three more short quotations from the same number of letters are worth mentioning. One of these was received on my return from a trip to the Hokkaido and started off, "I hope you are keeping well your tripe in Hokkaido." In another letter the writer made the remark, "I can never forget your kidneys." Although, on first reading, one may receive the impression that I was not unconnected with the butcher's business, it is no doubt superfluous to point out that the first remark was meant to imply the pious hope that I was having a good *trip* in the Hokkaido, whilst in the second extract quoted, the writer has confounded "kidneys" with "kindness," reminiscent of the British aviator in *Bull Dog Drummond* who tried to explain to the French *gendarme* that his machine had crashed in an onion field, which, to the bewilderment of the *gendarme,* he described as "*J'ai craché dans les rognons,*" which, of course, has a somewhat different meaning, namely, " I have spat in the kidneys."

The third and last quotation to be made is that from a letter which ended, " Hoping to have epistolary communication with you in eternity." One might almost imagine from this remark that the officer who wrote was a believer in Sir Oliver Lodge's theories.

As pointed out elsewhere, however, the foreigner's attempts at speaking or writing Japanese are no less comic to the hearer or receiver than are such efforts at English as those quoted above to the Englishman.

While on the subject of speaking and writing, one other point, which has not so far been noted, may be mentioned. During my attachment to the 34th Regiment the local newspaper correspondent used to pay frequent visits—generally about once a week—to the barracks to find out any points of interest in the doings of the regiment which might be mentioned in the papers. One case has already been recorded of how it was stated that I had taken part in a snow-march and had stuck it out very well, in spite of the fact that I had not even started on that particular march. That was not, however, the only occasion on which my doings, or reputed doings, were described in print, for it seemed that the " attached foreign officer " (myself) was frequently used as a sort of useful stand-by if there was nothing else out of the ordinary happening. On such occasions it was almost invariably the unfortunate " attached foreign officer " whose doings were dragged in to fill up space, and I have still got in my possession a number of cuttings in which such things as my diet, my favourite Japanese songs, my favourite Japanese food, and a hundred and one other little items are described in detail. Sometimes the reports were moderately correct, while at other times, as in the case of the snow-march, they were entirely fabulous. How they originated is a mystery to this day, but such is fame.

Newspaper reporters were not the only people who found their way into barracks, one noticeable thing being the number of visits carried out by boys and girls of the local schools, groups of 50 or even 100 children being brought by their teachers to see over the barracks and to be shown different phases of military training. Some there are, no doubt, who would say that the fact of such visits being made is but another example of militarism. They may perhaps be correct in their contention, but it always struck me personally as an excellent method of teaching discipline and loyalty to the children, a branch of education which is often sadly lacking in many of our own secondary schools.

In addition to these visits of school children to the barracks, officers were occasionally sent off to the local schools to deliver lectures in which the virtues of loyalty and courage were extolled. It will be seen, therefore, that the *seishin kyōiku* or "Spiritual Training," which is such a feature of camp and barrack life in Japan, is extended even to the primary and secondary schools.

In the case of the soldiers themselves this training is carried on up to a certain point even after they complete their period of Colour service, for most reservists, on returning to their homes, join the local *zaigo gunjinkai* or reservist associations, which have branches in pretty well every town and village. These organisations are, in certain respects, not unlike our own ex-Service men's associations, and have, as their main object, the duty of preserving the spirit of military *camaraderie* amongst themselves, and of instilling it into their friends and relations. During Grand Manœuvres and other such times the local *zaigo gunjin*, *i.e.* the members of the *zaigo gunjinkai*, turn out in force and help the authorities to find billets for the troops and to keep order in general. One of the duties of the commanders of regimental recruiting districts is to inspect these associations from time to time and lecture them on military subjects, while they, in their turn, help the conscription officials by teaching the elements of drill to future recruits, so that, when their turn comes to join the Colours, they already have a smattering of military knowledge. The soldierly way in which a new batch of conscripts march into the barracks on the occasion of their joining up is, in fact, a point which must give a favourable impression to any foreign military observer who happens to be present at the time.

Mention was made, a few pages back, of the local newspaper correspondent at Shizuoka writing up accounts of the regiment's doings. This book is not the proper place in which to discuss the subject of the Japanese Press, but a few words may be said as to military publications.

Although many of the regiments have official histories of their own, none, so far as I am aware, publish regimental magazines or journals of any kind. There are, however, a certain number of military publications after the style of our own *Army Quarterly* and *United Service Magazine,* the two most important being the *Kaikosha Kiji* ("Officers' Club Magazine") and the *Heiji Zasshi* ("Military Magazine"). Of the two, the former is by far the better, and is run by military officers. The *Heiji Zasshi,* on the other hand, is owned and published by civilians. The articles contained therein are of a very elementary nature, and are inferior in most ways to those of the *Kaikosha Kiji.* A noticeable point about it is that most of the articles are by anonymous writers, who, by their style, appear to be civilians or officers on the retired or reserve lists. Other military publications of this nature also exist, as for example the *Kenkyū Geppō* ("Research Monthly"), brought out by the Research Branch of the Infantry School. The circulation of such magazines is, however, more limited than that of the two mentioned above. They are, moreover, not obtainable by the general public, as they are by way of being confidential.

Although both officers and men are encouraged to read books and other publications dealing with military subjects, other literature is practically banned from barracks, especially anything of a political nature. If a soldier wishes to bring in anything to read, he has to submit it first to his company commander, who, if he thinks fit, will confiscate it. This censorship even extends to pictures which may be considered to exercise a deteriorating effect, and I remember, in one case, seeing an officer tearing a picture of a girl out of a magazine which one of his men had submitted to him for approval. It was simply an advertisement depicting a *geisha,* and there did not seem to be anything very demoralising about it, but, when I asked why it was being torn out, the answer was given that no pictures of girls were allowed in barracks, as they tended to make the men immoral. One wonders what would be thought of the morals of the British " Tommy " (and of many officers too for that matter), whose walls are not infrequently plastered with pictures of scantily attired damsels, culled from *La Vie Parisienne* and other choice literary works.

It is not, however, that the Japanese soldier is possessed of higher morals than those of his British *confrères,* but it is simply a further illustration of the fact that their respective moral outlooks differ. What appears to us to be immoral in many cases is, to them, quite harmless, and *vice versâ.* The Japanese, for example, think it very disgusting to see people kissing one another, while we think it very unpleasant to see people picking their teeth or clearing their throats in public, though both these actions appear quite natural to the Japanese.

Instances of differences of this kind in outlook might be multiplied indefinitely, the classical example of course being that of the system of "Licensed Quarters" as against uncontrolled prostitution. An Englishman is apt to look on the Japanese as very immoral owing to their *Yoshiwara,* whilst the Japanese who goes to England is, as a rule, generally shocked on first acquaintance with Piccadilly and Leicester Square at night, as one knows from talks with Japanese officers and others who have been there. Before, therefore, definitely dubbing the Japanese an immoral race, it is necessary to consider such points as these. It will then be seen that immorality is a comparative term, and that things which appear immoral to one standard are not so to another.

PART II

WITH JAPANESE TROOPS IN OVERSEAS GARRISONS

CHAPTER XVII

MAINLY CONCERNING LOCAL CHARACTERISTICS OF TROOPS

APART from independent troops, chief amongst which may be mentioned those forming the Formosan garrison and the four cavalry brigades, and apart also from auxiliary units such as the six aviation battalions, the M.T. unit, and the numerous other branches of the Service which go to make up the full complement of the Japanese army, the main force consists of twenty-one infantry divisions. Of these, two are stationed permanently in Korea, while the remaining nineteen may be regarded as "Home" divisions, as they are normally distributed amongst the four islands comprising Japan proper. Actually, however, there are never more than eighteen divisions in the home country at the same time, as one of the nineteen is always in South Manchuria on garrison duty, each of the "Home" divisions taking its turn there, two years at a time.

Of these so-called "Home" divisions, 14 are allotted to the main island, 3 to Kyushu, 1 to Shikoku, and the remaining one to Hokkaido. The term "allotted" is used advisedly, for, as mentioned above, there are never more than 18 of these divisions actually stationed in Japan proper at one time, as one of them supplies the garrison for South Manchuria. It might, therefore, be better to say that the 19 divisional areas of the home army are distributed as above.

Up to now the pages of this book have been devoted entirely to the troops in the main island, though, of course, much of what has been written concerning them would apply equally well to all units of the Japanese army. Nevertheless, just as conditions in our own army are different in India, Egypt, or any other foreign service station from what they are in England itself, so also do those in the Japanese army differ according to locality, military life in Japan proper being very different in many respects to what it is in Korea, Manchuria, Formosa, and other overseas garrisons. For this reason, therefore, it has been considered advisable to separate this book into three parts, the first one dealing with army life in the main island, the second attempting to show something of the conditions in other surroundings, whilst Part III. will be more or less a summary of the main points brought out in the first two parts and of some of the military problems confronting the Japanese army.

Unfortunately, I never had the chance of being attached to a unit stationed outside the main island, so that much of what will be written in this second part may appear to be superficial, as it mainly concerns Japanese military life as seen from without, and not, as was mainly the case in Part I., as seen from within. The conclusions drawn will, however, have one saving grace, namely, that they are based, not simply on hearsay evidence, but chiefly on actual experiences gained by semi-official wanderings through the areas of the garrisons concerning which these pages are being written.

Before going on to write about the Japanese overseas garrisons, a few pages may be devoted to the divisional areas of the remaining five divisions of the home army which were not included in Part I. Three of these five divisional areas, as mentioned above, are allotted to Kyushu, while the other two belong, one each, to Shikoku and Hokkaido respectively. Although not stationed in the main island, these can hardly be called overseas garrisons, any more than our own troops in Ireland are regarded as being on foreign service. Nevertheless, especially in Hokkaido, conditions in these three islands differ a certain amount from those obtaining in the main island, so it may not be out of place to jot down a few points noted in the course of up-country trips made through them.

The first of these trips was made in the summer of 1919, when some five or six weeks were spent travelling about through Shikoku and Kyushu by myself, and keeping as much as possible off the beaten-track, in order to see as much of the people and country of these parts as they really are, and not merely as they are shown for the benefit of the globe-trotter.

If parts of these particular chapters read too much like a tourists' guide, and seem to have but little connection with military matters, it must be pleaded that they have merely been included in order to show something of the country and people from which the Shikoku (11th), Kyushu (6th, 12th, and 18th), and Hokkaido (7th), divisions are recruited. Topographical, climatical, and other such conditions have, admittedly, a very decided influence on the characteristics of the human race, and, in order correctly to compute the fighting value of any particular body of troops, the conditions under which they, in their childhood, were brought up, is not by any means one of the least points to be considered. For this reason, therefore, the pages of the next two chapters will concern the country and the local people of the three smaller islands of Japan rather than the actual military life in them, points concerning which will merely be mentioned *en passant*.

Before going on to describe portions of the trips through these islands, a few words, *à propos* of what has been said above may be written as to the characteristics and fighting qualities of the troops in different parts of Japan.

Owing to the insistence on uniformity in all units of the Japanese army, there is, as a rule, but little difference in the standards set by individual units, there being no such things as "crack" regiments such as there are in our own and most other European armies. Owing, however, to the conscription system and the way in which Japan is divided into permanent divisional and regimental areas, local units have certain local traits more highly developed than is usual in our army, in which it is not by any means uncommon to find a number of London Cockneys in a Highland regiment or a mixture of English, Irish, Scots, and Welshmen in a regiment recruited in the south of England. Even in the regimental and battalion organisations the Japanese army is, therefore, more uniform in regard to the localities from which the men are recruited than is the case in our own army, and, when you come to the divisional organisation, the difference between ourselves and the Japanese is even more pronounced in this respect. The units of a British division are continually being changed by the movements of troops from one command to another, but in Japan they are always permanent members of the same division and the same brigade, the man in the ranks being likewise always taken from the same locality and having the same home station.

Any difference that exists in different units, therefore, is not to be found in the lower formations such as battalions and regiments, but in the higher ones such as the division, and this difference is due, not to lack of uniformity in training, but to local characteristics of the people living in any one particular divisional area. If, therefore, you have studied the local conditions of any one divisional area in Japan, you should be able to tell with a fair degree of accuracy the type of man to be found in the division recruited from that district—a state of affairs which it is quite impossible to tell in the case of any division of our own army, the units of which are being continually chopped and changed about.

Like in everything else, both systems have their good and their bad points. So far as co-operation goes, the Japanese divisional system is probably the better, as, in the event of war, the various components of any one division, having been accustomed to working together in their peace training, will probably be able to co-operate better than our own at the start. On the other hand, the British system is probably at an advantage from the point of view of flexibility, and, in view of their wider experience in varying conditions of ground and climate, the various units will be better prepared for whatever climatic or topographical conditions may crop up in the course of fighting.

The Japanese system of always keeping the same units in the same places strikes one as being a weak point in their training, for there is no doubt that the greater the number of the varieties of ground and local conditions under which a soldier can be trained, the better he is equipped for whatever country in which he may have to fight. Japanese officers to whom one mentions this generally agree, but they say they are handicapped in their wishes to remedy this fault:

(1) By the fact that the term of service for the men is only two years, and that there is not, therefore, sufficient time to move about much.[1]

(2) That by way of concession to those who are called up for service with the Colours, they are trained at places near their own homes.

(3) That the cost of moving troops about is too great.

The first two points are, of course, directly traceable to the conscription system, and the superficial observer might point to these, therefore, and say that they go to prove that it would be better to abolish conscription and adopt the voluntary system. The third point, however, may be used still better by the supporters of conscription, for it is but one more argument in favour of those who, like the majority of Japanese army officers, always, and probably with truth, maintain that Japan is too poor to afford the upkeep of a voluntary army, which is, of course, a very much more expensive thing than a conscript one.[2]

[1] The period of Colour service has now been reduced still further, namely, to 1 year and 10 months.

[2] The almost invariable answer given by a Japanese officer when questioned why any particular improvement is not carried out is, "Japan is too poor." Japan is often, with a certain amount of truth, accused of squandering too much money on her fighting forces. Fifty per cent. of the national expenditure, as it was in 1921, certainly seems too large a proportion to be spent on their behalf, but if the voluntary system took the place of conscription, the percentage would have to be increased still further unless the army were reduced very considerably. This subject of army reduction will be found treated in another chapter (Part III., Chapter XXVI.).

It follows from what has been said above, that Japanese divisions, though uniform in most respects, vary in some cases in fighting qualities. Taken as a whole, however, the majority of divisions differ but little, the only ones which appear to be above or below the average being the three recruited from Kyushu (6th, 12th, and 18th), the 1st (Tokyo) Division, and the 4th (Osaka) Division. The three former are rather above the average, and it may be noted in passing that the island of Kyushu, besides providing the three best divisions, also produces a larger proportion of army officers than any other area of its size in Japan, as will be seen by anyone who visits the *Shikwan Gakkō* (Officers' School) and inspects the statistics of that institution. Kyushu, and Yamaguchi Prefecture which faces it on the main island, are far ahead of any other part of Japan in this respect.

The other two divisions mentioned above, namely the 1st and 4th, are rather below the average if one is to judge by their actions in the wars with China and Russia. This is no doubt due to the fact that they are recruited mainly from the large industrial centres and are largely tainted with the worst qualities of commercialism. Being town-bred, they are probably of higher intellect than their brothers-in-arms in the divisions recruited from the mountainous districts of Kyushu and other parts of Japan, but they are more unruly and hard to manage and not infrequently join the Colours very much against their will; in fact, the statistics for Osaka and Tokyo show a greater proportion of malingerers to avoid military service than any other part of the country, and, in 1922, there were actually two cases of men committing suicide in Osaka with that object in view.

Three other divisions which call for special mention are the Guards, the 19th, and the 20th. The former is stationed in Tokyo, but, unlike the 1st Division, which is also quartered in the capital, the Guards are recruited from all parts of Japan and have no one particular area. The other two divisions mentioned are stationed permanently in Korea, the 19th with headquarters at Ranam in the north-east of the peninsula, and the 20th at Ryuzan, a suburb of Keijo

(Seoul). Like the Guards Division they are conscripted from all over Japan and, therefore, have no special local characteristic as have most of the Home divisions.[1]

From what has been said above, it will be seen that the majority of divisions and their respective units differ but little in regard to quality, although some of them have special local characteristics of their own. This uniformity is largely due to the fact that, although the N.C.O's and men of any one particular unit carry out the whole period of their service with the same unit, officers are continually being moved from one to the other, either for short periods of attachment lasting a week or so or for an indefinite number of years, few, if any, officers rising to field rank in the regiment in which they were granted their first commission. By means of this interchange of officers it is possible to keep uniformity of training and administration throughout the various units of the army.

In the following chapters of Part II. will be found an account of wanderings through various places in which Japanese troops are, or were, stationed both inside and outside of Japan, and of the impressions gained thereby at the time. The tourist-guide touch will be reduced as much as possible, but if at times it appears to be too much to the fore, the reader is asked to remember that it is introduced with the idea of showing something of the country in which those troops are stationed on account of the influence it exerts, or may exert, on them.

[1] The 7th (Hokkaido) Division should also be mentioned as rather different to the ordinary Home divisions. Most of its recruits are taken from the Hokkaido, but, as the man-power of that island is insufficient to keep the division up to strength, a certain number have to be drawn from the main island of Honshu.

CHAPTER XVIII

SHIKOKU AND KYUSHU

ALTHOUGH during the first eighteen or twenty months in Japan I had contrived to see a good bit of the main island, it was not until the summer of 1919 that I carried out visits to any of the other three principal islands and not until a year later that I tried still further afield.

Although there was little of military interest in the visits to Shikoku, Kyushu, and Hokkaido, a short account of them—mainly extracts from the diary made at the time—will be given in this chapter and the next, as a sort of " breather " before going on to record the impressions obtained as a result of visits to some of the oversea garrison areas.

During my stay in Shikoku, one of the places at which I stopped was Kotohira, noted amongst the Japanese for its shrine to Kompira Sama, the god of seafarers. Kotohira has a most fascinating old-world atmosphere about it—a funny old-fashioned Japanese town with its great shrines, its bands of pilgrims in old-time clothes, its curious old shops, houses, and inns, and but few signs of that horrible mixture of East and West which is only too common in most of the larger towns and cities of Japan.

There was, however, one jarring note to this old-world atmosphere, for, after climbing up the nine hundred steps which lead to the main shrine, two or three very artistic minor shrines being passed on the way, one was confronted at the top by a telephone-box and an automatic one at that. It seemed almost sacrilege to find this very inartistic sign of modern times, and I expressed myself on the subject to a young Japanese student who had climbed to the top with me, but he did not seem to see anything incongruous about it, for he only laughed.

The whole town is built on the side of a hill, stone steps taking the place of roads, which, together with the funny wee buildings on either side, and the strips of canvas stretched overhead to shade from the sun, combine to give it an old-world appearance, not unlike that of Clovelly and other such places to be found in Devonshire.

" The town is simply run for pilgrims to the shrine, it being reckoned that nearly a million visit there every year. There are two main shrines, the Asahi (Rising Sun) and the Kompira. The latter is really the principal one and is on the summit of the hill, surrounded by magnificent old cryptomerias, and commands an excellent view of the surrounding country. But both are very fine, and, in addition, there are numberless smaller shrines all the way up on either side. At these you see the pilgrims stopping from time to time, clapping their hands first in order to attract the attention of the gods.

" There are also two live sacred horses and several bronze ones. One of these latter, apparently a very favourite one, has a hole rubbed in its nose, as people with diseases think that by rubbing its nose they will be cured. Personally I should think they are more likely to get some fresh complaint, as people with leprosy, cancer, and heaven knows what not, all go and rub the beast, which would hardly tend to make it a good disinfectant.[1]

" One little stunt which some of the pilgrims do, is to run up and down (or rather walk) the nine hundred steps a hundred times. By so doing they are said to be assured of going to heaven when they die. Personally I should prefer the risk of going elsewhere by not doing it.

" Kompira is specially the god of sailors and seafaring people of all kinds, so there is a large building at the top filled with models of ships, life-buoys, paintings of wrecks

[1] Similar practices are carried out in other parts of Japan as well.

and naval warfare and suchlike things, some of which, especially the latter, are very interesting. The whole lot have been given by men who have been saved from shipwreck, battle, and other pleasant forms of sudden death, through, what they believe to be, the divine agency of Kompira Sama."

It was while looking at the paintings on the wall that I noticed one of a modern battleship, and in one corner of this painting was a picture of a naval officer whose face, obviously that of a European, seemed strangely familiar. On reading the Japanese inscription written underneath, it turned out to be that of Prince Arthur of Connaught. Prince Arthur has, of course, paid three visits to Japan, and is very popular amongst the Japanese; but it seemed strange to find a portrait of him hanging on the wall of an ancient Shinto shrine, in an old-fashioned Japanese town pretty well off the " beaten track " of the average foreign sightseer.

Some two or three most interesting weeks were spent seeing over various parts of Shikoku, partly on foot, partly by rail, and partly by coasting steamers, and always keeping off the beaten track as much as possible, and then I crossed over to Kyushu. " There was one other foreigner on board, a Russian colonel from Semeonov's forces, but he spoke neither English nor Japanese, so I had to try my hand at French but found myself very shaky at that language."

Beppu, where we landed and in the neighbourhood of which I spent several days, is an extraordinary place, literally built on boiling mud and water. Every house, every building, even the schools and the prison, have natural hot water laid on; in fact the difficulty is to get ordinary cold drinking water. It must mean a tremendous saving in fuel bills, because not only is it unnecessary to heat your water, but also you need no fuel for cooking, all cooking being done by digging a hole in the ground and using the natural heat underneath to boil, roast, or fry, or whatever else you wish to do. In front of every house are two or three of these holes covered with matting when not required; but when anything has to be cooked you see them remove the covering and put the kettle or saucepan, or whatever it is, into or over the hole. Rather useful in those days when coal was forty or fifty *yen* a ton and charcoal not much cheaper!

There are several kinds of hot water to be had there, and waters of various temperatures—some too hot to put your hand in, whilst others are just tepid. Included in the latter is natural hot water tasting like soda-water; in fact it is the only drinkable water there, and in the hills at the back you get the curious sight of waterfalls of boiling water, while small streams of hot water abound everywhere.

In addition to hot water being laid on in the houses, there are also large public baths of natural hot water, free to everyone who wishes to use them—men, women, or children (mixed), and it is said that, in consequence of free bathing and free cooking, real poverty is unknown there, though it is a largish town of 50,000 or so inhabitants.

The scenery all round Beppu is very fine—the well-wooded hills, 3000 to 4000 feet in height, forming a sort of semicircle with the ends terminating in the sea, while in front you get Beppu Wan (Bay) surrounded by hills on either side.

Up in these hills you find a number of *jigoku* ("Hells"), or ponds and craters of boiling mud, something similar to the *Ojigoku* ("Big Hell") up in the Hakone hills. One of the finest of them, *Umi Jigoku* by name (The Sea of Hell), is a large pond of clear bluey-green boiling water, and separated by only two or three yards is a larger pond of perfectly cold water.

It will be recalled that it was at Beppu that the foreign attachés were quartered during the Grand Manœuvres of 1920 mentioned in Part I. Much of the country which I visited during the summer of 1919 was the same as that in which the manœuvres were held the following year, though I did not know at the time that this was to be the case. Included in this was Usa, the site of the shrine to Hachiman (God of War), which has been mentioned before, and the Yabakei Valley, a place made famous to the Japanese by the writings of one of their old poets. The scenery up there is magnificent—quite a narrow valley, not more than a quarter of a mile in width on an average, and sometimes even less. But on either side are great precipitous hills, beautifully wooded, with great rocky crags in places, and fine rugged peaks, almost fantastic in shape. These rise 1000 to 2000 feet above the river (rocky like a Scottish burn) running in between. It is a wonderful sight—wild and silent—the only thing spoiling it being the road running through the valley, which somehow seems out of place. Japan is, in fact, a splendid country for scenery, the main trouble being that each new place you see seems to be more beautiful than the last and the English language does not supply a sufficient number of adjectives to describe it.

Several days were spent in the Yabakei district, but call for no special comments beyond the inevitable one that the scenery and the exercise were excellent, and that one had a chance of getting into touch with the country-folk, who were delightful to meet, less cultured perhaps than their kinsmen of the towns, but hard-working, simple, and honest, and hospitable to the last degree.

A week later I got to Moji and crossed from there over to Shimonoseki on the main island, spending a few days footing it round the neighbouring country and then going on to Miyajima.

Owing to that island being within the fortified area, photography is, unfortunately, forbidden. Apart from the beautiful scenery of the place, one point worth mentioning here on account of its connection with the Japanese army is a certain temple in which a detachment of Japanese troops was billeted just prior to their leaving for Manchuria in the war of 1894-5. Being confident of their own military prowess, some of them hung wooden ladles for serving rice (*meshi-toru*) on the pillars of the temple, the significance of this act being that *meshi-toru* also means "to conquer," and they felt quite certain that they were going to "conquer" China. The present-day visitor to this temple, or rather portion of temple, is greeted with the curious sight of a building stacked from floor to roof with wooden rice ladles, because it became the custom for visitors to the island to commemorate this action by depositing a ladle of their own in the building.

Of this visit to Miyajima and the subsequent trip through the Inland Sea on a small coasting steamer touching at Ujina, Yoshiura, and half-a-dozen other small but picturesque towns on the way, and the visits to other places in Shikoku and the neighbouring islands, which also took place, no more need be said. The beauties of the Inland Sea and the Sacred Island of Miyajima—an island where no man or beast is allowed to die or be buried, those on the point of death being taken across to the main island to end their days—all these things have been described a hundred times or more by others.

In regard to the personal side of this particular trip, as apart from the actual scenery, it can only be said that the people with whom one met were extraordinarily kind and hospitable, and, though I set off by myself, I never had any cause for loneliness, as at every place to which I went, I always came across someone—a student, an officer, a private soldier, a merchant, a farmer—who, apparently taking pity on a foreigner who was by himself but could speak the language of the country, would attach himself to me and make it his special business to look after me and show me round. With several of these chance acquaintances I became on very good terms, and for several months afterwards I used to receive letters or post-cards from them. For all their faults—and what nation is faultless ?—the Japanese are by nature kindly and hospitable, and anyone who wishes to prove this for himself, has but to learn the language and live amongst them in the country districts of Japan for short periods, for it is in the country and not in the big towns and cities that you see the Japanese at their best.

CHAPTER XIX

IN THE HOKKAIDO

HOKKAIDO, the northern island of Japan, is probably the least visited of the four principal islands which go to form what is commonly known as Japan proper. Owing to the fact that it is but sparsely populated, a suggestion is frequently put forward to the effect that the Japanese should make more use of it to relieve the question of surplus population in other parts of the country.

In order to see something of this island, which held out prospects of solving so vital a question, and in order also to see something of that rapidly dying out race, the Ainu, who are practically non-existent in any other parts of Japan, I decided to visit these parts as soon as I had completed the period of attachment to the Infantry School at Chiba. Towards the end of July, 1920, therefore, I set off northwards by the night express, arriving at Aomori about 3.30 p.m. next day after a hot, sleepless, and uncomfortable journey. Four and a half hours on the sea completed the first " lap," and some twenty-four hours after leaving Tokyo we settled down for the night at Hakodate. I say " we " because, on the train, I had met Captain Hasegawa of the 28th Infantry Regiment, who had been with me at Chiba, and who was then returning with his wife and family to rejoin his regiment at Sapporo. This officer had a brother living at Hakodate, and, on hearing that I was bound for the same destination, he had insisted on my going to stop the night with him and his family at his brother's house, where I was received with the greatest kindness and made as comfortable as one could wish.

The following afternoon we went out by tram to the hot springs at Yu-no-kawa, some five or six miles from Hakodate, and had a bathe there. As is very often the case at these hot springs, the bathing was mixed. Though I had been to a good number of such places since coming to Japan, I still could not help seeing the humorous side of it. On this occasion, for instance, I was squatting in the bath, clad in nothing but the proverbial smile, when a dear old lady, similarly arrayed, came and planted herself beside me and entered into a long conversation with me. In Japan that kind of thing seems perfectly natural and not in the least indecent, yet one could hardly imagine it happening in England.

From Yu-no-kawa one obtains a very fine view of Hakodate, which has a striking resemblance to Gibraltar. The town lies at the base of a fortified hill rising about twelve hundred feet above it, this hill being connected with the mainland of the Hokkaido by a narrow neck of low-lying land.

One noticeable thing in Hakodate was the number of Russian refugees to be seen. Most of them were of a pretty low type, but some of those one saw had fine intellectual faces and had obviously seen better days. Two such men passed us on our way to Yu-no-kawa, and one could not help feeling sorry for them. Both were fine well-built fellows, and, in spite of the dirty ragged peasants' clothes which they were wearing, their whole bearing showed them to be *sahibs*.

After three or four days spent in Hakodate I set off for Sapporo, some nine hours by train to the north, spending a day at Onuma on the way. Little need be said, however, of this part of the trip, interesting as it was to one who had not been there before. Suffice it to say that at Onuma there is a very picturesque lake ringed in by hills and overlooked by the Koumagatake volcano, while Sapporo is a large town unlike any to be found in the main island of Japan, for it is more foreign than Japanese in appearance,

Fine broad roads run at right angles to one another instead of there being just a confused jumble of roads and houses, as one finds in other parts of the country.

One of the main reasons for this visit to the Hokkaido was, as already stated, to see, if possible, something of the old aborigines, the so-called "hairy Ainus," who are now only to be found in this one island, despite the fact that at one time in the distant past they inhabited the whole of Japan and were, in fact, the original owners.[1] As the greatest living authority on this interesting race is Dr. John Batchelor, a medical missionary living in Sapporo, one of the first things I did on reaching that town was to call on him. I believe I am right in saying that, with the exception of a C.M.S. lady missionary, whom I subsequently met at the village of Piratori, Dr. Batchelor is the only foreigner who has mastered the Ainu language.[2] For over forty-five years he has devoted his life to working amongst the Ainu, who consequently look on him as almost a god, and refer to him as *Mishpa,* meaning "Chieftain," a name by which he is known even to those of that race who have never seen him. Though I had heard a lot about him I had never met him before. A fine old man with a long white beard and a thick crop of white hair, he has a most venerable appearance, and, in spite of being nearly seventy, holds himself as straight as an arrow and walks like a man of only half his age.

I saw a lot of him during the three days spent at Sapporo, as he very kindly invited me to go round to his house for all meals for which I was not otherwise engaged, and from

[1] The origin of the Japanese themselves is wrapped in mystery, though the main concensus of opinion seems to be that they are the descendants of Malay pirates, who settled down and married on the islands. They themselves claim to be descended from the gods. One fact, however, is certain, namely, that they drove back the previous possessors, the Ainus, so that now there are but few of the latter to be found anywhere except in the northern island of Hokkaido. Legend has it, however, that even the Ainus are not the aborigines and that, prior to their coming, Japan was inhabited by a race of pigmies dwelling in caves.

[2] Dr. Batchelor has the distinction of being the compiler of the only Ainu-English dictionary in existence. When one considers that the Ainus have no written language, the difficulties of compiling such a work may be well appreciated.

him I was able to pick up a great deal of information about the Ainus and their ways.

While in Sapporo, I got into touch with a number of Japanese, thanks to letters of introduction from Japanese officers and others, and Dr. Batchelor himself helped me in this respect also, one of those to whom he introduced me being a Kyushu woman, who was a fine type of what one imagines the old *Samurai* women must have been. On hearing that I was an army officer she pointed to a painting hung on the wall. It was a portrait of the Great Saigo, the famous Japanese soldier-patriot who led the Satsuma Rebellion of 1877. Drawing herself up with pride she said, "I also am of *Samurai* birth. My father fought by the side of the Great Saigo, and on seeing his chieftain killed he committed *hara-kiri* over his dead body." The way she said it was really extraordinarily impressive—very simply, yet with a look of the greatest pride in telling of how her father had ended his own life in order to be with his lord in the next world rather than surrender to his enemies. It somehow gave one an idea of the fine spirit of the *Samurai* of old, and how, even at the present time, the old pride is still there. The same lady showed me a short sword given to her, after her father's death, by her grandfather, with instructions to carry it on her always and be prepared to use it to safeguard her virtue. All *Samurai* women used to be armed with such a weapon for that purpose, but I had never seen one before.[1]

[1] It is interesting to note that this woman still held the old views on the subject of *hara-kiri* in spite of being a Christian. In this connection it may be stated that there is in Tokyo a Japanese Christian priest who served as a sergeant during the Russo-Japanese War. He was wounded and taken prisoner, but after being released on the conclusion of hostilities, he met with a very chilly reception from his friends and relations, and even from the members of his Christian congregation, who all maintained that he should have killed himself rather than let himself fall into the hands of the enemy. I know him personally and he is a splendid old fellow, but it is said that he has never lived down the reproach from his congregation even to this day. After the Russo-Japanese War many cases occurred in which repatriated prisoners were refused entry into the circles of their former friends and relations, but the special interest in this particular instance lies in the fact that the principle of "death

After leaving Sapporo I went on by train to Tomakomai and from there went by light railway to Sarubuto, arriving at the latter place after spending the best part of the day in trains. The country through which one passes on the way had only been opened up comparatively recently, and was quite unlike the Japanese scenery to which one was accustomed down south—huge cultivated plains and virgin forests with settlers' cottages planted down here and there, the houses likewise being unlike the ordinary Japanese ones. Sarubuto itself was typical in appearance of a township such as one sees in cinematograph films of "Life in the Wild West"—a few wooden houses close to the railway station—while most of the men that one saw were mounted and, incidentally, were wearing clothes similar in appearance to those worn by men in "Wild West" films.

At Tomakomai I had met a bearded old gentleman who turned out to be the head-man of Piratori, the village for which I was heading. I had expected to have to put up in Sarubuto for the night, as Piratori is some ten or twelve miles from the railway, and one has to order horses or a conveyance of some kind beforehand; but Kimura, the head-man, I found, had ordered a cart to meet him and he very kindly offered me a lift. As I had no particular desire to put up at Sarubuto for the night, I readily accepted his offer, but it was about the most uncomfortable and painful journey I have ever made or ever hope to make. The cart was an ordinary wooden one, such as is used for carting stones, and had no springs. It was more than half full of baggage, so we both had to sit huddled up native fashion. Instead of going at a walking pace, as carts of that kind do in England, the driver lashed up his horse and set off at a quick trot which, with the state of the roads and lack of

rather than surrender" holds good even amongst Japanese Christians. In our own army we have, of course, the tradition on the Indian Frontier of never allowing oneself to fall into the hands of the enemy when fighting the Frontier tribes, but that is largely due to the fact that you are likely to be tortured to death if you do, though the element of losing British *prestige* if any dead or wounded are left behind is also a factor in this "Frontier tradition."

springs, just about jolted one to bits. Combined with this there was a heavy drizzle of rain falling, so I put up an inward prayer of thanks when we drew up at the village of Piratori some two hours later.

Piratori is one of a group of half-a-dozen or so Ainu villages in that part of the Hokkaido, and it is only within the last few years that they have begun to open up the country round there. The light railway from Tomakomai to Sarubuto had only been opened for passenger traffic five years previously, though it had been laid some five or six years prior to that, for the transportation of lumber from the forest land cleared by the settlers who had been induced to go there. Before this line was opened to passenger traffic, it was a two days' journey on horseback from the nearest station, only a single path through dense forest and jungle then being in existence. These conditions still exist beyond Piratori, and my plan, made after consultation with Dr. Batchelor, was to make my way through there to the railway at Kanayama, a distance of sixty to seventy miles, and from there take train to Asahigawa.

It was said just now that Piratori was an Ainu village. As a matter of fact, it is rapidly becoming Japonicised and there are now more Japanese than Ainus there.

My first sight of an Ainu woman had been in Sapporo, where Dr. Batchelor was employing one as a servant. It gives one a bit of a shock at first to see the women of this race, as they tattoo the upper lip with a huge moustache stretching almost across the face, which, of course, disfigures them badly. The men have long black hair and thick black beards and, like their women-folk, have a plentiful supply of dirt about them.

The Ainus, however, are rapidly dying out and, according to Dr. Batchelor, there are now only about sixteen thousand left, and of these less than half are of pure Ainu blood, this being due to intermarriage with Japanese and the fact that many so-called Ainu are really Japanese adopted by Ainu women when still very young. Three Ainu women had come up to Sapporo a short time before my arrival there, and each had bought a Japanese baby for five *yen* apiece. Dr. Batchelor said he knew of many such cases. In his opinion it is only a question of time before the race becomes extinct, and that this will not take more than another fifty years, as the death-rate is very much greater than the birth-rate. The Japanese are doing their best to stamp out their language and to Japonicise them by intermarriage; they are rapidly drinking themselves to death; diseases of all kinds, especially consumption and ophthalmia, are rife; and various other reasons all go to bring about the eventual extermination of the race.

Dr. Batchelor had given me a letter to a Mr. Mukai, an Ainu Christian priest living at Piratori, and had asked him to guide me round the local Ainu villages through which I should have to pass on my way up to Kanayama, and to procure me a guide for the rest of the way.

Mukai was head of the C.M.S. Mission up there, and, except for one at Makawa, is, or at any rate was, the only Ainu ever ordained. He was a nice-looking fellow and spoke excellent Japanese, and his wife was an intelligent, good-looking girl, who, being a Christian of the younger generation, was not disfigured with tattooing. When one sees a couple like this, well educated and as civilised as a well-educated Japanese, it seems a pity to think that the race is being allowed to die out by drinking itself to death. This drinking is especially carried out whenever they kill or capture a bear, as the Ainu is, above all else, a bear-hunter and goes off into the hills round about with his bow and arrow (poisoned) in search of bears, which are still fairly plentiful in those parts.

Attached to the mission at Piratori was a Miss Bryant, who had lived among the Ainu for the last forty years or so. It must have been a lonely life for her, as there were no other foreigners living nearer than at Sapporo, a tiring journey of ten hours or so, and there were less than half-a-dozen even there. I went to look her up on my arrival at the village, and was surprised to find a tall, white-haired lady, dressed very correctly in black clothes such as might be worn by an elderly woman in England, and living in a room furnished in foreign style, looking as serene and calm as though she were living in a London flat. It seemed a curious contrast to the squalid little Ainu huts and their inmates which one had seen just a few minutes before.

She seemed very pleased to see me and told me that, except Dr. Batchelor, I was the first white man she had seen up there for two years. Dr. Batchelor, she said, generally came up two or three times a year, and in pre-War days an average of two or three foreigners would come annually, but since the War they had been very scarce.

One hears many things said against missionaries, but whether one agrees with them or not, one cannot help admiring the self-sacrificing life spent by those, like Miss Bryant, who willingly cut themselves off from the outside world in order to carry out the injunction, " Go ye into all the world and preach the Gospel."

I had originally meant to spend only one day at Piratori, but, owing to the heavy rain which had been falling recently and which, moreover, continued to fall, it was impossible to proceed further till four days later, as the rivers were all impassable. The first of the rivers to be crossed was only a short distance away and had no bridge. After three or four days of steady rain I had nearly decided to give up the trip to Kanayama, but on the night of the 10th the rain stopped, and by next morning the river, though still in " spate," had fallen four feet, and the rope ferry, the only means of crossing, was working once more. Accordingly I set off on foot about 10 a.m. with Mukai, the Ainu missionary previously mentioned, and an Ainu woman coolie, whom he had procured to carry my baggage consisting of one very weighty suit-case.

Personally I should not have cared to carry that suit-case much more than the length of a station platform, as it was a pretty good weight, being half filled with books which I had been using for studying the written language during my trip up north. Owing to the weight, I had tried to charter a man to carry it, but had been assured that the woman could easily manage it, and, sure enough, she strapped it on to her back and seemed to think nothing of it.

Owing to the state of the river from the heavy rain, the ferry had not been working for two or three days, and, even though the river had fallen several feet during the night, the force of the current was such that one could not help wondering what would happen if it caused the wire rope to snap. The boat would have been smashed to bits on the river boulders in no time, and it would have been impossible to swim in such a current. Luckily, however, no such thing occurred.

Amongst the passengers were the post-boy and his pony. Letters, it seemed, were delivered to the villagers on the other side of the river, the Sarugawa, once every other day —river permitting. This post-boy was a young Ainu of about fourteen years old by his appearance, and rode his pony beautifully, without stirrups. We saw several other young Ainu boys riding during the day and they were all the same. The Ainu is a born horseman and in that respect is a contrast to the Japanese, who is generally an indifferent rider.

About midday we reached the Ainu village of Niptani, but as we could get nothing to eat there, we had to push on to Nioi, another Ainu village some two *ri* (about five miles) further on, arriving there about 2 p.m. after passing Penakori, another village, *en route*. Heavy rain set in again on the way, so we were thoroughly drenched, as I had packed my raincoat, thinking that we had done with rain at last.

Just before reaching Nioi, the path came to a branch of the Sarugawa going off to the east, and we had to cross it by another wire-rope ferry. Huge tree trunks were being whirled down the river by the strong current, so the boat had to be handled with care to avoid being struck by any of them, which, of course, meant an extra charge for crossing the river.

At Nioi we put up at a small, and not over-clean, inn, owned by a Japanese and his wife, and in the afternoon followed the path down the east branch of the river to the

Ainu village of Nupkibetsu, looking at Porosaru and Nioikotan, two other similar villages, on the way, and getting back to Nioi about 8 p.m., having covered fifteen or sixteen miles on foot during the day.

Like Piratori, most of the so-called Ainu villages are rapidly becoming Japonicised, but Porosaru, Nioikotan, and Nupkibetsu are still pure Ainu, each of them consisting of forty or fifty huts made of reeds and straw, each house having its own store-house close by. These store-houses are also built of reeds, but are raised on four posts three or four feet above the ground as a safeguard against rats, etc.

We looked inside one or two of the houses. All were very dirty and filled with smoke, as the fire for cooking in an Ainu hut is in a hole in the floor in the middle of the hut, there being no arrangement made for getting rid of the smoke. Little wonder is it that ophthalmia and other diseases of all kinds are so prevalent.

Heavy rain set in again after we had arrived back at the inn, and carried on till about 6.30 next morning. Mukai had to go back to Piratori that day, so I left him and set off with the Ainu girl coolie about 8 a.m., heading up the main branch of the Sarugawa. About a mile from Nioi we had to cross the river again by a steel-rope ferry, and on the other side saw some Ainu dug-out canoes—very primitive-looking affairs, each made of a single tree trunk hollowed out.

About 9.30 a.m. we came to Osatsunai, another village of reed huts, and were there able to hire a pack-pony. The baggage was roped on to the pony's near-side while a large log of wood was roped on to the off-side to counterbalance it, and I was made to sit on top. Wretched wee beast! I tried to procure another pony, as I thought the weight was too much for the one animal, but the owner of the pony would not hear of such a thing, and assured me that it was capable of carrying much greater weights.

They are very strong, these country-breds, and are never groomed, stabled, or fed, but are just turned loose in openings in the forests when not being used and are then left to their own devices. Needless to say, a large number are killed yearly by bears with which these forests are infested.

As they wanted the pony back that evening, the Ainu girl came with me as far as Iwachishi, another six *ri* (about fifteen miles) further on, in order to take it back. Ainus certainly have plenty of "go" in them. This girl had already carried the heavy suit-case three or four miles on her back, yet she then did the fifteen miles to Iwachishi on foot in three hours, while I rode, and after a rest of an hour or so she set off back on the pony for the return fifteen miles.

About midday we reached Ikeuri, the last Ainu village on the way to Kanayama, after having passed through two others, Okotnai and Sorokessu, on the way.

The road, part of the way, ran through dense forest on high ground above the river, and was a bit dangerous in parts owing to landslides caused by the rain. In these forests were enormous great oaks and trees of all kinds with dense undergrowth, all very fine in their way, but the trouble was that they swarmed with horse-flies and stinging insects of all kinds.

At Niseu, a hamlet a mile or two before reaching Iwachishi, the river had to be crossed again. As the ferry-boat was too small to take the pony, I tried crossing a hundred yards or so up-stream, where I had been told there was a ford. The current was too rapid and the water too discoloured from the rain to see the bottom, so I got the pony to wade slowly across. It might have been a ford in ordinary weather, but, before I knew what was happening, I found a swirling mass of muddy water up to my pony's withers as he stumbled into a hole, the water coming over the saddle and soaking both me and my baggage. By good luck rather than good management I managed to hang on and keep the pony on its feet, or we should both have been swirled down by the current. The Ainu girl, who saw the whole thing from the bank, got a worse shock than either I or the pony, if one might judge from her expression.

About 1.30 p.m. we arrived at Iwachishi, a small mountain village. I had intended just to change ponies there and push on to Usappu for the night, but the innkeeper said that the path had been so badly cut up by the rain that it would be impossible to get there till after dark, and it was too dangerous after nightfall on account of bears. Judging, therefore, discretion to be the better part of valour, I decided to stay where I was for the night, and, as heavy rain set in about 3 p.m. and carried on till late at night, I was glad that I had taken the old man's advice.

On Friday the 13th I set off about 7.30 a.m. on a hired pony, with a pack-pony to carry my kit, and accompanied by a guide who was also mounted. About 8.30 we came to another rope-ferry, in which we were able to take the ponies across, one at a time. Up to this point the path had passed through patches of cultivated ground, but, once across the river, it became a mere mountain track, winding its way up through dense virgin forest and jungle.

About 9 a.m. we came to a point where the track was blocked by a huge tree fallen across it, so had to dismount and hack a way through the thick undergrowth with axes which we had luckily brought with us. A mile or so further on we came to a river with the bridge broken down, so once more had to set to work to hack a path through the jungle to a point twenty or thirty yards up-stream, where the banks were not so steep, and where we were able to ford our ponies across.

In places the track had all but been washed away by the rain, and, owing to its precipitousness in parts and the thick mud into which we sank from time to time, it was unsafe to remain mounted. The only thing to do, therefore, was to dismount and leave the ponies to follow by themselves, as the narrowness, steepness, and slipperiness of the path made it too dangerous to think of even leading them. Heavy rain, which had been threatening all the morning, set in about 10 o'clock to add to the general cheerfulness of things, and having been told that the woods were infested by bears, and that rain generally set them on the prowl, I began to wonder if there were not perhaps something in the belief that the 13th of the month, falling on a Friday, was unlucky, the date then being Friday, August 13th. Occasionally we came to a clearing in the forest with half-a-dozen or so settlers' houses in it. One or two to whom we spoke seemed surprised to hear that I was merely up there on pleasure, and said that they had never seen an *ijin san* (foreigner) up there before. No doubt (if they thought anything more about it) it only strengthened their belief in the madness of all Europeans, for who but a madman would come to such a place for pleasure.

The country all round there is very fine, with its magnificent wooded hills and overhanging precipices and wee mountain streams everywhere, but it must be a pretty lonely life, so completely shut off from the outside world as they are. For six months in the year the country is snow-bound, and, even allowing for best conditions, it is forty odd miles to the nearest railway station with only rough mountain paths in between.

About noon we arrived at the village of Usappu, where we procured a meal at the local inn. Unfortunately, there were no ponies to be had, and as the other two had to be returned to Iwachishi, I had to charter a coolie to act as guide and carrier, and had to pad it on foot to Shimukappu, another six *ri* further on.

About 1.15 p.m. we set off from Usappu, and shortly after got into thick forest and jungle again. The path the whole way was wide enough for a cart, and is, in fact, occasionally used by such, though it must be a slow and painful job, as it was badly cut up and very steep in places. Owing to the number of bears about it is unsafe to travel by night in that district, and I must admit that, even though we went by day, I was not sorry to have someone with me, as, owing to the thick jungle, a bear could come up to within a yard or two of you without being seen; moreover, there was something uncanny in the stillness of those huge mountain forests, with never a sign of life other than very fine butterflies and an occasional snake and, of course, the ubiquitous horse-fly. It was curious what little animal life there was to be seen up there. Apart from dogs and fowls in the villages and, of course, horses, I saw nothing but two eagles the whole of the trip.

About 6 p.m. we reached the village of Nojo, and an hour later arrived at Shimukappu, a village ringed in on all sides by densely wooded hills.

The following day (the 14th) I set off walking by myself about 6 a.m., as there were no ponies to be had, and, after a somewhat tiring five *ri* by a so-called road over another mountain pass, arrived at Kanayama about 11.30 a.m., thereby getting back to the railway again after a tramp of about seventy-six miles across country. It had been a very interesting trip, and I was glad to have done it, but I registered a vow never to try it again, at any rate not unless I became possessed of two sound limbs, instead of having only one on which to depend.

The last five *ri* was one of the most tiring bits, as the road was simply a sea of mud, over one's ankles half the way. Incidently, two bridges had been carried away by the flood, which meant fording one of the rivers, and in another place a large tree had fallen across the track. However, I met two woodcutters on the way, and as they also were bound for Kanayama, we walked the rest of the way together. I was with them when we came to the latter, and they promptly set to work to saw a passage through it. One of these two men turned out to be a reservist of the 67th (Hamamatsu) Regiment, which is brigaded with the 34th (Shizuoka) Regiment, so we found many mutual friends about whom to talk. It seemed funny to run up against a Hamamatsu man away up there in the north; in fact, I was greatly surprised to find that several of the settlers to whom I spoke during this trip were from the south. They all, however, said the same—that they went up to Hokkaido originally in the hope of making money, but that their main object then was to make just enough money to get them back to their own native provinces, as they could not stand the long cold winters of those parts.

To those who, by way of settling the surplus population question in Japan, point to the fact that there is plenty of room in the Hokkaido, these remarks should serve partly as an answer. There is certainly plenty of room for more to live there, but one cannot force any man to go off to a climate he dislikes intensely. It may be wrong for the Japanese to object, but the fact remains that they do. The case in point seems not unlike that of the outcry made by some of our own Liberal politicians shortly before the War, when they pointed to the iniquity of the Duke of Sutherland and others using large tracts of country as deer forest, instead of allowing it to be cultivated. It took quite a considerable amount of arguing to convince them that the land there could not be used for the cultivation of mangold-wurzels or any other kind of food-stuff.

Though it had been interesting to see something of the Ainus in their native surroundings, in view of the fact that pure Ainu villages are rapidly becoming things of the past, it was, of course, impossible to carry out anything like a study of their life and habits in so short a space of time. For those anxious to make a study of them, the numerous books and articles written on this subject by Dr. Batchelor should suffice. One or two short anecdotes in regard to the Ainus, told me by the Doctor himself, may, however, be of interest.

According to him, the Ainus, on the whole, are very lacking in common-sense. As an example of this he mentioned how, on one occasion whilst he was more or less in the wilds up-country, he sent an Ainu off to a village some distance away to see if there were any letters for him at the post-office. The Ainu returned next day with the news that there were several. "Why, then," asked Dr. Batchelor, "have you not brought them back with you?" The man looked hurt at such a suggestion. "Why have I not brought them back?" he queried; "Why, you only asked me to go and see if there were any for you. You did not ask me to bring them back." On another occasion, he told me, he asked an Ainu woman servant to post some letters for him. In perfect innocence she walked round to the front door and put them in the letter-box, where they were discovered by him a few hours later.

Japanese officers to whom I have spoken about the Ainus uphold this statement in regard to their lack of common-sense, and maintain that it is for this reason that they are never conscripted for any branch of the Service except infantry, in spite of the fact that their horsemanship would, one might imagine, make them more useful as cavalrymen. It is considered, however, that they have not sufficient intelligence to be drafted into the cavalry. Of course, even in infantry regiments Ainus are but rarely to be found, despite the fact that they come under the conscription regulations in the same way as the Japanese themselves.[1]

Even apart from the fact that the Ainus are rapidly diminishing in numbers, they are so hopelessly disease-ridden that only a very small percentage of the male population are passed by the conscription officials in the medical examinations. As an example of this, the head-man of Piratori told me that out of eighteen youths who had presented themselves that year for conscription, only two had been passed fit.

The only regiments in which Ainus are to be found are those in the 7th (Asahigawa) Division, and even in the units of that division the number is very small, amounting to only two or three per company. It is said that they are seldom promoted to non-commissioned rank, owing to the fact that the Japanese soldiers dislike having to obey such N.C.O's, as they consider all Ainus to be inferior to themselves.

Amongst the many curious things which Dr. Batchelor told me about this race of bear-hunters was that even the more civilised members frequently feel the call of the wild, and such as are living in towns or cities have to go off for at least a week or ten days each year to seek solitude in the mountains, there to commune with nature. During these ten days or so they practically revert to their old barbaric state, and spend the time fishing, hunting, running and rolling on the ground and shouting.

[1] It is interesting to note that this is the case, for, although the Koreans are now just as much Japanese subjects as are the Ainus, they are not conscripted either into the army or the navy.

C. A. W. Monckton, in his *Last Days in New Guinea,*[1] tells how the Papuans have a little habit of going mad for short periods, and that when in that condition they simply run amok and slay friend or foe alike with impartiality. The fit of madness soon passes, and after it has done so, and provided the gentleman in question has not been strung-up or jugged as a result of his escapade, he becomes once more a quiet and law-abiding member of the community. The Ainu, of course, does not go the length of murder when he gets his particular call of the wild, but it is possible that there may be some connection between the two cases.

As already mentioned, the Ainu is, above all else, a bear-hunter. It seems something of an anomaly, therefore, to find that the bear is regarded by him almost in the nature of a god.

In one village through which we passed we were shown a young bear in a kind of wooden cage. This bear, so we were told, had been brought in while still a cub, and at the outset had been treated as a member of the community, the women of the village treating it as though it were one of their own children, even suckling it at their breasts. Unhappily, however, for Master Bruno, he was, when we saw him, getting rather too large, and we were told that he was shortly to be despatched into another world.

It seems that all this is a part of the Ainu religion, if such a state of things can be called a religion, and when the time has come for him to meet his doom, great ritual is observed and prayers are offered for his soul. Poor Bruno! No doubt he would prefer not to be deified in this manner.

As mentioned earlier in this chapter, bears are responsible for a large amount of annual mortality amongst the ponies in that part of the country. They are said to be at their worst from September to November inclusive, but, except in wet weather, seldom show themselves during the day, and generally go on the prowl only at night. Though the Japanese farmers are always ready to defend themselves and their ponies, they never hunt them, but employ parties

[1] Page 152 *et seq.*

of Ainus for those worst three months of the year to do so. In winter, however, the Japanese search out dens in which the bears are hibernating and, by means of a long supple stick with a cleft at one end, induce the bears to come out. These sticks being supple can be made to bend round corners behind which the bear may be sleeping, and the cleft catches hold of the beast's fur. The pull on the fur, when the stick is twisted and withdrawn, causes the bear pain, whereupon he shambles out to ascertain the cause of the annoyance and is promptly shot. It does not seem a very sportsman-like method, though in reality it is probably no less so than the method of shooting tigers from the cover of a carefully prepared position free from danger.

The Ainu himself, however, likes to have a run for his money, and, even though the use of poisoned arrows is forbidden by the police, it is said that he still prefers this somewhat primitive method to that of the rifle, and as a result seldom kills the bear outright. If not too badly hurt, the bear on being struck gives chase, and it is then that the wily Ainu considers that life is worth living, for it gives him a chance of showing his skill both in the art of dodging and in further practice with his bow. Subsequently, provided Bruno does not get him, but that he brings Bruno's life to an end, he settles down to celebrate the occasion by drinking himself silly; for the Ainu hates to leave a cask of *sake* half-full, and is not content till he has drained it to the last dreg. This weakness for drink is the Ainus' greatest enemy and, as already stated, is one of the main reasons for the gradual extermination of his race.

Though it was only during the cross-country trip to Kanayama that I had a chance of seeing Ainus living in their more or less primitive state, I was taken to see an Ainu village and school on the outskirts of Asahigawa, whither I went by train from Kanayama. In this case, however, the village was largely Japonicised and was really nothing more than a show-place, though quite interesting in its way.

One of the officers at the Infantry School, during my

attachment to that institution, was a son-in-law of the Chief of Police at Asahigawa. Having heard that I was going up there on a visit, he had very kindly given me a letter of introduction to his father-in-law, with a request that he would afford me facilities for seeing places and things of interest in his district. Unfortunately, I could only spare one day at Asahigawa, but in the afternoon of that day I called upon the Chief of Police, who, on hearing that I was interested in Ainus, but had only a few hours to spare, provided me with a policeman as guide and sent me off with him by *kuruma* to the village mentioned above, which lay a couple of miles or so away on the outskirts of the town.

At this *buraku* (Ainu village) we were shown a varied assortment of Ainu ornaments, clothes made of wood-bark, arms, etc., included in the latter being a rather neat, though primitive, device for killing bears—a kind of bow and arrow with a trip-string attached to it. The bow is fixed with an arrow aimed at a point which the bear is expected to pass, the trip-wire being stretched across this point, so that when the bear shambles up against it, the arrow is released and so is the spirit of poor Bruno. The arrows have movable barbed heads made of bamboo, a hole being hollowed out in the head. Poison is inserted in the hole, and as the head is barbed and movable, it remains in the bear even if the shaft falls out. The poison is said to kill in thirty minutes, but until that happens the wily Ainu has sometimes to look pretty nippy, as the bear, if he has not lost too much blood, is apt to grow nasty and chivvy him.

After seeing the village, we were shown over an Ainu school by its Japanese headmaster. The curriculum appeared to be much the same as that of the ordinary Japanese primary school, all lessons being taught in Japanese, though the headmaster stated that the average Ainu child is about one year behind Japanese children of the same age in educational development. The school, like its Japanese counterpart, had a kind of fireproof brick shrine in its grounds containing a photograph of the Emperor.

The town of Asahigawa, like that of Sapporo, is laid out in modern style, with fine, broad, clean streets running at right-angles to one another. Thirty years ago the site of the present town was covered with thick virgin forest, but it now boasts a population of a hundred thousand or more. This rapid expansion is largely due to the fact that it has been selected as the divisional headquarters of the 7th (Hokkaido) Division, the whole division, with the exception of the 25th Infantry Regiment (Sapporo), being quartered in barracks on the outskirts of the town.

On my return from the visit to the Ainu *buraku* and school mentioned above, I found Captain Naka of the 27th Infantry Regiment waiting to see me. Captain Naka had been with me in the same class at the Infantry School, and having heard of my arrival at his regimental station, had come round to look me up and show me round the place.

As it was then nearly 6 p.m., the normal hour for the evening meal in Japan, we had dinner together at the inn at which I was stopping and then went off to the barracks belonging to his regiment. Unlike those on the main island the officers of the Hokkaido Division have special quarters provided for them in barracks, instead of having to find houses for themselves.[1] They are also better off in regard to their Mess, as, instead of the bare structures which serve that purpose in the main island regiments, they have quite comfortably furnished rooms, more like those found in our own army.

Amongst the trophies in the Mess of the 27th Regiment was a fine stuffed bear, which had been shot on the rifle range about five years previously while target practice was being carried out. The bear had apparently been sleeping in some high grass between the firing point and the butts, and was not seen till the sound of firing wakened it. The officer in charge thereupon ordered his men to fire at it and bowled it over. A stray bear or two wandering on to

[1] This is true also of troops in Korea, Manchuria, and Formosa, while in each case both officers and men receive additional pay similar to the foreign service pay in our own army.

a rifle range must certainly add a considerable amount of zest to the proceedings.

At the Mess I was introduced to several other officers of the same regiment, and found them very interested in the news that a certain Major-General Yoshibashi had committed *hara-kiri* by way of expressing his disagreement with the General Staff on the question of the use of cavalry. General Yoshibashi had been a cavalry commander and contended that the main *rôle* of cavalry should be shock action, while dismounted action was only of secondary importance for that arm of the Service. He also maintained that, as China and Russia were the only two countries in which Japan was ever likely to be called upon to fight, the number of cavalry units should be increased rather than decreased, there being plenty of scope for cavalry action in both of those countries. The General Staff, however, were opposed to all his views on this subject, so, by way of recording his own opinions of what was best for his country, he had committed *hara-kiri*.

While some of the officers to whom I spoke held the same views as General Yoshibashi, others sided with those of the General Staff in regard to the uses of cavalry, but all of them expressed great admiration for the action taken by the general in question, and regarded it as right and proper under the circumstances, whilst one officer remarked that, so long as Japan had men like him ready to follow his example if they considered it to be for the good of their country, Japan need never fear defeat. This is simply a further example of the extraordinarily high sense of duty still to be found in the Japanese army—a sense of duty which to us may seem extreme, but which is, nevertheless, rather wonderful in its way. Had General Yoshibashi been a British officer, he would, no doubt, have contented himself by writing to *The Times* by way of registering his disapproval.

Little more remains to be said about this trip to the Hokkaido, in fact too much detail has been given as it is, considering the ostensible purpose of this book. A visit to the picturesque hot-springs of Noboribetsu, followed by a further journey by rail to Muroran, where a morning was spent looking over the Government Iron Works, ended a most interesting four weeks, and on the afternoon of the same day I boarded the *Keijo Maru,* which docked at Aomori some twelve hours later, arriving there shortly after 4.30 next morning. A morning spent at Asamushi, a hot-spring a few miles down the line from Aomori, and then some twenty hours in a hot and stuffy train brought me back to Tokyo on the morning of the 20th. A few days later I set off once more on another month's trip, but this time of rather a different nature. An account of this will be found in the next chapter.

CHAPTER XX

IN SIBERIA AND NORTHERN MANCHURIA

SHORTLY before setting off on the trip to the Hokkaido described in the previous chapter, I had asked General Woodroffe for leave to visit the old Manchurian battlefields, going *viâ* Siberia by way of seeing something of the conditions in those parts as well. Accordingly, with his approval, the Japanese military authorities had been asked to afford me facilities for going wherever I wished, and in due course, armed with passports, introductions, and passes, I set off, a few days after my return from Hokkaido, for Tsuruga, and from there was provided with a passage on board a Japanese military transport bound for Vladivostock, where we arrived on the evening of September 12th, 1920. Major Marsden, who was at that time the British military representative at Japanese army headquarters, was away from Siberia at the time, but Sergeant Goldney, his confidential clerk, came to the ship to meet me, as also did a Japanese staff officer, who had been sent round by army headquarters to see if he could help in any way. Owing, however, to cholera tests, which had to be made first, no one was allowed to land until the following morning. It would fill too many pages to attempt anything like a full description of the doings of the next month, so that only such portions as may be of interest to the reader will be mentioned here.

No one who has stopped but a few days in a place has any right to express too positively his views on conditions obtaining there, and it is not intended to transgress that unwritten law more than necessary, but before proceeding further it may be as well to refresh the reader's mind with a brief outline of *faits accomplis* in order that he, or she, may be better able to understand how matters stood at that time.

In the summer of 1918 it had been decided by the Allies to endeavour to pull the loyal Russians together a bit and, with the help of men, money, and munitions, to build up a new Russian front against the Germans, and also to help the eastward movement of the Czecho-Slovaks, who, as may be remembered, were being obstructed by troops containing a large number of German and Austrian ex-prisoners of war. Contingents from various Allied countries had, accordingly, been despatched to Siberia with this end in view.

By November, 1918, the first cause for sending these troops had ceased to exist, and by the spring of 1920 the Czecho-Slovaks had all been repatriated, and all the Allied troops had been withdrawn except those of Japan, which, for reasons which need not be discussed here, were retained in Eastern Siberia. The British Military Mission had finally left in May, 1920, but, for intelligence purposes, and by virtue of the terms of the Anglo-Japanese Alliance, which was still in existence at that time, two British officers had been left attached to the Japanese army headquarters, with a sergeant as confidential clerk and a private as batman. One of these two officers was, as already stated, away at the time I arrived in Vladivostock, but he had very kindly armed me with letters of introduction to various friends of his at army headquarters and elsewhere and had sent instructions to the effect that I might use his house and his car for so long as I was in Vladivostock.

Unfortunately I was only able to spend three days in that city, but during those three days one heard and saw much of great interest. My diary for the period from September 12th to October 10th occupies over a hundred and fifty pages, so it is useless to attempt to write more than the briefest outline, and then, following the admirable example of certain famous chroniclers of ancient times, to say as they did, "And the rest of the acts of this officer and all that he did, are they not written in the diary which he kept at that time." By way of saving time and space, therefore, it may be as well simply to give extracts from that diary, and the reader's forgiveness must accordingly be asked, if the next few pages appear somewhat disjointed at times.

" Very interesting here (Vladivostock) just now owing to the extraordinary mixture of races, though it must have been even more so before the Allied troops were withdrawn. . . . A very cosmopolitan-looking crowd, clad in a wonderful assortment of clothes, both uniform and mufti. Quite a number of the Russians are wearing British uniforms. Difficult to tell in many cases which are civilians and which are soldiers. Those in uniform are a terrible-looking rabble, and there are some pretty fair toughs amongst the *dhroski* drivers, etc.—great hefty beggars with shaggy unkempt hair. The soldierly bearing of the Japanese troops and their business-like appearance is certainly in marked contrast to the unkempt rabble employed by the local government under the title of Militia, who have a cut-throat appearance and, if all the stories that one hears be true, are hand-in-glove with the very gentry against whom they are supposed to be guarding. Unsafe to go out unarmed after dark."

Though the Bolsheviks themselves at that time were not causing much trouble in the Vladivostock area, murder and robbery were rife, especially on the outskirts of the city, and one heard of several recent cases of kidnapping, the victims in most cases being moneyed men who were held up to ransom and only released on payment of large sums.

" As a result of the consular body appealing recently to the Japanese for the protection of their nationals, owing to the frequent cases of 'hold-ups' in broad daylight outside the town, the Japanese have arranged for a military escort for foreigners who wish to go out on Sundays motoring in the country. At 10 a.m. an armoured car sets off, and all who wish its protection fall in in rear, while a second armoured car falls in in rear of the whole party. At 4 p.m. the convoy has to return with true military punctuality. Sounds rather Gilbertian but is nevertheless true."

Japanese troops were, of course, in evidence everywhere. "Most of the principal buildings here seem to be occupied by the Japanese, the army headquarters itself being in a former hotel; in fact one might imagine that Vladivostock had been seized by them for good and all. I wonder!"

The above was written, of course, more than a year before the Washington Conference took place, and the world now knows that Japan had no such intention. This whole question of the Japanese occupation of Eastern Siberia has had its humorous side. The fact of the military authorities continuing to maintain troops there, after all the other Allies had withdrawn, brought forth violent criticism from all quarters, both home and foreign, and Japan was accused of occupying this territory in flagrant opposition to the wishes of its owners, as well as to those of her own people and of the other Powers. There was a certain amount of justification for this accusation, but the fact nevertheless remains that on several previous occasions when she had intimated her intention of withdrawing, alarm and despondency had at once manifested itself, not only amongst her own nationals living in those parts, but also among members of the other foreign communities who had business interests there, and even among many of the local Russians themselves, in spite of the fact that both Russians and foreigners alike never tired of hurling abuse at Japan for her continued occupation. This may sound something of an anomaly, but nevertheless it was so, and is explained by the fact that everyone living in those parts was apprehensive of what might happen once the disciplined forces of Japan had withdrawn their protection.

The Japanese may be disliked and distrusted, but their presence, while it lasted, spelt comparative safety for those living in the area under their control.

True, however, to her promise given at Washington, Japan at last issued definite orders for the evacuation of Siberia by her troops, and the world had the curious experience of seeing some of the leading Russians from those parts going over to Japan to request "the continued occupation of Siberia by Japanese troops in order to prevent disorders and lawlessness," the mayors of Vladivostock and Nikolsk being included in this deputation. Not content with this, the Vladivostock Assembly authorised the appointment of delegations to the principal Powers, asking them to request Japan to leave her troops in Siberia. Amongst those thus sent to America and then to Europe were Merkulov, the former Premier, Professor Miroliulov, Chairman of the Assembly, and Bishop Nester of Kamchatka. Had it not been for its note of tragedy, the whole thing would have had a humorous atmosphere about it, for, first Japan was abused for staying on, and then, when she at last decided to leave and thereby put an end to being the object of execration and obloquy, she had delegations sent, not only to her, but to Europe and America as well, begging her to continue doing that for which she had previously been ostracised. True it was that those delegations represented but a small minority, but they were despatched all the same.

During those three days spent in Vladivostock I came to know a good number of the Japanese officers at army headquarters, owing to letters of introduction with which I had been provided, and all, without exception, showed me the greatest kindness.

"Tuesday, 14th. Spent morning at G.H.Q. and had lunch there, setting off immediately after in one of the Staff cars with a couple of Japanese officers to look over the Russian forts on the hills at the back of the town. On the way passed a prisoner-of-war camp filled with Turks and Austrians. Poor devils! Think of still being prisoners after all these years. Am told that a number of them have gone off their heads as a result of their long imprisonment. However, the Japanese are caring for them now and seem to be treating them very well." (A long account of the forts and the surrounding country then follows, as well as various other notes on the day's doings.)

"Wednesday, 15th. Lunched with Colonel Yamamoto of the General Staff at the Central Hotel. Lieut.-General

Takayanagi (Chief of Staff) was really the host, but sent a message of apology to say that he could not come, as he was too busy conferring with the delegates of the Verkhne-Udinsk Government who had recently arrived in Vladivostock."

The British community in those parts consisted of only a dozen or so at that time, and in addition to them I also met a certain number of Russians, whose views on the situation were extremely interesting to hear. Amongst these latter was General Moissieff, father-in-law of one of the two British officers previously mentioned. He was not, as his title might imply, an army officer, but was, or rather had been, what used to be known in Russia as a "Civil General," that is to say a high official ranking as a general. "Prior to the Revolution he had been attached to the Czar's head-quarters, and after the murder of the Czar he had joined Koltchak, who appointed him head of the Siberian Railway. Later he was appointed Minister of Ways and Communications, but the day before he was to have taken over this new post the Koltchak Government collapsed, amongst those murdered being the very minister he was to have succeeded. He himself narrowly escaped with his life through the help of Mr. Hodgeson, who was at that time acting British High Commissioner in Siberia. The latter had left by the last train, taking with him the few remaining British residents, and got General Moissieff's private railway coach hitched on to the train."

It would take too long to recount the numerous anecdotes of the War, as seen by him at the Russian Imperial Head-quarters, and of the Revolution, as told by himself and his family during an afternoon and evening spent at his house, but it gave one a most interesting insight into the feelings and emotions of the old royalists, and the terrible experiences through which they have had to go.

The General and his family at that time were living some fifteen miles or so out of Vladivostock, and to reach their house it was necessary to go by local train—a train composed entirely of fourth-class carriages—great barn-like conveyances with wooden seats. Though only a distance of fifteen miles, it took nearly an hour and a half to get there, but considering the cost of the fare the marvel was that any train could be run at all. The return ticket cost only four *roubles*. The quotation for the *yen* (at that time worth about 2s. 6d.) on that particular day was standing at four hundred and twenty *roubles* (it went down to three thousand a few days later), so that the cost for travelling some thirty miles worked out at just about a farthing. Owing to the *rouble* having become all but valueless, most, if not all, the business in Vladivostock city was being conducted in Japanese *yen*, but for reasons best known to themselves (the motive was said to be patriotic), the post office and the local railway continued to deal in the former currency of the country and had, up to then, steadily refused to accept the *yen* as their monetary standard.

In regard to this local railway, another quotation from the diary may be of interest as showing the condition of affairs at the time.

"Returned to Vladivostock by the 8.40 p.m. train. . . . This train likewise consisted of fourth class cars only, and was even more desolate in appearance than the former one. I do not wonder that people are a bit chary of travelling after dark in these parts. There was only one other passenger in the car with me, this car being a great barn-like affair with ten rows of seats and a semi-partition between every other one, with a passage running down one side. Each seat could hold six people comfortably, as the line is a five-foot gauge with broad cars, yet the sole illumination for the whole car consisted of three guttering candles on a ledge above the corridor, so that the entire place was in darkness except for this somewhat eerie flicker, which tended to make the darkness and stillness more pronounced and uncanny. Little wonder that so many murders take place in these trains at night-time. I felt glad that I had taken S . . .'s advice and had brought my automatic with me."

After a most interesting four days in Vladivostock, I set off by the 11.30 a.m. train for Harbin, having been provided with a railway pass by the Japanese army headquarters. For the next thirty-six hours we jolted along in a somewhat leisurely manner, the train eventually reaching Harbin at 10.30 on the evening of the following day. The car in which I travelled was labelled "1st Class," and must have been very comfortable when new, but (to quote from the diary) "it is very dirty now and badly in need of repairs. Unpleasant 'stable-companions,' reminiscent of days in the trenches, abound. The guard, a Russian, is also a dirty-looking ruffian, and his uniform gives him the appearance of a French Revolution gaoler as depicted in books or on the stage. . . . The lighting of this train is very primitive and consists only of one candle per compartment. During the day, when passing through tunnels, the train is in darkness. There are electric bulbs, but they do not work."

About twelve hours after starting we reached Pogranitchnaiya on the Manchurian frontier, and had to wait an hour and a half while thorough inspections were made, "first by Japanese soldiers, then by Chinese passport officers, then by the Russian Customs' officials, and finally by the Chinese railway guards, who at this point replace the Russians. Truly travelling is no fun in these parts!"

From that point onwards every station at which we stopped appeared to be guarded by Chinese troops, a dozen or so with fixed bayonets lining up to attention in extended order for so long as the train was in the station. At the larger stations there were also Japanese troops of the 16th Division, with R.T.O's, mostly subalterns, as well. As the train never seemed in a hurry to leave any station, I got out at some of these places and had talks with the Japanese on guard. At Imienpo, where we stopped about forty-five minutes, I had a long talk with the R.T.O. and the subaltern in charge of the local Japanese detachment, both very good fellows. "In talking about the Chinese troops on guard, who appeared specially numerous at this point, they said they were quite untrustworthy, as most of them are nothing more nor less than mountain bandits, and one could never tell which side they would take in the event of a raid on a train by *Hunhutzes* (Manchurian bandits)—a form of amusement carried out from time to time, the last big one in those parts having been in April. The late commander of these (Chinese) troops, so K. . . said, is himself now leader of a band of *Hunhutzes*. Some of them certainly had pretty cut-throat-like appearances, as had also many of the men loafing about the station. As the line is frequently attacked in the Imienpo sector, an armed guard of a dozen or so of these gentry was put on the train before she left the station."

The above is an extract from the diary, and shows the type of gentlemen found in many units of the Chinese army. This is simply one amongst many striking differences between Japan and her large, though feeble, neighbour, China. In the former country, the profession of arms is regarded as one of great honour, whilst in China, on the other hand, the soldier is regarded as a necessary evil and, far from being looked up to, is considered a thief and a murderer—a reputation not infrequently well merited.

When at last Harbin was reached, I found that the Japanese headquarters there had detailed an officer and two N.C.O's to meet me and look after me, a kindly thought on their part, as accommodation was scarce and I spoke neither Russian nor Chinese, the two chief languages there.

The next three days were spent in and around Harbin, a subaltern from the *Etappen* headquarters being told off to take me in tow the first day, and to introduce me to the local Japanese commanders and others. One thing which could not but leave an impression was the friendly way in which one was met and treated, especially by the more senior officers. Not only at Harbin, but at Liaoyang, at Port Arthur, at Seoul, and at other places also, I was introduced to the garrison commanders, who one and all showed the greatest hospitality and friendliness. Had I been the Military Attaché himself, or some senior officer on an official mission, such an attitude might have been expected, but being nothing more than a very junior captain with no special official standing, it struck me as being an extreme act of courtesy on their part to treat me as they did, and

I could not but feel grateful for all the arrangements they made for showing me round the various places of interest, both military and otherwise.

Harbin itself is an interesting place, divided as it is into three parts—Russian, Japanese, and Chinese, respectively—each part truly characteristic of its own particular country.

Amongst other points of interest to which I was taken during my stay there was the railway bridge over the river Sungari. At each end of this bridge, which was about half a mile in length, were two small forts, which had been erected by the Russians in 1916 and had been held by them until the spring of 1920, when their garrison had been disarmed and turned out by the Japanese, owing to their Bolshevistic tendencies.

At the time of my visit, two of these forts were being held by the Japanese, one on each bank, the other two being held by Chinese troops. I was shown over the Japanese one on the right bank—a three-storied concrete building with loopholes for rifle and machine-guns. An underground passage connected it with the Chinese fort, but this had been temporarily blocked. Both Japanese and Chinese soldiers were guarding the bridge.

There were two other British officers in Harbin at that time, one of these being Brigadier-General Beckett, the British representative on the International Railway Board,[1] while the other was a Captain S . . , who was on his way through to Pekin from Irkutsk, whither he had been to try and get food and provisions through to British prisoners in Bolshevic hands. This latter officer, an Australian by birth, had a regular penchant for ramming his head into any place which might give him the chance of, as Gilbert would say, " Awaiting the sensation of a short, sharp shock, from a cheap and chippy chopper on a big black block." It would take too long to recount all his doings, but they include, amongst other things, a term at sea with the merchant

[1] The Railway Board mentioned here was the one appointed in 1918 to look after the interests of the Chinese Eastern Railway and to keep it in running order.

service, a spell of gun-running during the Russo-Japanese War, a hand in the defence of Port Arthur in 1904 and also in a couple of South American "scraps," a spell of sheep-farming, participation in the Abor Campaign, and, lastly, after the outbreak of the late War, service in "Mespot" and Siberia. When I met him again a year later in London, I found that he had been scrapping in Ireland, had resigned his commission in the army, and was then making plans for joining an expedition to the South Pole. Incidentally, he had his hand swathed in bandages at the time, and on being questioned, explained that he had recently had a fight with the cook at his boarding-house, who had suddenly gone mad and had set to work with a hatchet to slay anyone within reach. Some people never seem happy unless they can contrive to get themselves into trouble somehow or other.

Like many others in those parts at that time, Captain S. . . . had his quarters in a private railway coach and General Beckett was similarly placed. Though somewhat cramped for space, these two officers had contrived to make their temporary dwelling-places quite comfortable and homelike.

Although one could not expect to learn much about conditions in those parts in the few days at one's disposal, the very fact of seeing the places for oneself and of hearing at first-hand from those who were in a position to know, helped to give one a better idea of what was going on than any amount of reading in the papers or in official reports and despatches. Lack of space forbids the recounting, in any sort of detail, all that one saw or heard during those few days at Harbin, but a few extracts from our old friend the diary may be of interest. Commenting, for instance, on the wide use of railway-coaches: "It is a curious sort of country in that way. Everyone who is on some special mission seems to have his own railway-coach in which he lives. If he wants to go off somewhere up or down the line, he just gets his coach hitched on to a train going to that place, and when he arrives there he is pushed off into a siding, where he remains till he wants to go somewhere else. In the case of Harbin, these sidings cover a very large area and are packed with railway-coaches belonging to foreign missions of every kind and description, about every nation under the sun being represented, each coach having on it a painting of the national flag of the country to which it belongs."

In another place, referring to the various Russian cliques, the following note occurs :

"Went along in the afternoon with S. . . . to the Café Ural, a tea-shop run by wives of former Russian officers. . . . Most of the other men there were officers of Kappel's army who, being fed up with Semeonov, have come down to Harbin—fine-looking fellows most of them and all wearing proper uniforms, not the half and half sort of garments which are so much in evidence here in Harbin and in Vladivostock. . . . There is a rumour that Semeonov himself is coming here to-day, but P. . . . thinks it unlikely, as he would be killed almost for a cert. if he came."

The following extract serves to show the distinctive national features of the main divisions of Harbin itself :

"Captains S. . . . and G. . . . of the Japanese Military Mission had me to dinner and then took me off to a *geisha* show. Seemed funny to get inside the place and find everything pure Japanese—the *tatami*, *shoji*, *geisha*, *hangyoku*, and the food itself, all just as you would find them in Japan. That is the curious thing about this place. You go to the Russian quarter and feel that you are in Russia ; you go to the Japanese quarter and you think you are back in Japan ; you go to the Chinese quarter and you are in China. It is like living in three different countries at the same time."

Referring to Chinese troops, who were much in evidence in Harbin, this passage occurs :

"Cannot say I think much of the Chinese soldiers here—dirty, sloppy-looking beggars with both arms and equipment in a filthy state. Like those on the train journey from Vladio, their rifles are of every pattern under the sun—Japanese '30th' and '38th' year,[1] German mausers, and

[1] 1897 and 1905 pattern rifles.

an assortment of weapons which appear to have been made in the Stone Age. The Chinese police here, both civil and military, all carry rifles of sorts and swarm everywhere. Thinking I might be able to see something more of the Chinese soldier, who, in spite of his dirty appearance, looks as if he might be good material if properly led, trained, and disciplined, I called on Captain Lan Ching Shan [1] at his barracks, but found he was away."

These few extracts are taken more or less at random from a mass of notes occurring in the diary of that period, and may help to give what is commonly called local colour to the impressions left on one by a short stay in Harbin in the early part of the autumn of 1920.

[1] A Chinese officer with whom I had travelled part of the way and who had asked me to call on him.

CHAPTER XXI

SOUTH MANCHURIA

LEAVING Harbin at 1 p.m. on September the 20th in company with three Japanese officers, we reached Kuao-Cheng-Tsu, the frontier station of the war area, some eight hours later, and, after a long and thorough inspection of passports, we reached Chang-Chun about 10 p.m. At that point we had to detrain, owing to its being the terminus of the five-foot gauge and the place where the four-foot eight-inch gauge of the South Manchurian Railway begins.

It was during this stage of the trip that I had an insight into two points typical of the Japanese military system; the one dealing with the old *Samurai* spirit of " death rather than surrender," and the other with the method of watching the movements of others. The following two extracts from the diary record the two incidents in question:

" Captain N. . . (one of my three travelling companions) had, in addition to his war sword,[1] a shorter but serviceable-looking weapon with an edge like a razor-blade. On questioning him on it, he said his father had given it to him as a parting gift when he left for Siberia, with instructions to use it on himself if ever he should be faced with the alternatives of death or surrender. He mentioned this in the most matter of fact sort of way, as if it were the most natural thing for a father to say to his son."

[1] The sword carried by the Japanese officer in peace-time is merely an ornament—a " tailors' sword " as one might say—but as soon as he is mobilised he discards this purely ceremonial weapon for a heavy, keen-edged war-sword, a family heirloom as often as not, of beautifully forged steel.

The other incident occurred while waiting in the office of the R.T.O. at Chang-Chun for the train to Mukden. We had an hour or so to wait, and the R.T.O., a young cavalry officer, had very kindly asked me into his office for a rest and a drink.

" While waiting in the R.T.O's office, a dirty-looking fellow in Chinese clothes walked in and said something to X. . . . (the R.T.O.), which I did not catch, and then sat down on a chair. Was somewhat surprised when he turned to me and started to speak in Japanese, whereupon X. . . . laughed and explained that he was a Japanese *kempei* (*gendarme*) in disguise. Tells me he has been out here some years on the game, his chief job at present being to keep an eye on Bolshevik agents entering the country, by mixing in crowds at railway stations and elsewhere and pretending to be a Chinaman."

Leaving Chang-Chun and its friendly R.T.O. at 11 p.m. we arrived at Mukden about 8.30 next morning, and for the next few days I took up my quarters at a very comfortable foreign-style hotel, in front of which was a large open space with a stone obelisk in the centre to commemorate Japan's crowning victory over the Russians at that spot. It seemed curious to think that only fifteen years previously that part of the town was non-existent, it being then nothing more than a barren plain and the scene of some of the fiercest fighting.

Lack of space once more makes it necessary to confine oneself merely to a few extracts. As these pages are meant to deal mainly with sidelights on the Japanese army, the extracts selected from now onwards will have to be based on that subject, whilst descriptions of the country itself, and of its Chinese and Manchu inhabitants, together with impressions thereof, will have to be cut down to a minimum and in most cases entirely omitted.

At Mukden was stationed the 3rd Railway Garrison Battalion,[1] so one of the first things I did after my arrival

[1] By the terms of the Treaty of Portsmouth the Japanese are entitled to maintain six battalions of Railway Guards along the line from Chang-Chun to Port Arthur, in addition to one complete division in the leased territory of the Liaotung Peninsula.

there was to call at the headquarters, knowing that they had been advised beforehand of my coming. The commander of the independent troops, Lieut.-General Kishii, happened to be in Mukden that day, and on hearing of my arrival he sent for me and, in the course of a very cordial reception, promised to give me all the assistance I might want.

Unfortunately, for two days out of the five spent at Mukden heavy rain made it useless to attempt to see anything of the old battlefields in the vicinity—the main purpose of this part of the trip. It gave one a chance, however, of getting into touch with the Japanese, both military and civil, in those parts, as well as with some of the local British and American community, and of hearing the views of each. Neither was exactly complimentary to the other, but one came away with the feeling that much of the misunderstanding which existed between the Japanese and English-speaking community was due to the language bar and to the spirit of give and take being chiefly conspicuous by its absence on both sides.

The Japanese have at times acted in a spirit contrary to the so-called "Open Door" policy, but at the same time there is no doubt that many of the anti-Japanese stories that one hears in Manchuria and other parts of the Far East are greatly exaggerated, and that trade jealousy is responsible for a great many of them. It is not meant to imply by this that the Japanese themselves are free from blame; indeed, many of the best type of Japanese greatly deplore the trade immorality of their countrymen in Manchuria and elsewhere; but it is a pity that many of our own merchants and others stray somewhat from the truth at times in their desire to compete with their counterparts from Japan.

On September the 23rd and 25th, the whole time was spent in company with a subaltern from the Garrison Battalion, riding over what had been, fifteen years previously, the scene of some of the bloodiest fighting in the Manchurian campaign of 1904-5. This subaltern had been told off to act as my guide, ponies and a mounted orderly having likewise been provided by garrison headquarters. The orderly carried ball ammunition in case of trouble, as armed bandits are apt to make themselves unpleasant in those parts.[1]

The first of these two days was spent in looking over the scene of the battle of the Shaho, while on the second we rode out to the old Russian position near Likuanpo, some six or seven miles to the west of Mukden. In both cases the country itself was barren and arid in appearance, whilst the *kiaoliang*, which was ten feet or so in height on all sides, restricted any view one might otherwise have had. The roads, if they could be dignified as such, were simply rough muddy tracks, and one can well imagine the difficulties experienced by Russian and Japanese alike in moving even infantry in those parts during the rainy season.

On the way we passed through numerous squalid little Chinese villages with mud walls, whilst everywhere one went, offensively ugly black pigs were encountered.

Although interesting to see over the actual sites of the fighting of fifteen years previously and to be able to visualise more clearly the course of events which one had previously studied at Sandhurst and elsewhere, one could not but wonder how matters would have fared had the contending forces been equipped with air-craft, tanks, gas, and all the modern appurtenances of war which played so important a part in the War which burst on the world about nine years later. Events would probably have shaped very differently, for instance, at Mukden, had the science of aviation been developed even to the extent it had reached when, ten years later to the day (March 10th, 1915) the British attacked and captured Neuve Chapelle.[2] Had the Russians on that occasion been in possession of an air force, it would have been difficult, if not impossible, for the Japanese to deceive them, as they did, into believing that the main attack was to take place against their left flank.

[1] General Chang-tso-lin, the Chinese Governor of Mukden, was himself formerly a bandit. I had previously received a letter of introduction to his Japanese military adviser, Col. Machino, on whom I called, but much to my regret I did not meet the General himself.

[2] The crowning victory of Mukden took place on March 10th, 1905.

In regard to the use of air-craft in Manchuria for war purposes, it is of interest to note that experiments carried out by Japanese aviators go to show that even large bodies of troops moving through *kiaoliang* are invisible from the air. As, however, the *kiaoliang* is cut down to about two feet in height in the early autumn of each year, and does not start to grow again till about June, it could only be used as cover against air-craft for three or four months in the year. Anyone who has studied the history of the 1904-5 campaign will remember the use made of this cereal by both sides in affording cover to an attacking force.

But little now remains to remind one of the fierce fighting which raged in those parts during the latter part of 1904 and the opening months of 1905, beyond a few old and much dilapidated field-works, and here and there a stone cairn erected as a memorial, in some cases by the Japanese and in others by the Russians. It was instructive to notice the respect paid by the Japanese to these reminders of those who had died in battle, both the subaltern and the orderly standing to attention before these silent witnesses and, after baring their heads solemnly, bowing to them.

On the 26th I left Mukden and went on to Liaoyang, where I was met by an officer who had been sent to guide me to the divisional headquarters[1] where the divisional commander, Lieut.-General Shiki, received me with the greatest friendliness. Interest was added to this visit by the fact that the building used as divisional headquarters, the one to which I went, was the same as that used by Kuropatkin as his army headquarters during the battle of Liaoyang.

The next two days were spent in further expeditions to former battlefields, including a visit to the famous Shou-sampo position and to the Yentai and Manju Yama, a mount and an armed mounted escort being provided in each case. As in the case of the battlefields round Mukden, few traces were left to indicate the heavy fighting of fifteen years before,

[1] The 16th (Kyoto) Division was at that time stationed in Manchuria.

but it was all very interesting. Moreover, the guides provided were excellent company and, knowing the country thoroughly, were able to explain the various stages of the fighting.

The fact of passing a patrol of Chinese police armed with rifles on one occasion elicited the information that armed bandits were numerous in these parts. A few days later, when visiting the scene of the battle of Chin-Chow, I had a long and interesting conversation on the subject of Manchurian bandits with a Japanese civil official who on that occasion accompanied me as guide. According to him the actual Leased Territory of Kwantung is free from these gentry who cause so much trouble north of Pulantien. Actually, he said, quite a number of these bandits come down south into the Leased Territory, but they only do so in order to live and rest on the spoils of their exploits further north. So long as they create no trouble in the Leased Territory, the Japanese leave them alone, but once they begin making trouble, steps are immediately taken to suppress them. Knowing this, and knowing that if they want loot they can obtain it without trouble further north, these gentry are content to become peaceful citizens so long as they remain in territory administered by the Japanese.

From this it would seem that it is possible to move about in safety anywhere within the Leased Territory, but that north of that it is unsafe to go off any distance from the railway line without an armed guard. The fact that on each occasion that we went off on visits to battlefields we were accompanied by one or more armed orderlies, though we never went more than ten miles off the line, shows the state of unrest existing in those parts sufficiently well. On two of these occasions we met patrols of armed Chinese police on the lookout for bandits.

Foreign merchants in those parts, when travelling up-country, generally have to take Chinese troops with them as escorts, but, if all one hears is true, these troops are not much use in the event of trouble, as many of them are ex-bandits themselves, and run away, like the " Duke of Plaza-Toro " of *The Gondoliers'* fame, or else side with the bandits when attacked. The fact that the famous Chang-tso-lin, the Chinese Governor of Mukden, is himself an ex-bandit, gives some idea of the type of man employed by the Chinese in those parts.

While on the subject of bandits it may be mentioned here, for the benefit of those who have not heard it, that one of the most common allegations made against the Japanese in Manchuria is that they sell arms and ammunition to these bandits and urge them to keep the country in a state of unrest, so that they (the Japanese) may have an excuse to interfere and thereby extend their control—a species of peaceful penetration. Official Japan vehemently denies these accusations, and an unbiased observer would probably accept this denial, as investigations generally tend to show that there is little or no foundation for such stories; in fact they remind one of the story of the Angels of Mons, or the one about the Russian troops passing through England in the early days of the War. It is always "someone else who had heard it from someone else." It is quite possible, however, that in some cases individual Japanese, who are out to make money, perpetrate misdeeds of this kind, for in all probability it is just as lucrative a business to carry on an illicit traffic in arms with Manchurian bandits as it is to smuggle wines and spirits into the United States at the present time. The bandits are ready to pay large sums for arms and ammunition, just as are their *confrères* amongst the tribes on the Indian frontier.

Although, however, Japan may be justified in denying all responsibility in regard to the arms traffic amongst the Manchurian bandits, it is nevertheless an open secret that she made use of these gentry during her war with Russia, and during my stay in Mukden I came to know a certain Japanese civilian sufficiently well to get him talking on the part played by himself in this connection. His story sheds an interesting light on what he referred to as part of the "unwritten history" of that war, and, as I have good reason for believing the authenticity of his statements, it may be of interest if a brief summary of what he said is inserted here.

This Japanese graduated from the Imperial University in 1902 and was at once sent off by his government to make a survey of Manchuria and to get into touch and obtain friendly relations with the bands of *Hunhutzes* in those parts. While still carrying out this work the war with Russia broke out, and he was given a captain's commission and employed on special duty.

Shortly before the battle of Mukden he was sent off as second-in-command to a force of *Hunhutzes* about five thousand strong. The *rôle* of this force was to carry out raids on the Russian left flank away among the hills, in order further to make General Kuropatkin think that this was the threatened flank. The force consisted chiefly of infantry, though a small body of cavalry was attached to it, and two guns were dragged about in conspicuous places in order to make the Russians think that artillery was being brought up on that flank. These guns were of very old pattern and were never actually fired, but were simply employed in order to deceive the Russians. At the same time Chinese agents were employed to spread about rumours of a large force of artillery having been seen, in order further to increase the Russian fear for their left flank.

The official histories of the Russo-Japanese War intimate that the Japanese made use of the *hunhutzes* at times, but, so far as I know, none of them make mention of this force, a force which, under the circumstances, must have helped very considerably towards the overthrow of the Russian army on that occasion.

To return, however, to Liaoyang, or Ryoyo, by which it is known to the Japanese.[1]

[1] One of the difficulties of travelling in Manchuria is that every place has two or more names, the one being the Japanese pronunciation of the ideograms used and the other the Chinese way. Thus Mukden is called Hoten by the Japanese, Liaoyang becomes Ryoyo, and Dalny is known as Dairen, and so on *ad infinitum*. The written ideograms are the same in each case, and the difference in the pronunciation is brought about in the same way as that by which the figure "7" is pronounced "seven" in English, *sept* in French, *shichi* in Japanese, and so on, though in each case it conveys the same meaning when written as a numeral.

It so happens that in this town there has existed for many years a Presbyterian Mission, the members of which attend not only to the needs of the souls of their converts, but also carry out excellent medical work amongst them. How I got into touch with these good people need not be mentioned here. Suffice it to say that it was not without a feeling of home to find oneself suddenly and unexpectedly in the midst of half-a-dozen or more of one's own countrymen (and women), most of whom had obviously not been born south of the Tweed. This is no place to go into details, but should these pages by any chance fall into the hands of any of those patient workers in that far-away, arid, and *very* dirty Chinese city, I hope they will accept this small token of gratitude from one to whom they all, and especially Mr. and Mrs. Douglas, showed such kindness. Sir Ian Hamilton, in his *Staff Officer's Diary*, recounts how he met with great kindness at Liaoyang from these very same men and women, and one of the latter, from her remarks to me on the subject, professed to be rather hurt by his mentioning her by name. It never struck me at the time that one day I might possibly add to her grievance by having her once more mentioned in print. Should these lines ever meet her eyes, I trust she will bear no malice, as they are written only in a spirit of admiration and gratitude.

After three days at Liaoyang, a night journey brought me to Dairen, which I had fixed on as a good central spot from which to make visits to Port Arthur, Chin-Chow, and other places made famous in history by the fighting of the Japanese, first against the power of China, and subsequently, ten years later, against that of Russia.

There are no Japanese troops in Dairen itself, but at Port Arthur, which is a train journey of rather more than an hour to the south, are the headquarters of the Kwantung Command as well as the headquarters of the Civil Administration of the Leased Territory. The country between these two places is, for the most part, hilly, but it was difficult to make out from the train, even with the aid of a map, the various succession of positions held by the

Russians as they were gradually forced back on to the main line of forts.

It was on the morning of October the 1st that I set off for Port Arthur. As in the case of other places visited, an officer had been sent down from headquarters to meet me at the station. Having been taken round to call on the Commander-in-Chief (General Tachibana), and other officers at the army headquarters, and also on the Civil Governor (Mr. Yamagata, an adopted son of the late Marshal Prince Yamagata), we set off to see the places of chief military and historical interest.

It would take too long to describe the whole of this visit, as we went from one fort to the other, and, with the help of maps and what one had studied in the histories of the campaign, it was possible to obtain a fairly accurate idea of the ghastly carnage which had been necessary to bring about the fall of such a position—strong by nature and rendered almost impregnable by every known device of man.

In the visits to the battlefields around Mukden, the Shaho, Liaoyang, and elsewhere, there was little to show the casual observer how the tide of battle had raged over those flat, dusty plains, dotted about with an occasional squalid hamlet, or small copse, or over the mountainous country to the east and north-east, but here at Port Arthur, every surrounding hill-top, with its almost ubiquitous fort, enabled one to visualise the bloody encounters of fifteen years previously, even their names bringing back to one deeds which had stirred the world to its depths—Peiyushan, the hill under cover of which the Russian Fleet was able to hide itself from direct observation until the Japanese captured "203 Metre Hill" by means of almost superhuman efforts; Kikwanshan, against the north fort of which General Samejima himself led a "forlorn hope" with successful results; the Bodai and Erlungshan forts, with their wide, concrete-sided ditches, which the Japanese had to cross after getting raked with fire while advancing up the steep *glacis* and through the deep electrified barbed-wire—all these and many more stand there to this day, their crumpled and battered forts and guns in most cases just as they were on that first day of January, 1905, when General Stoessel and his staff marched out to capitulate to General Nogi at the village of Suishiying, after a siege of 159 days,[1] during which the Japanese had lost twenty-three thousand in dead alone. It is no reflection on the deeds of our own army or those of any of our Allies, to say that bravery such as that exhibited by the Japanese in their attack on, or the Russians in their defence of, Port Arthur, has never been excelled and seldom equalled. Mistakes were made on both sides, just as mistakes were made in France, Mesopotamia, and elsewhere, and one may be tempted to say, "It was magnificent, but it wasn't war," for Nogi undoubtedly made a great mistake in underestimating his enemy's powers of resistance, apparently thinking that he could carry all these positions as easily as they had been carried ten years previously in the war with China, when half a day had been sufficient to break down all resistance. But even the greatest generals are apt to make mistakes, and though Nogi has been accused of recklessly throwing away the lives of his men, he achieved immortal fame for both them and for himself, for they knew full well that he never demanded of them that which he was not willing to do himself. It is now a matter of history how, on being told of the death of his two sons in the attack on "203 Metre Hill," he continued to direct operations without any sign of emotion, and how, eight years later, on the death of his Emperor, he proceeded, with his wife, in accordance with the old *Samurai* spirit, to disembowel himself in order to join his lord and master on his journeys to the next world.

Although space forbids a detailed account of the visit to the former battlefields in and around Port Arthur, one more point may be added in regard to the impressions gained on that occasion.

From the accounts, both official and otherwise, published about the siege of that town, one gets the impression of a

[1] Though the siege proper actually lasted 159 days, the first stages of the investment may be said to have opened 81 days before, namely May 6th 1904, when the Japanese occupied Feng-Wang-Chen.

large land-locked harbour rather on the scale of the Grand Harbour at Malta, or like that of Hong-Kong. Anyone visiting Port Arthur for the first time must be struck, therefore, by the comparative smallness of the harbour in which the Russians were bottled up during the siege, and how narrow is the entrance which the Japanese endeavoured to block. Land-locked it certainly is, and a more wonderfully strong natural fortress it would be hard to find, ringed round, as it is, with hills, with others in rear running in regular belts across the peninsula, with comparatively level ground in between, strong lines of defence all provided by nature and all asking to be fortified; but it seems almost inconceivable that so many war vessels of all types, as the Russians had, could have found shelter inside the harbour itself. Although Hirose and many another brave man lost his life in his efforts to block the entrance, the wonder is that anyone who took part in those gallant expeditions ever escaped with his life, for the narrow entrance must have been simply raked with fire from Peiyushan, directly opposite it, and the batteries on Golden Hill on the east side at practically point-blank range, to say nothing of the numerous other forts, such as Erlungshan, commanding it.

A stone tower, two hundred and eighteen feet in height, now stands on the summit of Peiyushan as a monument to the dead. Close by is a tomb, underneath which there are vaults containing the bones of as many as could be found of the twenty-three thousand Japanese who made the great sacrifice whilst carrying out the successive attacks which finally led to the capitulation of the Manchurian fortress. It is a fitting spot for such a memorial, for it is one of the main keys of the whole position, and, though it was never actually captured, it served the Russians to maintain their fleet in comparative safety until the successful assault by the Japanese on "203 Metre Hill" on November 30th, 1904, exposed the anchorage to direct fire.

Another monument to the dead which calls for special mention is that on Itszshan, which, together with other forts, was delivered to the Japanese on January 4th, 1905, as guarantee of capitulation. There are Japanese commemorative tablets on most of the more important positions, but the monument on Itszshan is peculiar in that it was erected to the dead of both sides in the presence of the late General Nogi, representing Japan, and a Russian general officer representing the empire of the former Czar—a fine tribute in its way as showing that there is no enmity existing between the dead.

But enough has now been said about Port Arthur and its battlefields.

General Tachibana had, when I was taken to see him earlier in the day, asked me to dine with him at his official residence that evening, an invitation which I readily accepted. There were five other Japanese officers present, including Major-General Hamaomote, the Chief of Staff, but the dinner was quite informal and very friendly.

General Tachibana himself has had a distinguished career, and has since then come still more into the public eye by virtue of his appointment to succeed General Oi as C.-in-C. of the Japanese forces in Siberia. It may, therefore, be of interest to note that, from remarks made by him on the occasion of this dinner, one could see that he held all the old *Samurai* traditions about fighting to the last and no surrender. In a discussion, for instance, as to whether or not Stoessel had been justified in surrendering Port Arthur, he was most emphatic that no military commander could ever be justified in giving up a fortress, and maintained that, if ever he himself should be in a similar position, he would fight to the last and then, if need be, take his own life rather than surrender to the enemy. By the quiet, though emphatic way in which he said this, one could well believe that it was no empty boast that he made.

On the day following this dinner, I paid a visit to an officer friend of mine in the 38th Infantry Regiment, which was stationed at that time at Port Arthur. The barracks occupied by the regiment had originally been erected by the Russians in the days before they had been ousted by the present owners of this natural fortress. One could not help, therefore, contrasting these quarters with those normally occupied by Japanese troops in their own country, the difference being particularly marked in the case of the officers' quarters. Except in Hokkaido, officers in Japan have to find their own quarters, which are generally very simple and inconspicuous ; but in Manchuria special ones are provided, and in the case of Port Arthur these are palatial in size, each married officer having a fine large stone-built house for himself and his family. Outwardly they are pretentious-looking buildings, but one no sooner enters one of them than it is seen that the Japanese officer is really no more luxurious in his style of living there than he is in his own country, for the rooms are furnished with the barest necessities only, whilst simplicity is the keynote of the whole household.

The same evening I returned to Dairen, and then spent the following day going over the old Chin-Chow and Nanshan battlefields which lie about an hour's journey to the north. As there were no troops near there, the Port Arthur authorities had provided me with an introduction to the Civil Administrator of that district, and he it was who accompanied me on this occasion and acted as guide.

Like the other battlefield sites visited, it was very interesting to see over the ground and to run through the various phases of the fighting with the aid of maps and plans, but it would only be tedious to the reader to go into any details which, if he wishes to know them, can be found in the official and other histories of the war. Two things only will, therefore, be mentioned in regard to this particular visit, the first that, like at Port Arthur, one was struck by the difference in regard to topographical features, as described in the various histories of the Russo-Japanese War, and those obtaining now. In place of the "barren treeless heights" mentioned therein, there are now comparatively well-wooded hills. Later on, while passing through Korea, the same thing was noticeable. All this has been brought about within the last ten or twelve years by the Japanese, who are still hurrying on the work of re-afforestation.

The second point is in regard to the two monuments which stand on the summit of Nanshan. One of these is erected to the Japanese who died in gaining the victory, while the other commemorates the death of the Russian defenders. Up to the time of the outbreak of the World War in 1914, a service had been held at each of these memorials every year on May 26th, the anniversary of the battle, for the repose of the souls of the dead Since 1914, however, the Russians had been kept too occupied with their new war to send representatives to Nanshan, so the Japanese took it on themselves to carry out the service for them—a tribute to the bravery of their former enemies. Whatever may be said against the Japanese for their so-called " Militarism," commercial dishonesty, or anything else of which they are so often accused, it must be admitted that, in actual warfare and its aftermath, they shew up very well indeed. Not only is this the case, but, as Sir Ian Hamilton pointed out at a banquet held in London in the summer of 1921, there is one thing in which you can trust Japan implicitly, and that is in a military pact. A Japanese merchant may break his word if he finds it convenient to do so, but a military agreement which has once been ratified will never be broken, however advantageous it may appear for Japan to do so. One has only to consider the late World War to see a modern example of this. When war broke out in 1914, the majority of the military party, the real rulers of Japan, were frankly pro-German in their sympathies and were fully convinced that Germany would win. But in spite of this they remained true to their alliance with Great Britain, a nation on the side which they honestly thought would be the losers. Japan is not by any means a country of saints, but she is certainly a country whose military word can be trusted.

Had the Anglo-Japanese Alliance terminated prior to the outbreak of war in 1914 instead of not till 1922, it seems quite within the limits of possibility that Japan might never have joined the Allies and she might even have joined against them, in which event our Eastern possessions would have been in a very precarious position, which would have necessitated the despatch of naval and military forces to save them—forces, moreover, which we could have ill afforded at the time. Furthermore, the transport of the Australian and New Zealand troops to England would have been almost, if not quite, impossible, and in a hundred and one other ways Britain would have been badly handicapped and the whole course of the War altered in consequence. These and many other points must be taken into consideration by those who make it a practice to sling mud at one who, for some twenty consecutive years, faithfully played her part of the bargain in connection with the Alliance between the two island empires. The somewhat lame excuse of those who are habitually railing against the iniquities, real or imaginary, of the Japanese race, is that in doing so they are only doing what part of the Japanese Press did during certain phases of the War, when there was an unpleasantly anti-Allied feeling expressed. It was certainly regrettable, but it must be remembered that two blacks do not make a white, and it was, after all, only a section of the Press that developed this tendency; and what country in the world has not got its "Yellow Press" or its equivalent?

Before closing the chapter on this trip through South Manchuria it may not be out of place to mention one or two typical cases of anti-Japanese feeling which were very much to the fore in those parts at that time.

One thing which was causing very bitter feeling amongst the Chinese in South Manchuria just then, was the way in which the cholera inspection was being carried out at the port of Yingkou. All 2nd and 3rd class passengers, without certificates to shew that they had been inoculated for this fell disease, were herded together, irrespective of sex, in the railway examination room, and were made to strip to the waist and be inoculated then and there. The Japanese, of course, think nothing of stripping in this way, but in Chinese eyes it is as degrading as it would be to Europeans. It is unfortunate that in cases of this kind the Japanese, especially the subordinate officials, are so lacking in tact, for that is what it really amounts to. It naturally angers people, and foreigners out there who do not understand Japanese customs and characteristics are ready thereby to put a wrong construction on everything done by them and to believe every story they hear, if it is against the Japanese. In the case just mentioned, for instance, it has to be remembered that the Japanese thinks nothing of divesting himself (or herself) of all garments, and probably, in fact most certainly, thinks foreigners must have very low minds to see anything wrong in doing so. On the other hand, a decent Japanese is simply disgusted if he sees a man kissing his wife when seeing her off at a railway station or elsewhere. To the Japanese the act of kissing is simply a disgusting show of animal affection and therefore not to be tolerated in public.

The cholera inspection incident mentioned above is given as an example of how the Japanese, through lack of tact, are apt to engender feelings of hostility against themselves. The two stories which follow, therefore, are given to shew the other side of the picture—how a number of normally intelligent members of the foreign communities in Manchuria and other parts of China have got into a habit of believing anything they are told, if it discredits Japan, or will put a bad interpretation on every Japanese action. Both stories, it may be said, were heard at Mukden, where the anti-Japanese feeling appeared to be particularly strong.

The Japanese, in order, so it was said, to extend their control in the country, would send off disease-ridden prostitutes to out-of-the-way Chinese villages in order to spread disease amongst the villagers. The disease would become so bad that doctors would then have to be sent off to cope with it. As Chinese doctors are scarce, Japanese ones would be sent, and, as the country is in a very disturbed state, it was always necessary to send troops to protect them also. In this way Japan was gradually extending her influence throughout the country.

This story is typical of many I was told while in Manchuria, and it is difficult to understand how intelligent people can believe such stories without even questioning them, but the fact remains that they do so.

The other story, told me by foreigners in Mukden, was that the Japanese troops, knowing that Chinese are frightened when they hear firing at night-time, purposely fired off guns at night to frighten them. On making inquiries into this from Japanese officers stationed there, I found, as was to be expected, that no firing ever took place at night, except occasionally when carrying out night exercises such as troops of all nationalities have to perform at times.

These two stories are taken at random from many of those heard, the latter in particular showing how a bad construction is put on even the most trifling incidents in which Japanese troops are concerned.

The Japanese may not be guiltless of many of the charges made against them, but when one hears such stories as the two just quoted, it makes one wonder how much truth there is in the others. The stories of their torturing the Koreans, for instance, may be true in certain cases, but, from the way in which the foreigners in Mukden and such places talk, one might imagine such cases to be universal.

So much had been heard of the alleged Japanese atrocities in putting down the Korean insurrection the previous year, that it was interesting to hear the Japanese side of the question. In the course of conversations with Japanese officers on the subject, they pointed out that, in many cases, the Koreans were equally if not more brutal, and that it was due to these brutalities that the Japanese acted harshly on some occasions. In the famous Suwon incident, for instance, Koreans set fire to a Japanese school, destroyed the police station, and killed two policemen, one of these two receiving more than fifty wounds in his body. This, according to the officer who told me, was all done before any troops arrived, so one can well imagine the feelings of the troops on finding what had happened. These troops were, as is known, subsequently punished for their harsh treatment of the Koreans, and no doubt deserved the punishment they received, but the statement made by this officer showed that the Koreans themselves were not by any means blameless, though the majority of foreigners in Manchuria and Korea overlooked this point and only told the one side of the story—the side against the Japanese. This is only one instance, but many others could be quoted in which only the anti-Japanese side was known to the foreigners.

The reason for this seems to be that only very few foreigners living in Manchuria and Korea can speak Japanese, and therefore they do not come into contact with the Japanese. Those in Korea are mostly missionaries who work amongst the Koreans and only get to know the Korean point of view, while those in Manchuria only hear the Chinese point of view. The Japanese, owing to their difficult-to-understand characteristics and, very often, lack of tact, only add to the foreigner's convictions that all their actions are wrong.

It is also undoubtedly true that the Japanese who find their way to those parts, especially those living in Manchuria, are not by any means the best type. That the Japanese authorities themselves realised this fact and were, in certain respects, rather perturbed about it, was shown by the following incident :

In a conversation with Mr. Kobayagawa, Civil Administrator of Kinshu (Chin-Chow)—one of the three districts into which the Kwantung is divided for purposes of civil administration—he told me that he was taking a party of twenty representative Chinese from Kinshu district to Japan about the end of the month. Actually there were about three hundred thousand Chinese in this district, and this party, all of whom were going voluntarily, were being taken to Japan in order to meet high Japanese officials and leading business men, and to be shewn both the industries and the beauties of the country. The main point of this visit was, according to Mr. Kobayagawa, to shew the Chinese that they must not judge the Japanese by the type only too common in Manchuria. On further questioning, he said that a similar party of Chinese educationalists from his district had been taken to Japan in April of that same year, and it had been so successful that it was expected that the other two districts of the Kwantung would probably follow the example shortly by also sending parties of representative Chinese to Japan. This was all done, of course, with a view to setting up better relations and of doing away with the anti-Japanese propaganda which was at that time so rife in those parts.

That the military were equally anxious to obtain a better understanding, also appeared to be evident. While at Liaoyang, for instance, Lieut.-General Shiki, Commander of the 16th Division, received me in a most friendly way and asked me about my impressions of Manchuria, and on the following day one of his A.D.C's asked me to tell him frankly what was the opinion of foreigners in regard to Japanese administration in those parts, and in what way they considered it could be improved. From the way he said it, I had little doubt that he had been instructed by General Shiki to make these inquiries, and as the General gave one the impression of being both straightforward and friendly, the only construction to be placed on this question was that he had a real desire to find out foreign opinion with a view to obtaining better relations. This may not be correct, but it was the impression I received.

There are two side to all questions, and although out there the foreigner regards the Japanese with suspicion, the same feelings seem to be held by the latter towards the foreigner. In a conversation which I had with another general officer while in Manchuria, I was asked for my opinion of the foreigners in those parts, and the officer to whom I was speaking expressed his own opinion, which was anything but complimentary towards them. He said that he had spent some years in Europe, and during that time had made many friends there, but he considered that those who came out to China and Manchuria were certainly not, on the whole, representative of the best type. His opinion was backed up by two other senior officers who were present, and who had also been to Europe. It is probable, however, that the reason for their holding such views was due largely to mutual misunderstanding. Owing to the language difficulty and the difference in customs, the Japanese and the foreigners in those parts seldom have much chance of meeting and getting to know each other, and neither, therefore, gets to understand the view-point of the other —regrettable but almost inevitable under the circumstances.

CHAPTER XXII

KOREA

On the evening of October 4th, I boarded a Japanese freighter at Dairen, bound for Antung. Except for those going steerage—mostly Chinese—the only other passengers on board were two Japanese ladies.

About 1 p.m. next day we came to the mouth of the Yalu, which forms the natural frontier between Manchuria and Korea. After steaming up-stream an hour or two, we picked up a pilot who took the ship up as far as Sandoro, which we reached about 4.30 p.m., and where I was met by a *gendarme* corporal, who had been sent down from Antung to meet me. Owing to the shallowness of the river above Sandoro, the next two hours or more were spent in a steam-launch, which took us on up to Antung, where we landed and put up for the night.

Antung itself is in Manchuria, and in order to get into Korea it is necessary to cross the river by the railway bridge, which has passport offices at either end, and is always guarded and patrolled by Japanese troops.

The following day the *gendarme* corporal arrived in the early hours of the morning and intimated that he had fixed up a programme, which we proceeded to put into effect by setting off about 7.30 a.m. in a couple of *rickshaws* for Shingishu (New Wiju) on the Korean side of the Yalu. This meant crossing the railway bridge mentioned above, and it was a curious experience to pass in the space of a few minutes from a town in which the distinctive dresses of the Chinese and Manchus were predominant into a country in which the dress was entirely different.

The Korean dress is a curious-looking garment, everyone, men and women alike, being clad in white. Outwardly the Koreans look clean on account of this, but, if all that one hears be true, they are somewhat of the nature of " whited sepulchres," as they seldom change their under-clothes and they wash themselves still less frequently. The Japanese, of course, are just the reverse. Though the outward appearance of the lower classes often is dirty, they all " tub " every day and are, therefore, generally clean so far as their bodies are concerned.

My stay in Korea was, unfortunately, too short to make it possible to write much about it, so the diary must be pressed into service again. On the subject of dress the following comments appear:

" There seem to be three kinds of head-dress among the men—a black gauze one very similar in appearance to that of a Shinto priest ; a small sort of top-hat perched on the top of the head, reminding one strongly of the kind worn by George Robey or some such comedian ; and a large soft straw one which acts either as an umbrella or a sunshade, according to the weather. Most of them wear long baggy white trousers, shaped like those worn by the Turks and tied at the ankle, and smoke long thin pipes.

" Most of the country women wear a sort of close-fitting bodice in two parts, the upper part above the breasts and the lower part below, thereby leaving the breasts exposed. From the waist downwards a very full skirt is worn with sort of long white drawers reaching to and tied at the ankles, reminiscent of the clothes worn by women in England in the middle of the last century."

Korean time is one hour ahead of Manchurian, so, although Shingishu is only half-an-hour's *rickshaw* ride from Antung, it was 9 a.m. by the time we arrived there. From that point we set off for Wiju, a town some seven or eight miles upstream, the intervening distance being covered in a motor vehicle of somewhat archaic appearance.

On our arrival at Wiju, we went straight to the *gendarmerie* headquarters, where we were very hospitably received by the *gendarme* adjutant and by a subaltern in charge of a detachment of the 77th Infantry Regiment stationed in the town.

During my attachment to the Infantry School, I had made great friends with a captain of this regiment, so I asked the subaltern about him, and found that he was commanding another detachment of the regiment at Kokai, about two hundred miles north-east of Heijo (Ping-Yang), where the regimental headquarters were stationed. The only means of communication between these two last-named places was by road, which fact gives one some idea of the lack of communication which still exists in Korea. It goes to show, too, the difficulty that there must be in carrying out military training when regiments, such as the 77th, are split up into small detachments at such great distances from one another as those at Wiju and Kokai, the former being over a hundred and fifty miles from its regimental headquarters, while the latter is separated by as much as two hundred miles.

This splitting up of regiments into so many detachments in Korea is one, amongst many, of the difficulties with which the military authorities have to contend. Owing to the disturbed state of the country—" The Ireland of Japan," as it has sometimes been called—and also to the fact that, owing to the lack of communications, it is difficult to move bodies of troops rapidly from one place to another, it has been found necessary to have small detachments dotted about throughout an area almost as great as the main island of Japan itself. In this main island, however, there are normally no less than fourteen divisions plus independent troops, whilst in Korea there are only two divisions. In the former case, moreover, the inhabitants are friendly, communications are comparatively good, and there is no hostile frontier to guard. Compare this with Korea, most of whose seventeen million inhabitants are, at the best, only friendly on the surface and through force of circumstances, whilst a large number of them, in conjunction with Manchurian bandits, are for ever hanging about along the frontier line on the lookout for chances to give trouble. This unsettled condition of the country, therefore, combined with its lack of communications, makes it imperative for the military units to be split up to such a degree as seriously to hinder the carrying out of training in some cases.[1] There is talk at the present time of withdrawing many of the smaller detachments which are spread about throughout the peninsula, but it seems unlikely that the frontier garrisons could be withdrawn with any degree of safety, this borderland between Manchuria and Korea being a constant thorn in the flesh of the Japanese.

Owing to the not infrequent occurrence of "sniping," which takes place from time to time in those parts, the police and *gendarmes*, as well as the troops up there, always carry ball ammunition. Only a short time before I arrived at Wiju a fight had taken place a few miles away, and some forty outlaws—Koreans, Chinese, and Russians—were reported to have been killed, it being said that the latter were Bolshevik officers in disguise.

Much trouble is also experienced by the Japanese in their efforts to put down the smuggling of opium across the frontier. In that part which is formed by the Yalu, the river is, of course, a great protection in the warm months, as there is only one bridge over it, namely, the one from Antung, and the fords are all marked down and guarded; but for five or six months in the year the river is icebound, so the difficulties of guarding it effectively during that period are greatly increased.

Along certain parts of the frontier small forts of the blockhouse type have been erected, but although my former regimental commander, Colonel Kimura, who had recently been transferred to the command of a regiment at Ranam in north-eastern Korea, had invited me over to stay with him, and might have been able to make arrangements for me to see something of these frontier posts, I was unfortunately unable to spare the time, as I had to hurry back

[1] Companies on detachment are normally relieved every year whilst platoons change over every three months.

to Japan in order to see to various things there before returning to England.

To the best of my belief there is only one British officer—in fact only one foreign officer—who has ever been shown over these frontier posts, and that is Captain R. D. Bennett, M.C., of the Middlesex Regiment. He it was with whom I came out to Japan in 1917 as a Language Officer. In April, 1920, he was sent off for six months to the Japanese army headquarters in Korea, and this attachment entitles him to the distinction of having been the first foreign officer ever attached to the Japanese army in Korea, and, it may be added, the only one so far. I had hoped to find him still at Seoul when I reached there a day or two later, but found that he had just completed his six months' attachment and had returned to Japan a few days previously.

Although unable to see anything of these frontier posts, the days spent in Wiju district were not without interest. The primary object of the visit was to see over the site on which was fought the famous battle of the Yalu, and, as I had had to study this particular battle in detail for examination purposes in pre-War days, it was extremely interesting, which fact no doubt accounts for the following comment which I find jotted in my diary at the conclusion of an account of the doings of that day:

"Little did I think when I sweated up the details at Sandhurst of this jolly old battle that I should ever actually see the scene of it all, let alone make an official tour of it."

The whole story of the forcing of the river by the Japanese is too well known by students of history to bear repeating here, so no further comments need be made on the subject of the battle itself. The country all round was wild and rugged, and one could well imagine the difficulties which must have attended Kuroki's army in forcing their way through those almost roadless mountains.

After having shown me over as much of the site of the former battlefield as could be seen from high ground in the vicinity, the two officers accompanying me took me off to lunch at a local Japanese inn, Ito, the corporal, being invited to join us. One thing that struck me very much on this, as on other occasions, was the good feeling existing between officers and men. In this particular case the two officers treated the corporal as though he were an equal once they were all off duty, and I had noticed similar cases previously.

Later in the afternoon I said farewell to the two officers and set off with Corporal Ito on the return journey. The Governor of Heianhokudo, who had his headquarters at Wiju, and to whom I had been introduced on my arrival there that morning, had very kindly lent us his car to take us back. He also provided us with a policeman, though why we should have been honoured with this latter gentleman I do not quite know, and I could not help wondering what people would think if they saw me wedged in between an armed *gendarme* on my right and an armed policeman on my left. No doubt I would have been taken for a Korean agitator caught red-handed. However, if political prisoners are treated as I was, they would have little cause for complaint, for both the *gendarme* and the policeman were excellent company, especially the former, and when I left by train for Seoul that night, both he and his sergeant-major came to the station to see me off, and we parted swearing eternal friendship.

A friendly *gendarme*, it may be said, is always a useful adjunct when travelling in Korea, as he is able to save one no end of trouble with passport officials, Custom's officials, and others—at least Corporal Ito did this for me, for his word seemed law. But though he got me through all the formalities with officials of the kind enumerated without the least trouble, the train had not proceeded far when a smiling face appeared at the entrance of my compartment, and the owner thereof announced that he also was a passport officer. He was a most friendly individual, and without hesitation proceeded to inform me of all my movements since I had landed at Vladivostock a month before. As I noted in my diary at the time, "All these good people seem to keep sort of *dossiers* in which to enter up the various activities of foreigners in general." However, this particular passport officer was so very frank in telling me of all my doings, and was so extraordinarily friendly, that one could not feel annoyed by it ; in fact, he seemed to see the humorous side of it all as much as I did, when I chaffed him for keeping an eye on my movements as though I were a dangerous Bolshevik.

I had originally intended to stop at Ping-Yang for a day or two on my way south, but time was limited, so I went straight through to Seoul, where I was met at the station by an officer from the army headquarters.

The morning was spent in being taken round to pay visits at the army headquarters and the headquarters of the 20th Division, at both of which I was again much struck by the exceedingly friendly welcome extended. General Oba, the C.-in-C., was away at the time, but Major-General Ono, his Chief of Staff, and several other senior officers were there, and all without exception shewed the greatest kindness.

Captain Harada, the officer who had been told off to act as my " bear-leader," had been given the loan of one of the headquarter cars for the day, so that we were able to see more in the limited time at our disposal than would have been the case otherwise ; but though it was all very interesting in its way, there was little or nothing to call for special mention in these pages.

In the evening Lieut.-General Johoji, the divisional commander, gave a farewell dinner to Surgeon-General Haga, who was about to retire from the Service, and invited me to it as well. Though served in foreign style, the dinner took place at 6.30 p.m., as is usual in Japan, and was over by 9 p.m.

In the morning we had visited, amongst other places, the barracks of the 78th Infantry Regiment, as one of the officers of this regiment had been in the same set with me at the Infantry School, and had asked me to look him up if ever I went to Seoul. He and an officer of the 79th Regiment, who had also been at Chiba with me and who had come round to the barracks on hearing that I was there, had asked me to dinner with them that evening, but, as I had already accepted the invitation given by General Johoji, I had had to decline. However, on my arrival back at my quarters that evening, I found both of them awaiting me, and they insisted on taking me off there and then to a Japanese restaurant, where we had a most cheery evening and eventually got back about 1 a.m.

During this trip through Siberia, Manchuria, and Korea, I ran across quite a considerable number of officers whom I had known at Chiba and elsewhere, and it really did one good to find how genuinely pleased they seemed to see one. Whatever faults the Japanese may have as a nation, lack of hospitality or forgetfulness of former friendships are certainly not to be included amongst them.

Little or nothing more need be said about this trip, for the following evening I left Seoul by the night express for Fusan, which we reached some ten or eleven hours later. A sea passage of about the same duration took us to Shimonoseki and so back to Japan, after crossing the Straits of Tsushima, the site of that great sea-fight at which Admiral Togo destroyed Russia's last remaining hope by the destruction of Rodjesvenski's great armada on May 27th, 1905.

At Shimonoseki I unexpectedly ran across two Japanese officers, one of whom I had known before, and, as they were also travelling to Tokyo that night, we joined forces and journeyed up together. It turned out that they had been down in Kyushu fixing up quarters and making the necessary arrangements for the accommodation of the foreign attachés in the coming Grand Manœuvres, which were to be held there some three weeks later.

As I was to leave for home as soon as these manœuvres were over, the intervening period, after my arrival back in Tokyo, was spent chiefly in packing up, in farewell calls, and in a more or less concentrated and final effort to rub up my Japanese for the interpretership examination which was due to take place in London on my return there.

CHAPTER XXIII

SHANTUNG

SHORTLY before leaving Tokyo for the 1920 Grand Manœuvres described in a previous chapter, it had struck me that a trip up to Peking *viâ* Tsingtao might be worked in *en route* to England. Thanks to the Military Attaché, the Japanese War Office promised to afford me facilities for seeing over places of military interest at Tsingtao, and provided me with a letter of introduction to the army headquarters there.

Leaving Shimonoseki about midday on the 15th, we reached the port of Tsingtao some forty-eight hours later, after a fairly good passage, except for an unpleasant ground swell after getting into the Gulf of Pechili.

On coming alongside the quay I was met by an officer who had been sent down to look after me and take me back with him to the army headquarters, where I was received by Major-General Hikida, the Chief of Staff, who was at that time acting Commander-in-Chief in place of General Yui, who was temporarily absent in Japan.

I was also introduced to the other headquarters' officers and, on the following day, one of them, a cavalry major, was told off to shew me over the main points of military interest in the neighbourhood.

Although Tsingtao is said to be quite a gay place in the summer months, owing to its being a popular summer resort, it had a deserted sort of appearance at that time of year, in spite of possessing some fine roads and buildings, relics of its former Teuton owners.

Before going on to describe the impressions gained during the two or three days spent there, it may be as well to place the reader, as it were, in the picture, by refreshing his memory with a rough outline bearing on the Shantung Question.

Although this question is now practically a thing of the past, thanks to the Washington Conference, it was still a very thorny problem at the end of 1920 when I went to Tsingtao. It was partly due to a desire to see something of this bone of contention and to more or less get into the picture myself, by way of being better able to understand the question, that led me to decide on going up to Peking *viâ* this erstwhile German fortress.

This is no place in which to discuss the rights and wrongs of the case, but for the benefit of those who may have forgotten the main outline, it may be as well to summarise briefly the course of events.

As a result of the Sino-Japanese War of 1894-5, Japan, by way of indemnity, received certain territorial concessions in addition to a considerable sum of money. No sooner had she been granted this territory than Russia, France, and Germany forced her to forego the most important territorial gains, on the grounds that it was very wrong of one country to seize part of another. The hypocrisy of the whole thing was shown later when Russia proceeded to obtain the lease of the Liaotung Peninsula—the very territory from which, by her hypocritical talk, she had ousted the Japanese.

Though Germany and France, unlike Russia, did not take any of the actual territory previously ceded to Japan by China, they had no scruples in seizing bits which they wanted, and it was Germany's action in 1898 that led up, some twenty years later, to one of the most vexed questions of the Far East—a question which is still not entirely settled.

In 1898 Germany forced China to lease Kiaochou Bay and certain of the surrounding country, in compensation for the murder of two missionaries. Sixteen years later, by which time Tsingtao, at the entrance to this bay, had become one of the finest fortified ports in the Far East, this territory was captured by Japanese troops assisted by a British detachment of some two thousand men.

After the fall of this fortress the British withdrew and left the Japanese in possession, and from that time onwards the so-called Shantung Question developed until the climax was reached in 1919, when the Chinese delegates, backed by American opinion, refused to sign the Versailles Treaty, owing to the fact that the former German leased territory in Shantung had been allotted to Japan as her share of the spoil instead of being handed back to China. One could very naturally sympathise with the Chinese in their chagrin at seeing a portion of their country handed over to Japan, but it must be said for the latter country that they, the Japanese, considered that they had an equally good claim to it in view of the fact that they had taken it from the Germans and not from the Chinese, and, moreover, they expressed their willingness to return it to China at a price. No doubt from a purely moral point of view this was wrong, and Japan would probably have been wiser if she had foregone her claim to bargain and had, in a spirit of generosity, returned it to China, trusting that the latter, out of gratitude, would pay her something for it. This, it may be said, would have been the really ideal and generous attitude to have adopted, but one cannot altogether blame the Japanese for not doing so.

In the first place they argued more or less as follows :

"Supposing we, the Japanese, had not taken Tsingtao and the neighbouring territory from the Germans, China would not have had it returned to her until 1997, when the lease expired, and probably not even then. As it is, however, we have taken it from Germany by perfectly fair means and have, in addition, expended a considerable amount of blood and treasure in doing so. Moreover, we are quite prepared to return it to China if she pays us for it, so that she will get it back sooner than would otherwise have been the case. The Chinese, on the other hand, have helped in no way whatever to regain this bit of their country, so why should we return it to them free, when it is we who have borne all the trouble and expense."

The Chinese, of course, contended that, as they had come into the War in 1917 on the side of the Allies, they ought to have this territory returned to them by way of compensation, and their powers of oratory were such that they enlisted the sympathy of America in their cause. This had the effect, however, of making Japan all the more determined to exact the uttermost farthing, for she remembered (all too bitterly) how she had been cheated out of the fruits of victory twenty odd years before, when Germany, Russia, and France had combined to force her to return Port Arthur, for which she had paid so dearly, and Russia had then proceeded to annex that same territory for herself. Undoubtedly this was at the back of Japan's mind when she found America supporting China's claims in 1919, and, however honest America may have been in her intentions, there is no doubt that many Japanese saw, or thought they saw, in her interference merely a repetition of the events of the closing years of the last century.

Even apart from that, however, Japan felt that she was being unfairly discriminated against, as was shown by the arguments made by Japanese with whom one discussed the subject, a very common argument being to the following effect:

"Why is it that we, who won Tsingtao fairly under the rules of war, should be regarded as the incarnation of all that is bad, and that everyone does his utmost to prevent us from receiving what is justly due to us, whilst Germany, when she seized the same territory for no other reason than the murder of one of her nationals, should not have had a word of protest said against her?"

Whatever one thought about the rights and wrongs of the case—and there were many of each on both sides—one could not but see the logic of the Japanese point of view. Other Powers might seize hundreds of thousands of square miles of someone else's territory and no one would raise a murmur, but as soon as Japan wanted to take a few hundred square miles, the whole world was up in arms denouncing her as militaristic and imperialistic. It is rather a case of "Job's Comforter" to try to point out to a Japanese, with these injustices rankling in his mind, that what could be done with impunity twenty or thirty years ago is now, owing to the awakening of the conscience of the civilised world, impossible. He realises, only too well, that this so-called "conscience" has been brought about by the fact that the countries obsessed with it are merely so because, for the time being, they have all that they themselves require, and it pays them to prevent less satisfied people from butting in in such a way as possibly to disturb their own interests.

This little diatribe is not meant either to endorse or to condemn Japanese policy in Shantung and other parts of China; it is merely put forward to show something of the Japanese line of thought on such matters. It is, unfortunately, only too true that mistakes—often of a serious nature—have been made by Japan in her dealings with China, but the events of the last twelve months or so have clearly shown that she is honestly endeavouring to rectify those mistakes, and, in any case, before condemning her for her faults, imaginary or otherwise, it might be as well to apply the old test, "Let him who is guiltless throw the first stone." The country which has never committed a blunder or injustice of any kind has not yet appeared in this world.

All the Japanese troops which were in Shantung have now been withdrawn, but in November, 1920, when I went to Tsingtao, there was a garrison of about four battalions of infantry with headquarters at Tsingtao, Fengtzu, Kaomi, and Tsinanfu, respectively, their main function being to guard the railway running from the first to the last named place—the so-called Shantung Railway. The headquarters of the whole force was at Tsingtao, as also was that of the Civil Administration, the chief of the latter at that time being Dr. Akiyama.

Before proceeding to Tsingtao one had, of course, read a good deal in papers and magazines, both Japanese and foreign, about the various aspects of this vexed question ; but just as a few days spent in Siberia and Northern Manchuria, talking with people on the spot, had helped to give one a better perspective of the Siberian situation than months of reading on the subject had done, so also was one able to obtain a better idea of the Shantung Question, by spending a few days at Tsingtao and hearing the view of those on the spot.

As a result of discussing the matter with both Japanese and foreigners there, one came away with the impression that the former were certainly antagonising the latter, and thereby automatically ranging them on the side of their adversaries in the Shantung debate, but that this was largely due to lack of tact on their part and mutual misunderstanding, owing to the language difficulty and divergency of interests. As is often the case in such matters, it was obvious that the petty official was largely to blame, for, in spite of the unfortunate anti-Japanese attitude of most of the foreigners whom one met, they all spoke very highly of the higher military and civil authorities. If the Chief of Staff and the Chief of the Civil Administration were typical of the higher officials there, this can be well understood. The former I met several times and the latter once, at a dinner given by General Hikida when some twenty or so military and civil officials were present, and a more charming and courteous couple it would be hard to find anywhere.

Judging from newspaper talk, one might imagine that the so-called " militarists " of Japan were the incarnation of all that is evil. If these " militarists " are the higher commanders whom one meets in Siberia, in Manchuria, in Korea, in Shantung, and elsewhere—as one is led to believe they must be—they must each be possessed of two very different characters, as in Robert Louis Stevenson's famous story of *Dr. Jekyll and Mr. Hyde.* Judging from one's own experiences, it certainly seems that they more often adopt the personality of the former than that of the latter.

As it would take too long to describe in detail all that one heard and saw in the two or three days spent at Tsingtao, resort must be made once again to the diary.

"We set off in the car about 9 a.m. (Major T. . . and N. . ., who had come round to call for me). Motored out to the Iltis Forts, situated on top of a hill about a mile and a half to the east. These, and the fort on Hui Hsing Point, are the only forts left standing, the Japanese having dismantled all the others since their occupation of Tsingtao, by way of showing the world that they do not intend to fortify the place." [1]

From the top of Iltis Hill you get a fine bird's-eye view of the battle area. To the S.E., the German right flank, is the Yellow Sea, in which the British and Japanese warships operated, while a couple of miles to the N.W. is the harbour and Kiaochou Bay, in which the German fleet took refuge behind the mine barrage and operated against the attacking British and Japanese, the left of the German position resting on the bay. It was from there that the famous *Emden* escaped in order to carry out her raids. The Germans had three main forts on the hills running across this neck of land, the width from coast to coast being about three miles, but they also had a number of strong redoubts on the smaller hills—or rather hillocks—to the front. The attackers never actually reached these main forts, as the white flag was hoisted on November 7th, 1914, when the attackers, after one week's bombardment, assaulted the line of redoubts. The Shizuoka Regiment, the 34th, the one with which I carried out my first period of attachment, was on the extreme right of the attack, while the British force, consisting of the 2nd South Wales Borderers and half a Sikh regiment, was to their left.

The three main forts have a clear view of the country for a distance of two or three miles across low-lying ground which the attackers had to cross, another range of mountains running across the peninsula to the back of this strip.

The Germans really had three lines, the first being the range of hills to the N.E. and the last the line of redoubts and a wall running across from one side of the peninsula to

[1] Japan has now, of course, withdrawn altogether and handed Tsingtao back to the Chinese.

the other. They certainly had a strong position, and one can see that, had they been really keen to do so, they ought to have been able to hold out much longer than they actually did.

"After having the details of the attack explained to me, we went inside the fort, which is an absolute warren underground with numbers of huge concrete rooms and a tunnel, about a hundred and twenty yards in length, connecting the eastern part with the western. Two 10.5 cm. guns, destroyed by direct hits, still remain.

"From the fort we motored to Tai-tung-chen across the front of the German position and then out to the original first line position and through the mountains to the N.E. Very fine rugged scenery, reminding one of pictures of the Khyber Pass and other suchlike places, the hills being strewn with boulders. The Germans had a company up in these hills at the start, and it seems surprising that they did not emulate the Afghan method of fighting. A few sharpshooters up in those hills, hidden behind boulders, could have played 'Old Harry' with any force advancing through this long narrow defile. All they seem to have done was to destroy one bridge, and, as the river was fairly narrow at that point, a new temporary one was soon erected.

"Motored out to the foot of Laoshan,[1] a rugged, rocky hill about 4000 feet in height, some fifteen or twenty miles from Tsingtao, the road only going as far as this. Got into a Chinese *kago* and was carried up one of the smaller hills, from which you get an excellent view of the gorge below. On the top and at the foot of this hill are several burnt-out stone buildings,[2] which were originally summer hotels and villas belonging to local Germans, who destroyed them as soon as war broke out, in order to prevent the Japanese making use of them.

"On the subject of the future of Tsingtao, Major T. . . . intimated that he was all for handing it back to China, but both he and Y. . . agreed that so long as Japan holds it

[1] It was at Laoshan Bay, just to the south, that the Allied forces landed.

[2] Including the Mecklenberg Hospital.

she must also retain the Shantung Railway to Tsinanfu, in order to prevent raids on it by bandits. In reply to my remarks that the Germans had found the guard of four hundred Chinese sufficient for this purpose, N. . . argued that the state of the country was more unsettled now than it was at that time, owing to the revolution and also the civil war betweeen the north and the south." [1]

On November the 20th, I left Tsingtao and went by rail to Tsinanfu, army headquarters very kindly supplying me with a free pass. Leaving at 8 a.m. we reached our destination at 6.30 p.m. the same day. In view of subsequent events the following extract from the diary is perhaps worth noting:

"The first half of the journey is very uninteresting—miles and miles of dead level country on either side as far as the eye can see, but the country gets a bit hilly during the second half—though they are dreary, treeless hills and not the fine, well-wooded, rugged type you get in Japan, nor is there any touch of colour; everything is a monotonous drab shade. At every station down the line one sees Japanese troops or *gendarmes* and one can quite imagine that they alone put people's backs up. One can well be in sympathy with the Japanese in their attitude towards the Shantung Question, so far as Tsingtao and the leased territory is concerned, but it would seem to be to their own advantage to withdraw the troops along the line, as they are not needed there and simply act as a sore to the Chinese and foreigners. If the Japanese did that, the Chinese would only have themselves to blame for their troubles in the Shantung, and the anti-Japanese foreigners would have their main argument knocked on the head."

It must be remembered, of course, that the above was written in 1920. Since then the Washington Conference has been held, and one of the results has been practically to settle the Shantung Question, so that now these Japanese

[1] This extract seems of interest in view of the most recent developments in the settling of the Shantung Question, and in view of the bandit outrages at Lincheng and elsewhere.

troops along the railway, which so offended the Chinese and others, have been withdrawn, as a result of which there is a much better feeling between the two nations. I had only time to spend a few days at Tsinanfu, the capital of Shantung Province, but it was quite long enough, as may be gathered from the following extract:

" Went out to the old native city with G. . . after lunch. Very thick walls round the city, with large gates which are kept closed at night, as at Mukden, Liaoyang, etc. Roads filthy, shops filthy, people filthy, everything filthy and unsanitary—absolute breeding-places for diseases of all kinds. . . . They (the Chinese), are cheery-looking rogues, but disgustingly dirty. I asked G. . . if they would ever learn the value of sanitation. He replied in the negative, adding that it would be a bad thing if they did, as they breed like rabbits and the only thing that keeps down their numbers is that so many hundreds of thousands of them die every year from these same unsanitary conditions. A curious way of looking at it, but there is no doubt a lot to be said for it."

G. . ., who made this comment, was a foreigner with whom I was staying at the time. It calls to mind a remark made to me by a Japanese officer with whom I was discussing the possibility of Japan going to war with America—a topic very much to the fore just then. According to him the rapid increase of population in Japan, combined with the fact that other countries were refusing to help to ease the congestion, would sooner or later lead to war. Although, of course, as he pointed out, it would be preferable to win, it would not matter very much really whether Japan did so or not, as the question of surplus population would be settled in either case. If she won she would be able to get colonies for herself, whilst, if she lost, she would have no need for colonies, as all the surplus population would have been killed off.

In Tsinanfu there was a battalion of Japanese infantry at the time I was there, whilst within the barracks in which they were quartered one could see the aerials of a high-power wireless, said to be in direct communication with Tokyo. The clean, tidy appearance of these barracks and their inmates was in strong contrast to the Chinese soldiers whom one saw about everywhere, "slovenly-looking beggars without arms or equipment, and wearing padded clothes. Nice and warm in cold, dry weather, but must be like sponges when it rains and quite impossible to get dry again. From all accounts, however, no Chinaman in these parts, whether soldier or civilian, ever thinks of going out in the rain. In fact, in the recent operations [1] heavy rain set in, and both armies ceased fighting for five days in order to keep themselves dry. That is what one might call 'gentlemanly' warfare."

In spite of its dirt and its smells, Tsinanfu is an interesting place in its way, and some of the means of transport which one sees in its streets are, to say the least, comic.

"I was very amused with the large wheel-barrows used here as a method of conveyance. Most amusing to see a couple of Chinamen squatting quite unconcernedly on one of these barrows, one on either side of the big wheel which is in the front centre, the while a sweating coolie trundles them along, the barrow emitting fearsome squeaks and groans, as the use of oil on an axle seems to be unknown in these parts. G. . ., as a matter of fact, tells me that John Chinaman prefers not to use oil on it, as he has an idea that the squeaking helps to keep away evil spirits."

One short entry made *à propos* of Tsinanfu gives in a nut-shell one of the main reasons for Japan's desire to retain what she had won in the Shantung. "Trade in these parts is expanding enormously of late and G. . . thinks there is a very big future before it."

Japan's great handicap is her lack of raw material, and she is faced with the problem of either finding an outlet for her surplus population or else obtaining sufficient supplies of raw material to give them employment in their own country. The Japanese have too many home ties to make

[1] Chang-tso-lin's operations against the Anfu Party, whom he helped to drive out of Pekin in the summer of 1920.

good colonists, so the best thing for them is to obtain sufficient raw material to keep themselves employed at home. Shantung is one of the richest provinces in China and offers Japan the very chance for which she is looking. By holding on, therefore, to Tsingtao and the one and only railway leading from the coast to the capital in the heart of Shantung, she was able to exploit the resources of the province to the best advantage. Politically and militarily this was of great importance, but there is no doubt that Japan's main thought was of its economic value, and much the same is true of her hold on Manchuria. True, she was able to dominate Pekin itself by her simultaneous hold of Tsingtao and Port Arthur, enabling her practically to guard the one and only entrance to the Chinese capital from the sea—a matter of very considerable military and political importance, constituting, as it did, something in the nature of a strangle-hold on her large but feeble neighbour ; but at the back of all this there was probably, one might almost say undoubtedly, the great outstanding necessity for procuring a free and unhampered supply of raw materials for her industries.

Although one cannot by any means endorse all Japan's actions in China, one must admit that the latter has brought many of her troubles on herself, not only in her endeavours to play off one country against another, but also by her unlimited corruptness, especially amongst the official classes, almost any single individual of whom, like the Turk, is always willing to sign away concession after concession and mortgage his country's resources up to the hilt, provided he himself makes sufficient personal profit out of the transactions. From a moral standpoint one would say that Japan has no right to exploit this weakness of the Chinese race, but it is more than likely that nine countries out of ten, if they found themselves in the same predicaments as Japan, would do likewise. Japan requires the raw material, and she sees it there ready to hand, but with its owners either too lazy or too inefficient to make use of it. What more natural, therefore, than that she should make a bid for it herself.

Apart from this, however, there is yet another point to be brought out in favour of Japan *vis-à-vis* China. In those parts of the latter's territory in which she has, or has had, a footing, enormous improvements are visible, especially in regard to sanitation and education. The Japanese quarters of such places as Tsingtao, Dairen, Port Arthur, or Mukden are as clean and orderly as you could find anywhere, and the Chinese living therein are gradually coming to realise the value of cleanliness, many of them even adopting the bath-house system which is such a feature of Japanese life. Hospitals and schools have also been provided for them and their standards of living have been raised. The Chinese *rickshaw* coolie of Dairen, for example, has been smartened up and made to feel a little self-respect, which, from what foreigners who knew Dairen twenty years ago say, he never had in the days of Russian occupation when he was left to his own devices. In the case of Korea, of course, improvements are even more noticeable, and it is only fair to admit that in most, if not all, the places which Japan has administered at one time or another, conditions have been improved and the lot of the natives has been bettered in many ways in spite of—in some cases—the unnecessarily repressive measures adopted. The old question naturally arises: "Which is preferable? To be independent but misgoverned and poverty-stricken, or to be under foreign domination but well-governed and prosperous?" Opinions differ, and the reader is at liberty to select his own.

CHAPTER XXIV

NORTH CHINA

" LEFT Tsinanfu early in the morning and arrived at Tientsin in the evening, passing through the famine-stricken area on the way—huge level plains with barely a sign of vegetation, all the crops having failed this year. Millions are said to be starving . . . Noticed a few poor blighters with nothing but a few shreds of sacking on them by way of clothes and it is pretty chilly here at night. . . . Don't wonder people living in these parts are subject to nervous breakdowns. More dismal, dreary country is hard to imagine. Just limitless stretches of drab-coloured, sandy, hill-less country, with hundreds of little sand-heaps dotted about everywhere, especially over the last thirty or forty miles of the line to Tientsin, all these mounds being graves, and no stone or anything to identify their occupiers."

The above extracts are given by way of drawing a contrast between the country in those parts of North China and that of Japan with its well-wooded hills and its magnificent mountain scenery. There are, of course, some beautiful parts of China, but after seeing something of Manchuria and then of Shantung and Chihli, one began to feel thankful that a kindly fate had sent one to Japan as a Language Officer instead of to China.

Apart from its own particular charm, it may be that, after seeing something of the depressing scenery around it, one arrives in Pekin and at once succumbs to its beauties and to its whole atmosphere of extraordinary interest, historically, politically, artistically, and in every other way.

Be that as it may, the fact remains that, after a visit to the Chinese capital, one is almost inclined to revise one's former opinion as to the kindness of fate, for the Language Officer in Pekin is to be envied.

On the way to Pekin I had stopped a couple of days at Tientsin, where the 2/55th Coke's Rifles were stationed at the time, the officers very kindly putting me up at their Mess.

Those who have served in Tientsin speak of it as a very good station, but for the casual visitor there is not much of interest about it, and one is not altogether sorry to leave the place. Pekin, on the other hand, only another three hours further on, is one of those cities like Kyoto, which, once you get there, you never want to leave, and in my own case, although I had only meant to stay one or two days and then go on to Hankow, I ended in stopping a week, which meant having to give up any idea of visiting Hankow if I wanted to catch the boat on which my passage was booked from Shanghai.

Although the globe-trotter, who spends a week or two in a place and then proceeds to write a book about it, always rather annoys one, you almost begin to sympathise with him when you try to write a book yourself and come to the point where you feel you must record your own impressions of a place like Pekin, of which you realise you know all too little and really have but little to say that has not been said by hundreds of people before you. However, although the entries made in the diary during those few days spent in Pekin cover some thirty pages of foolscap, only such parts as deal mainly with Japan or with military matters will be quoted, to which must be added the hope that they will not be too disjointed.

"Met a very cheering sight on entering our Legation compound, viz. a British 'Tommy' on 'sentry-go'—the first I have seen for over three years. One company of the 2nd Wiltshires detached from Hong Kong is on duty here as Legation Guard."

During my stay in Pekin the Military Attaché very kindly

put me up, though I generally messed with the officers of the Legation Guard—a very excellent set of fellows.

"The British Legation compound is an enormous place with quarters for all the Legation staff and also for the Legation Guard and others, the whole enclosure being surrounded by high, loop-holed walls, reminiscent of the Boxer Rebellion and very different from the peaceful appearance of the Embassy in Tokyo. All the Legations here are much the same in that respect, all being guarded by troops and prepared for defence in case of trouble . . . The Alston's[1] house is a wonderful old place, it having originally been a Chinese palace and built in the old Chinese style with huge red lacquered pillars and carvings of all kinds."

Amongst others whom I met in Pekin was a certain Wing Commander of the R.A.F. who was there at the time as an adviser to the Chinese on aviation.

"They were some of his machines which Chang-tso-lin seized recently. It seems that these machines were sent out to China on condition that they were not used for military purposes by either side.[2] They promised this, but, as H. . . says, everyone knew quite well that the Chinese would never keep to this agreement, and of course they did not. The more one lives and learns, the more one is forced to the conclusion that all countries, our own not excepted, are a set of hypocrites. We vilify the Japanese for supplying armaments to the two opposing forces, yet we do it ourselves, only that we are such hypocrites that we pretend we don't. The long and the short of it is that everyone is out for his own ends, and the more one hears the more convinced one becomes that half the anti-Japanese propaganda in these parts is simply due to the fact that we and other countries are jealous of Japan's position out here, and if we were in her place we would probably do just the same. Several people with whom I have spoken on the subject hold pretty much the same view, I find."

[1] Sir Beilby Alston, British Minister to Pekin, 1920 to 1922.

[2] This, of course, refers to the Civil War which was in full swing at the time.

One hears a great deal about the honesty of the Chinese as compared to that of their neighbours from Japan. In commercial dealings perhaps there may be some truth in this assertion, but the following entry, made after talks on the subject with various foreigners who have lived many years in Pekin, seems to point to the conclusion that dishonesty is not by any means confined to the Japanese.

" They admit that however much you may like individual Chinese you can never respect them, as they are full of corruption and deceit from highest to lowest and are absolutely untrustworthy, unless you have the upper hand, and heaven help the man under them. Their recent treatment of the Russians is a case in point. Incidentally, they seem to have made a bad mistake by the issue of their mandate denying all rights to Russians in China, as they had made no provisions for enforcing the mandate, and from all accounts they would willingly withdraw it if they could, but are afraid to do so for fear of losing face. What a bugbear that fear is to all Orientals, not excepting the Japanese, as instanced in the Shaw case."

While in Pekin, one got some side-lights on the subject of the Chinese army, as will be seen by the following extracts.

" The Chinese army seems to be a thing of beauty and a joy for ever. B. . . tells me that even the Chinese War Office itself knows neither its strength nor its dispositions. Their method of fighting must be truly marvellous. In the recent show, for instance, one of the generals had his favourite concubine captured by the opposing side, so the fighting was stopped for a bit in order to carry out negotiations for the lady's release. This was finally fixed up and she was returned to store in exchange for some of the rolling stock belonging to his army."

" In another case two opposing forces of artillery agreed to fire to the left of each other instead of at each other, but one of the generals, on seeing this, ordered his men to fire actually at the enemy. As soon as he had gone, however, his men sent over a note of apology to the enemy, and it was then agreed that in future they should only fire at each other when there were generals about."

"The two opposing forces very often agree beforehand when and where they are to fight and which side is to retire, the side retreating being paid by the others to do so. The amusing part is that, as a result of these agreements, *communiqués*, telling of the capture of some important place, are often published several days before the 'victors' arrive."

While in Pekin one saw Chinese soldiers posted with bayonets fixed wherever one went. This was due to the fact that the authorities were on the lookout for Anfuites, some of whom were known to be hiding in the Legation Quarter—that home of refuge for political refugees for many years past. In conspicuous places throughout the city were pasted photographs of the Anfu leaders with notices offering rewards for their arrest. The one most wanted had $100,000 on his head. This was General Hsu, commonly known as "Little Hsu" in order to distinguish him from another official of the same name. It was with considerable surprise that, on glancing over the portrait gallery of "wanteds" pasted on a large wooden gateway, I recognised this particular gentleman as having been leader of the party of Chinese officers who attended the 1918 Grand Manœuvres in Japan.[1]

Although "Little Hsu's" portrait was still being exhibited, he had, in point of fact, made good his escape a short time before. If all accounts are true, this was effected by the Japanese Legation, who were, in consequence, somewhat in disfavour with the new Chinese Government. The story goes that "Little Hsu" had fled for refuge to the Japanese Legation and that they had in due course managed to smuggle him safely out of the country by the simple expedient of sending him off to Tsingtao concealed in a large trunk or packing-case labelled "military stores," and from there he had been shipped over to Japan in a Japanese cruiser.

General Higashi, who was at that time Japanese Military Attaché in Pekin, was commonly credited with having been

[1] *Vide* p. 31.

mainly responsible for having him smuggled away in this fashion, but whether such was really the case or not no one seemed to know for certain.

Before leaving Japan I had been provided with letters of introduction to him and to Major-General Minami, the commander of the Japanese troops in North China, but, unfortunately, I was unable to see either of them, as both were out when I called, though I had a talk with the former's assistant.

The Japanese G.O.C.-in-C. North China had his headquarters in Tientsin, where most of the troops were stationed, and, though I was unable to meet him, I saw quite a lot of his second-in-command, Colonel Ueno, whom I had known previously in Japan, and who had invited me to look him up if ever I went to Tientsin. This last-named officer had, in pre-War days, been in England and had been attached to the East Surreys in Aldershot for a time.

As Chinese politics have so close a connection with Japan, it may perhaps be permissible to quote from the diary an entry made at the time in regard to the Anfu troubles mentioned above.

" When China joined the War she decided to raise three divisions to send overseas, their organisation and training being managed by a War Participation Bureau. These divisions were still being formed when the War ended, whereupon they were sent off to Mongolia and renamed the Frontier Defence Force, ' Little Hsu ' being sent off there as Governor-General. Mongolia, after the 1912 revolution, had become autonomous, but ' Little Hsu,' after becoming Governor-General, by various means of intimidation made them agree to give up their autonomy and once more become an integral part of China, which meant the deposing of the Living Buddha.

" As soon as he had forced the signing of this agreement, Hsu had the documents sent off to the Central Government at Pekin, the Chinese officials despatched to take the news being given orders to go at full speed. The party went off in nine cars and were so anxious to get the news through quickly that several of the cars got smashed up on the way and two of the officials were killed. Hsu, of course, gave out that Mongolia was hugely delighted to 'return to the fold,' but in reality he simply forced her to do so, the Mongolian delegates signing the document under threat of death if they refused. About this time Hsu and his friends of the Military Party formed the Anfu Club, the main object being to keep the country unsettled in order to give themselves a free hand. After a time, however, the people began to rise against all this tyranny, and Wu-pei-fu, a general from Hunan, who had been fighting for the North against the South, championed their cause, marched on Pekin, and defeated the Anfu Party, the Anfu troops deserting their leaders. It was at this time that Chang-tso-lin, on the pretext of restoring order, brought his troops up by rail from Mukden and, amongst other things, seized the aeroplanes which had been sent over from England."

Some eighteen months after the entry just quoted was made, Chang-tso-lin and Wu-pei-fu came to blows, the latter being the winner. In view of this fact the following entry made in November, 1920, is of interest.

"According to B. . ., Wu-pei-fu's troops are about the only ones in China with any discipline. B. . . mentioned this to Wu one day and complimented him on the fact, whereupon Wu replied, 'Yes! I intend to make them a match for the Japanese and then we will fight them and drive them out!'"

Wu shewed in his fight with Chang that he was a very capable general, but if he ever hopes to make his troops a match for the Japanese, he must, amongst other things, make sure that their pay is not, as is the case with most Chinese troops, several months in arrears.

Undoubtedly the Chinese have some very good points, and, in their relations with Japan, it is only human nature to sympathise with them up to a point in their *rôle* of underdog. On closer examination, however, after studying Chinese history and talking with those best qualified to know, one is apt to have doubts as to whether the Chinese are such misused people as they are often made out to be. One hears a great deal of talk about the Japanese ill-treating the poor, harmless Chinese, but when one looks closer into the matter, the conclusion reached is that no one is more cruel to the Chinaman than one of his own countrymen who happens to be in a higher position than himself, and China's treatment of Russians, ever since the Russian consular jurisdiction was withdrawn in 1920, goes to show that John Chinaman, whenever he gets the upper hand of anyone, is little better than a savage. Add to this that bribery and corruption are rife from the highest to the lowest; that very often Chinese soldiers go months, even years, without pay, and then, to make up for it, are allowed to loot and plunder whole towns and villages; that China's one aim and object in life is to play one nation off against another by fair means or foul—consider all these points and many more besides and one is bound to admit that "poor misused China" is something of a myth, or at any rate that she has brought most of her troubles on herself.

An American, with whom I was speaking not so very long ago, drew attention to the fact that the Chinese at the Versailles Conference were so much finer than the Japanese because they talked so much and so well, but this hardly seems classifiable as a virtue, as it is merely a question of linguistic ability. You might as well say that a politician or "tub-thumper" is a better man than a brilliant soldier or sailor, or a scientist, who is a hundred times more useful to his country but cannot even make an after-dinner speech.

One is following in the footsteps of the globe-trotting author if one professes to be an authority on China or the Chinese after merely spending a few weeks in the country, but it can do no harm to quote one more entry to show the impression left on one after talking with numbers of those who are qualified to speak, and after seeing a certain amount with one's own eyes.

"The Chinese seem in many respects like the Turks—cheery, smiling individuals, but rotten to the core. The coolie class appear to have many good points and the soldiery look as though they might be excellent material if properly led, equipped, and disciplined. But from all accounts the word ' honesty ' is unknown among the official class, who simply grind down all those under them. Inefficient to the last degree, they are always open to bribery and corruption. Much the same is true of the Turk, who, before the War, one looked on as a bit of a waster but quite a good sportsman. His treatment of British prisoners of war brought about a change of opinion, and any sympathy we may have felt for him has been swept away by the proofs of his cruelty. ' Johnny Turk ' and ' John Chinaman ' seem to be the same in that respect, as all accounts appear to prove pretty conclusively that the latter is capable of atrocities and cruelties of all kinds to any poor devil whom he happens to get in his power."

This indictment may sound a bit harsh and is possibly unfair, as it was written after only a few weeks in China, but it was nevertheless the impression left after conversation with people of all kinds who were in a position to know, and many of whom, in spite of admitting these vices, nevertheless had a real affection for the Chinese, who have, of course, many virtues to counteract their weak points. Compare this state of affairs, however, with that ruling in Japan.

In the case of the peasant class, apart from personal cleanliness, there is probably not much to differentiate between those of the former " Dragon Empire " and those of their small but powerful island neighbour. Hard-working and industrious, and capable of withstanding the greatest hardships without complaint, simple folk not overburdened with imagination, the peasant classes of both countries are kindly dispositioned and hospitable and only ask to be left in peace to enjoy the fruits of their labours. In both cases they form the bulk of the population, China and Japan being agricultural countries, though industrialism is spreading rapidly in the latter.

The peasant class in Japan is perhaps more happy in this respect, for taxation is regulated and the peasant has not the ever-present fear, as has his Chinese *confrère*, that his hard-earned savings may be seized at any moment by professional bandits, or their amateur counterparts in the army, and that even his property may be destroyed and his life threatened through one of the same two agencies.

This leads us to a comparison of the armies of the two countries, and all traces of similarity, such as those to be found between the peasant classes, disappear. China, in spite of her army of over a million, has no true martial instincts, and her soldiers are little more than an armed mob of hooligans—soldiers one day and bandits the next. The officers are little, if any, better, and are mainly recruited from the coolie class themselves. The money due to the soldiers is, in most cases, many months in arrear, and a general thinks nothing of keeping for himself the pay intended for his men. When, as a result, they show signs of getting restive, he appeases their wrath by giving them permission to loot the neighbouring towns and villages ;—great fun, no doubt, for the soldiers, but rather hard on the unfortunate civilian victims.

There is a Chinese proverb which says, "You don't make horse-shoes of good iron and you don't make soldiers of good men." The meaning of this is, of course, that it is only the lowest set of Chinese who take to the army as a profession.

From time immemorial this has been the case with the Chinese army, and, although great leaders such as Kublai-Khan and strategists such as Wu and Sun [1] have arisen amongst them, the army officers on the whole have never been of a type to earn the right to the generally accepted synonymous classification of "gentlemen." The term, "officer and gentleman," could never be applied to them as a class.

Enough has been said in the preceding chapters to show

[1] Wu and Sun lived some 2400 years ago, but the science of war as laid down by them at the time is, in principle, almost identical with that of the present day. Anyone interested in the subject is recommended to read the translation of their works made by the late Lieut. Col. Calthrop, R.A., and published by John Murray under the title of *The Book of War*. He will find his trouble well repaid, for the pages are full of interest.

how very different the Japanese army is from its Chinese counterpart and how greatly the type of officer in the former differs from that in the latter in training, in outlook, in efficiency, in class, and in every other respect.

Coming next to the merchant class it must be admitted that, if all one hears be true, the Chinese is the more honest and trustworthy in his dealings, and it is probably largely due to this fact that the idea has got about that the Chinaman is the better man, for it is, after all, the merchant rather than the soldier or the politician with whom most foreigners, either in Japan or in China, come into contact, and it is but natural for a man to judge a country by those of its countrymen whom he knows.

Some there are who, no doubt, will say that their dealings with Japanese officials in Manchuria or North China show that it is not only the merchants that are to blame; but, while admitting that the so-called "Open Door Policy" is not always strictly observed by Japan, it will generally be found, on close examination, that the foreign merchant is up in arms against the Japanese in China because their interests conflict with his own, and the unbiassed observer is bound to admit that, for the same reason, American business men in China are often just as unpopular with their British *confrères* as are the Japanese, and *vice versâ*. There is nothing so provocative of ill-feeling as conflicting interests in business, and it is a truism that over-keen trade rivalry bears with it the germs of war. The Chinese merchant is probably more honest in business than his Japanese counterpart, but undoubtedly one of the reasons for the latter being so unpopular with foreigners in China is, as has been said, that his interests conflict with theirs. Unfortunately, however, from what one hears, even the old-time proverbial honesty of the Chinese merchant is becoming a thing of the past, especially in southern China.

One more point in regard to the Japanese merchant, which cannot be too often reiterated, is that, in slanging him, one is apt to forget that his whole environment for hundreds of years past has tended to lower the degree of his honesty. The *Samurai*, the peasant, the artisan, the merchant—this, for centuries prior to the opening up of Japan in the middle of last century, was the order of priority in social standing in Japan. Not only was the merchant the lowest in the social scale—always excepting, of course, the outcast *Eta* class—but he was made to feel it and was made to put up with all kinds of indignities at the hands of the nobility and of the two-sworded *Samurai*, who even, so history records, on some occasions, in order to test the blade of a newly-acquired sword, would try its effect on the body of a luckless merchant who happened to have offended him. Thus, in the 45th article of Ieyasu's *Legacy*, a code of justice drawn up by that great warrior-statesman some 300 years ago, the following passage occurs.

"The term for a rude man is 'other-than-expected-fellow,' and a *Samurai* is not to be interfered with in cutting down a fellow who has behaved to him in a manner other than is expected."

Such being the case, it is hardly surprising that the merchant class, looked down on and disregarded, should have gradually, in the course of centuries, come to lose all sense of self-respect and shame, and should, as a result, have become dishonest in his dealings. Moreover, his first contact with so-called Western civilisation was not altogether conducive to raising his code of commerical morality, for he became himself the victim of the most blatant frauds and underhand deceits from European and American adventurers imaginable.[1] Things came to such a pass that the late Sir Rutherford Alcock, at that time British Consul-General at Tokyo, had to take disciplinary measures to suppress this great injustice which was becoming a blot on British prestige.

Dishonest practices amongst foreign merchants in Japan are not unknown even to this day, but they are now more few and far between. Similarly the Japanese merchant class

[1] The nature of these incidents is too long to describe here, but for those interested in the subject the Appendix at the end of *The Allies*, by Major General Sir H. Colvile, is recommended for their edification.

has begun to realise that honesty pays in the long run, and, although the late War showed all too clearly that there were still many black sheep amongst them ready to take dishonest advantages by exporting very inferior goods much below sample, indications are not lacking to show that matters are improving, commercial missions to Europe and America, such as that carried out by Mr. Takuma Dan and his party of Japanese business men towards the end of 1921, doing much to bring about that desirable state of affairs.

The Japanese officer class is still apt to look down on the merchant class, but the latter has now become such a power in the land that it can afford to disregard this fact, especially as the power of the former is correspondingly on the decrease. Moreover, the former class distinction is rapidly disappearing, and one now finds many members of the old *Samurai* families in the large business houses and, similarly, many naval and military officers come from the ranks of the one-time despised merchant class.

When in 1872 the system of conscripting young men from all classes was initiated, many of the old *Samurai* families cried out in horror at this innovation, for formerly no one but members of the *Samurai* families had been permitted to bear arms. But, as the late Marshal Prince Yamagata pointed out in Okuma's *Fifty Years of New Japan,* the decision of the authorities to break with tradition in this particular instance proved their wisdom, for, in the civil war which broke out shortly afterwards, the conscript merchants and peasants showed up better than did their volunteer *Samurai* brothers-in-arms.

All this, however, is leading away somewhat from the original theme, which was to draw a comparison between the Japanese and Chinese according to classes. The peasant, the soldier, and the merchant have now each been dealt with in turn, and it only remains, therefore, to consider the question of the official class.

The reader may very possibly disagree with the judgment passed a few pages back in regard to Chinese cruelty, and it may perhaps have been unfair to compare it with that of the Turks, but there is one point in that denunciation of the Chinese with which even their best friends will probably agree, namely, the criminal inefficiency and procrastination of the official class and their hopeless corruptness. Putnam Weale and other writers of his stamp, paid "advisers" to the Chinese Government, may rant and rage about the iniquities of the Japanese, but the fact remains that most of these "iniquities" are brought about by the total lack of honesty and hopeless corruptness of the average Chinese official, who is ready to sell his soul—let alone his country—for money, and then retire to live comfortably on the proceeds. Japan, knowing this weakness of the Chinese, may be wrong to take advantage of it, but she is only doing what hundreds of individuals of all nationalities are doing in Pekin every day, for the city swarms with concession-hunters and paid "advisers"—"parasites sucking out the life-blood of the country through the medium of its corrupt officials." One has but to read the works of Bland or any other unprejudiced observer, or talk with those best placed to know—better still, turn to the whole history of the country—and one will soon realise to what depths of corruption the Chinese official will go, for it is probably hardly an exaggeration to say that the number of high officials in China who have never accepted a bribe could be counted on the fingers of one hand. The humorous side of the whole affair is that every official is ready to impeach his opponent on the charge of bribery and corruption, irrespective of the fact that he is steeped in both himself. He will accuse the man in power of taking money from the Japanese or anyone else, but, when he himself rises to power, he will think nothing of doing exactly the same thing himself. Moreover, a Chinese official will be given charge of a large sum of money for distribution in a famine area or for improvment of education or the building of a new railway, or a general will be given money for the payment of his troops, but in nine cases out of ten none of these sums of money will reach their intended destinations untouched, and a very large percentage will find its way into the pockets of the official or the general *en route*.

Cases of bribery and corruption are not unknown in Japan, but to nothing like the extent to which they obtain in China, and they are probably not more common in Japan than they are in a great many other countries. Certain it is that ministers of state and other high officials do not seize money destined for other purposes, and one never hears complaints of salaries being left unpaid as is so very often the case in China. Nor can the Japanese official be termed either indolent or inefficient. True, the service of communications is not as good as it might be—the telephone, the telegraph, and the post—nor is the condition of most of the roads good, but those and other items are not due to the inefficiency of those in charge so much as to lack of the necessary funds and experience, and it is probably merely a question of time before all these matters are righted. Modern Japan has, after all, only been in existence for some sixty years, and she cannot therefore be expected to bring everything up to the standard to which it has taken other first-class Powers several hundreds of years to attain, for it is largely a question of money. Her army and navy are amongst the most efficient in the world, whilst her railway and shipping services leave little to be desired. Some of her other services are perhaps not quite up to standard, but they too will no doubt become so before many more years have elapsed.

There are those who say that it is because she spends, and has spent, so much money on her fighting forces that Japan is prevented from improving her other services. There is a great deal of truth in this, but it must be remembered that Japan was wise in setting herself to mould a really efficient fighting force before attempting anything else. Her army and navy have been to her as a shield behind which she has been able to shelter and get on with improvements in her other services. Had she set to work on her other needs first, and left the construction of a fighting force till everything else was completed, it is more than probable that her programme would never have been carried on very far and to-day she would be in much the same position as China—a plaything for the other Powers and a mere pawn in the game.

Japan, like other countries, has her faults, but before reviling her or dubbing her as "the Germany of the East," one should at least give her her due.

This is no place for the discussion of the morals of the Japanese, but while on the subject of their faults and failings, and as "John Paris" has of late brought this question very much to the fore by the publication of that cleverly-written but sordid novel, *Kimono*, it may be mentioned in passing that a wholly erroneous idea is obtained from a perusal of its pages. The impression left after reading it is that every Japanese inn is a brothel: in fact, "John Paris" makes this statement as though it were a fact. One also gets the idea that the "Jonkina" and the celebration of carrying the so-called "queen of the prostitutes" through the streets of the Yoshiwara were every-day events in Japan. As a matter of fact the "Jonkina" is danced no longer, and the Yoshiwara procession is likewise a thing of the past, as also is the placing of dressed-up *joro* in cages for the passers-by to see—an episode which the author of *Kimono* describes as though it were still done.

Even the Japanese *geisha* are not synonymous with prostitutes any more than the English chorus girl is necessarily a lady of easy virtue. That there are inns which allow practices which are not above reproach no one can deny, but it is probably only a small proportion of the whole. Japan has her vices the same as any other country, but the immorality ascribed to her in the pages of *Kimono* is grossly exaggerated, and it would be just as fair to judge England by a novel dealing with the morals of Piccadilly and Leicester Square at night as to pass judgment on Japan as a nation based on the pages of *Kimono*.

However, all this talk has led far away from the subject with which this chapter was started, and before bringing it to a close there are one or two more points to be mentioned in connection with this visit to Pekin.

One very noticeable fact was the cheapness of most things compared with what one had been accustomed in Japan, where, for example, the price even of a five-minute ride in a *kuruma* was outrageous. Here in Pekin one could hire a *rikisha* for an hour and pay twenty-five cents. But the outstanding feature of low prices was the cheapness of ponies. Every foreigner in Pekin keeps one or more as a matter of course, as the cost of a pony is merely nominal, and polo and riding, in consequence, are within the means of most, and are not merely the pastimes of the rich.[1] It is in this, amongst other things, that the Language Officer in Pekin is to be envied by his brother officers in Japan ; also in the fact that excellent shooting is to be had in the vicinity without much difficulty, whereas game of any kind is scarce in Japan

From a purely military point of view, however, the L.O. in Japan is better off, for he can mix with Japanese officers and carry out attachments with units of the army in a way which cannot be done in China. In the former country, moreover, there is much to be learnt by a study of its army, whereas in China this is impossible, unless it be to learn how things should *not* be done. Taken all round, therefore, the L.O. in Japan probably gains more from the purely professional point of view ; and, moreover, even though he is practically debarred from riding or shooting, he has, as has already been pointed out earlier in these pages, many compensating advantages.

[1] Quite good ponies can—or at any rate could, in 1920—be bought in Pekin for 60 or 65 dollars.

CHAPTER XXV

IN EUROPE AND ELSEWHERE

THERE remains but little more to be said about actual experiences. The week in Pekin went all too quickly, much of the time being spent in sight-seeing, including, of course, the Great Wall of China, the Temple of Heaven, and the Summer Palace, about any one of which many pages could be written, for each has an extraordinary fascination of its own.

As everyone in Pekin, almost without exception, keeps one or more ponies, and as people were very generous about lending their spare ones, there was no difficulty about borrowing one to ride out to most of the places of interest in the vicinity, and on one occasion I even came in for a ride with the local " drag," the " pack " of which itself was a very scratch affair, made up of dogs of every breed imaginable (and some of no breed at all), nevertheless it was great fun.

A thirty-hour train journey, mostly through flat, bare, uninteresting country, brought one to Pukow, from which point a ferry crosses the Yangtze to Nankin on the opposite bank of the river.

As luck would have it, H.M.S. *Colombo* was lying off the city in midstream, and as I had met some of her officers in Japan a few months previously, the day and a half spent in Nankin were anything but dull.

A night in the train is all that is required to take one from there to Shanghai, where, on the evening of December 4th, I embarked on the *Kamo Maru* and six weeks later landed in England.

Though there was much of personal interest in these visits to Pekin, Nankin, and Shanghai, as well as in the voyage home, no more than has already been written can properly be held to fall within the scope of these pages.

Shortly after returning to England I was attached to the Far Eastern intelligence section at the War Office, and there I remained until, much to my regret, I was invalided out of the Service in March of the following year (1922).

During that period, however, as the work involved was mainly in connection with Japan, it gave one an excellent opportunity for keeping in touch with current events in that country, both military and political, in a way that would have been difficult, if not impossible, without actually living in the country at the time.

It was a period of Japan's history full of incidents, not only of local interest but of international significance, the outstanding event of which was the holding of the Washington Conference and all that it entailed. It is still too fresh in everyone's memory to bear more than a passing reference, but no harm can be done by emphasising once more that its effects have been, and are likely to continue to be, so far reaching as possibly to change the whole course of history. War between Japan and America, which seemed practically a certainty in considerably less than a decade had no such conference taken place, may now be regarded as outside the realm of possibility ; Japan's policy *vis-à-vis* China has been completely changed, thereby removing yet another germ of war ; the naval forces of all the principal Powers have been able to stop the insensate race for superior armaments ; the Anglo-Japanese Alliance has been terminated and replaced by an agreement of a wider scope ; and Japan has shewn herself willing, by her voluntary evacuation of Siberia, of Shantung, and of Hankow, and in a hundred other ways, to remove, in the interests of world peace, causes of friction in the Far East, each in itself the embryo of a potential war. These are but a few of the singificant results of the Washington Conference in so far as they affect Japan. Will it be any wonder, therefore, if historians of the future regard the last month and a half of 1921 as one of the most outstanding periods of the world's history?

Several other events of importance to Japan, such as the Crown Prince's break with tradition in visiting Europe and in other ways, occurred during the year 1921, but, as most of them were mainly political, little more concerning them need be said here.

One more event, however, which may be mentioned in passing, was the death in February, 1922, of the aged soldier and statesman, Marshal Prince Yamagata, as he, probably more than anyone else, was responsible for building up the Japanese army to its present state of efficiency, and may be regarded as the father of the Military Party which has held so prominent a position in Japan for many years past.

Probably few men in history have exercised so much influence in the councils of their country as he did, and since the death of Prince Ito in 1909, and up to the time of his own death, he was regarded—and no doubt rightly so—as the real "power behind the throne."

Of all the able men produced by Japan since her introduction to the outside world, some sixty odd years ago, the name of the late Prince Yamagata stands in a place of its own. In the closing years of his life he was, perhaps, too conservative and in some cases influenced both the army and the nation itself in a way detrimental to the true progress of both; but, when one considers the untiring efforts of his younger days in preparing Japan for the high position she now holds in the councils of the world, it is little wonder that his name became one for which his fellow countrymen had such great respect.

Before bringing this chapter to a close, one more thing may be mentioned in regard to the Japanese army in other lands.

Just as, in the case of our own army, we send "Language Officers" to study the language and military affairs of our Far Eastern ally, so the Japanese have a system of sending officers to study in England.

The Japanese, as a rule, send to Europe only those who

have been through the Staff College, and who are, therefore, well equipped for making the best of the advantages offered.

Not only are *p.s.c.* men sent off on language study and for attachment to British military units, but the Japanese have an excellent system of sending officers off on so-called "pigeon tours" of Europe and America. Those selected for these tours are generally those who have done specially well while at the Staff College, or else have been particularly hard worked and need a change, or those who wish to supplement some special technical knowledge by studying it in other countries as well as in their own.

As a rule parties of six or eight officers are sent off at a time, and spend about six months travelling round Europe and America seeing points of military interest. The first two or three months are generally spent as a party, after which they split up into ones and twos. They stop a few days each in America, England, France, Belgium, Germany, Italy, Austria, and Czecho-Slovkia, etc., after which each officer or small group spends the rest of the time in one or other of the countries already visited.

Several such parties came through England during the time I was at the War Office, and it generally fell to my lot to act as "bear-leader" and take them down to the various military centres at which programmes for their visits had been previously made out. Some of those who came over to England in this way were old friends whom I had known in Japan, and it was always interesting meeting them again and hearing the latest news of other mutual acquaintances in their army.

In addition to those going on these "pigeon-tours," officers sometimes have leave, granted them by the army authorities, to further their military studies in Europe and other countries at their own expense, and in some cases officers are encouraged to save up sufficient money to enable them to see something of the continent adjacent to Japan. Particularly is this so in the case of those seconded for service in Formosa.

The period of duty in that garrison is generally limited to four years, during which time they receive extra pay, just as, in the case of our own army, units serving overseas are granted foreign service pay.

Officers serving in Formosa are encouraged to save this extra allowance, the unit commander acting as a kind of saving's bank. On completion of their terms of service they receive in one lump sum the money thus accumulated, and are encouraged to use it in a trip to Hong Kong, Canton, or elsewhere, in order to widen their experience.

Besides those proceeding to China in this fashion, one or more officers are sent each year at government expense to study the language. These officers are selected from those who have undergone a course at the School of Foreign Languages in Tokyo, the ones taking such a course having in their turn been selected from candidates from all units of the Japanese army.

After a year these officers are generally attached for a time to the General Staff or other such institution, where their knowledge of a foreign language can best be used to advantage.

Next to passing through the Staff College, selection for such purposes is greatly sought after.

In addition to the places already mentioned, a not inconsiderable number of officers are sent to China to act as military advisers and instructors, most of those selected being members of the General Staff, and, rightly or wrongly, they are often accused of meddling in politics to the considerable embarrassment of their government, who in their turn are accused by foreign countries of carrying out a dual diplomacy, As this question will be dealt with more fully elsewhere, nothing more need be said here.

Reference has already been made to those officers sent to England to study the language and military system in the same way that British officers are sent to Japan, but no mention has been made up to now of the Japanese Military Attaché himself, or of the Assistant Military Attaché.

In the normal course of events there would be no special

reason for mentioning by name the two officers who held these positions during the time I was in London, but for the benefit of the reader, who may have been puzzled by the dedication written at the commencement of this book, an explanation may well be given.

The Japanese Military Attaché at that time was Major-General Matsuo Itamy, K.C.V.O., whilst the Assistant Attaché was Major Jiro Kawase.

The former is now back in Japan and is at present head of No. 11 (Military Intelligence) Section of the General Staff. The latter died suddenly in May, 1922, to the great regret of the many friends which his cheery disposition had won for him.

My work constantly brought me into touch with both these officers and particularly with the latter. Both in official dealings and in social intercourse they commanded one's friendship and respect, and if all Japanese were as frank, helpful, and open-hearted in their dealings as were these two, there would be no cause for the misunderstandings which arise from time to time between their countrymen and ours.

A few days prior to the announcement of his death, I had received a letter from Major Kawase, in which he spoke of transferring his work to his successor before his departure for Japan.

Apparently, whilst employed in handing over this work, he died suddenly, as is shown by the following letter received shortly afterwards from his successor :

" With great sorrow, I am writing to you a few lines about the death of the late Major Kawase. I am sure you cannot believe the Major's death, which was so sudden that no body had forseen his sadness. He was working with me in the office with great busyness for working out the Change of Attaché, and left office at 6 with me. After having dinner near the office, he came back there and carried on his job, then he suddenly fell down which caused to break his brain, and left the world for ever. No word can be found for expressing the great loss of his death. He was, as you know, such a fine grolious, jolly chap that he died on carrying his job. He has four children of course, and his wife. I cannot bear to think of his widow's grieve. As I am very busy I shall give my writing up.

Yours sincerely,"

It is as a slight tribute, therefore, to one who was described by a brother officer as a " fine, grolious (glorious), jolly chap " that these pages are, in part, dedicated to the late Major Jiro Kawase, I.J.A.

PART III

BROADER ASPECTS OF THE JAPANESE ARMY

CHAPTER XXVI[1]

HISTORICAL SKETCH OF THE JAPANESE ARMY

IN previous chapters an attempt has been made to show something of the life and thought of the Japanese army as it is at the present time. Some may be interested in the history connected with the building up of these land forces, and, for this reason, it is proposed to devote this chapter to giving a brief outline of the growth of the military organisation in Japan.

From very early times the Japanese have been a warlike race, and, as far back as the second century, there is the record of the Empress Jingo carrying out her famous expedition against Korea, although it must be admitted that there is a great mixture of legend and myth connected with the historical facts of that invasion.

It is wrong, however, to suppose, as many people do, that the power of the military really dates back as far as that, because, in point of fact, history records that, in the seventh century and for many hundreds of years after, the soldier in Japan was regarded in much the same light as is his counterpart in China at the present time, namely, a necessary evil. It was, in fact, the introduction of the Chinese organisation of society into Japan shortly after A.D. 645, with the soldier and scholar first in rank, that

[1] The main historical facts recorded in this chapter have been taken from the following works, to which due acknowledgment must be made: Murdoch's *History of Japan*; Brinkley's *History of the Japanese People*; Okuma's *Fifty Years of New Japan*; Ballard's *Influence of the Sea on Japan*; and "The Times" *War in the Far East.*

brought about this state of affairs, although it is true that, whereas in China the latter was respected more than the former, in Japan the position was reversed.

Owing to these Chinese views, the War Department, as it existed at the beginning of the eighth century, was looked down upon by the country at large. Murdoch points out in his *History of Japan* that "a privileged military class was an outcome of feudalism," and that "the appearance of feudalism in Japan was contemporary with its appearance in Europe and proceeded from similar causes." It will be seen from this, therefore, that it is wholly erroneous to imagine that the military have been all-powerful from the very beginning of history.

Before going on to more modern times a few more facts concerning the land forces in those early days may be recorded, as they have a very distinct bearing on the army of to-day.

Conscription existed in Japan as early as A.D. 686, at which time one-fourth of the able-bodied freemen were selected for a service of three years, "and a few years later the proportion was increased to one-third." These troops, however, seem to have been merely armed civilians—a national militia rather than a standing army—and it was not until a century later that a definite military caste came into existence. The originator of this caste—the *Samurai*—was really one Tamura Maro, who gained great fame by his exploits and fine leadership against the Ainus, with whom the Japanese at that time were constantly at war.

About the same time that conscription was adopted in Japan, the science of fortification was learned from Korean refugees, but it was not until some four centuries later (about 1085) that any attempt was made to study military science, and even then it seems to have been of a very elementary nature, for, at the time of the Mongol invasion in 1274, history recalls that the Japanese, although they successfully expelled the invaders, were at a disadvantage owing to inferior weapons and old-fashioned tactics, depending too much on single combat and individual conspicuousness. What they lacked in scientific knowledge they seem to have made up in courage.

In view of what has been said in previous chapters regarding the Japanese army of the present time, this fact is well worthy of note, as it seems almost like a case of history repeating itself. In *matériel* and in tactics employed, the Japanese army is some way behind the land forces of the other world Powers, but there is no doubt that the men themselves are excellent fighters.

Some two hundred and fifty years prior to the Mongol invasion, a raid had been carried out on Japan by a force of Manchurian pirates, who had first attacked and captured the island of Tsushima and had then landed on the coast of Kyushu. On that occasion, however, the topographical features of the country had been favourable to the Japanese tactics, of which individual combat was the main feature as opposed to the massed tactics of their enemies. In that case, therefore, the present-day method was reversed, the tendency now being to adopt massed formations.

Though there was almost continuous internal strife subsequent to the Mongol invasion, no fighting took place with a foreign force until more than three hundred years later, when Hideyoshi set to work to carry out his invasion of Korea.

There are many people who consider Japan's rapid rise to world prominence during the last fifty or sixty years as a very remarkable event, almost incomprehensible, especially in regard to the capacity for military organisation exhibited by her; but one need only look back into her history to see that this particular asset of hers has been in existence for many centuries past, and this campaign of Hideyoshi's serves as an example. In 1592 to 1593, for instance, Ukida, acting on Hideyoshi's behalf, had an army of no less than 205,000 combatants under him in Korea, although, as Professor Murdoch points out, "Europe had never seen more than 60,000 men in the field together under one flag in that century."

By way of showing the "traditional national aptitude for

warlike enterprises and the inherent capacity for organisation" which has helped to bring about Japan's rapid ascent to the rank of a first-class military power, the same authority quotes several other occasions in mediæval times when Japan had armies of over 100,000 men in the field at one time, and some of these are well worth quoting.

Towards the end of the twelfth century, for instance, Yoritomo launched an army of 240,000 men to deal with Fujiwara Yasuhira in the extreme north of the island, and a few years later the Hojo Regent concentrated an army of 100,000 on Kyoto to deal with the malcontents there.

Another occasion on which large forces were put into the field was in the war of Onin (1469), when one of the contending chiefs began the strife with 160,000 men whilst his opponent had 90,000; and in one of the many internal wars in which Nobunaga was engaged in the sixteenth century, that old warrior mobilised an army of about 185,000.

Several other instances could be given, but the above should be sufficient to show that Japanese commanders, for hundreds of years past, have been accustomed to organise and lead very large bodies of armed men.

As this is only meant as a rough historical sketch of the Japanese army, too much time must not be spent on these earlier episodes, and they are only mentioned to show the kind of foundation on which the army of the present day has been built. One other point may, however, be included before passing on to more recent times, namely, that, as far back as 1180, there was an organisation known as the *Samurai Dokoro*, which was largely of the nature of a General Staff, though with more extensive functions. The chief interest of this body, from the point of view of comparisons, lies in the fact that, like its counterpart of to-day, it was one of the most influential organisations in existence.

Turning to more modern times, we find that from the termination of Hideyoshi's expedition up to the date when Japan was forced out of her seclusion by the arrival of Commodore Perry some two hundred and fifty years later, no fighting with external foes took place. During that period there was little or no improvement in military arms and equipment nor in the tactics employed, and, as a result of the lessons learned from the bombardment of Kagoshima and Shimonoseki and from other similar incidents, the Japanese very soon realised that, if they were to retain their independence, they must train and equip their armed forces on European lines. A lead was given by some of the more powerful clans, and in 1862 the foreign military system was adopted by the Shogunate, three corps being organised, the total strength of which amounted to 13,625 all ranks

Internal trouble, which broke out shortly afterwards, convinced the country that the old military system was no longer suitable, and, in consequence of this, the Shogunate engaged a French military mission under Chanoine in 1867 to make a thorough reform of the army, an example which was followed by all the clans.

On the restoration of the monarchy, which took place in 1868, the central government found itself faced with the problem of which European system to adopt, as some of the clans followed the English, some the French, and others the German, whilst others again were using the Dutch system as their model. It was not until after careful study that the French system was finally decided upon as the best, and accordingly, in 1872, a French mission under Marguerie was brought to Japan, and as a result of their efforts a well-organised force of some 40,000 to 50,000 men was produced a few years later.

In the year prior to the arrival of the French mission, the Imperial Guards had been organised and four garrisons with detached posts were formed, the troops raised by local clans being disbanded; but it was not until the following year that the system of conscription was adopted, and the last traces of feudal times—the confining of military service to the *Samurai* class—abolished.

This opening up of the military profession to all classes may be regarded as one of the most important events in the building up of the modern Japanese army, and, like all other reforms, it met with bitter opposition at the outset. Subsequent events, however, proved the wisdom of the decision, and set at rest the fears of those who had hitherto imagined that no one who had not been accustomed to warlike pursuits could make a good soldier. It was merely a case of history repeating itself, and might be likened to the Sikhs, who were changed from a people of peaceful occupation to one of the most warlike races of India; or again, a more recent instance, when a certain "nation of shopkeepers" showed itself capable of bearing arms and helping to vanquish one of the most military nations of modern times.

The credit of the initiative in the move to enlist men other than those of the military class into the army is really due to the Shogunate and to the Choshu Clan, who had successfully experimented with foreign methods upon some farmers.

For many centuries it had been the custom for military leaders to treat the science of war in much the same way as the possessors of certain inventions at the present time guard the secrets of their manufacture. Military science had, in fact, been passed on from father to son or from one military leader to his right-hand men in a way that prevented the rules of war from becoming common property, and from this it came about that the generals of those days earned for themselves the respect born of the fact that they alone knew the secrets of their profession and that none but they had the ability to impart that knowledge to others.[1]

Chief among the rules of war, which were handed down from generation to generation in this way, were the teachings of Sun and Wu, two somewhat disreputable but brilliant Chinese leaders who flourished some two thousand five hundred years ago. The teachings of these two, which

[1] In *The Book of War*, which is a translation of the works of Sun and Wu made by the late Lieut. Col. Calthrop R.A., the translator says in his introduction: "Like other arts, mystery was formerly supposed to surround the art of war, a belief that was encouraged by the strategists; and for a considerable time the few copies of this book that were brought over from China to Japan were jealously guarded by their possessors."

might still be profitably studied by military students, formed the basis of all military knowledge in Japan from very early days right up to the middle of last century, when the advent of European methods brought with them a complete revolution in the science of war as hitherto known to the Island Empire, though even now the main principles remain the same

During the period in which the French mission was modernising the Japanese land forces, numerous reforms took place and military educational establishments were founded, and in 1877, five years after the arrival of its instructors, the new army had its first serious test in warfare. In that year it was called upon to suppress the Satsuma Rebellion which had broken out, not against the Emperor, to whom the Great Saigo, the rebel leader, was steadfastly loyal, but against the government, whom Saigo accused of acting contrary to the best interests of the country.

The experiences gained in the quelling of this rebellion, which lasted eight months, and of a smaller one which had broken out in Saga Province three years previously, helped the Japanese commanders to see the strong and the weak points of the new organisation and enabled them to rectify some of the latter. A punitive expedition to Formosa, which had been carried out about the same time, also helped in this respect.

Amongst outstanding points brought out by the Satsuma Rebellion were the necessity for an efficient commissariat and for a system whereby the wastage of troops caused by fighting and disease might be made up. The fact that fully trained conscripts from the so-called non-fighting classes were vastly superior to semi-trained volunteers from the old *Samurai* families was also fully demonstrated, and, moreover, it was during these same operations that the telegraph was proved to be of such great value. As a result of this a military telegraph corps was organised in 1880.

The same year that the telegraph corps was formed saw the departure of the French military mission, and for the next five years the Japanese worked by themselves, depending on what they had learned from the French and on the results of investigations carried out by officers who had been sent abroad to France and other European countries for military study.

In 1885, however, a German military mission was invited to continue the work of their French predecessors, the leader of this mission being Major Meckel, one of the best products of the school of Moltke. To him and to those under him the Japanese army owes a great deal, and it is little wonder that, even to this day, they feel grateful to the country which lent them their services.[1]

Meckel's mission remained in Japan until 1894, by which time the army had been raised to a strength of about 150,000 organised into seven divisions, together with a certain number of independent units. War was declared with China a few months later, and it is interesting to note that no further military advisers from foreign countries were employed until a quarter of a century later, when, in 1918, a French military mission under Colonel Faure came to Japan for the purpose of organising the army aviation corps.

The war with China gave Japan the opportunity of testing the efficiency of her new but well-trained forces, and the results more than justified the hopes she had placed in them. The Chinese suffered complete defeat, as a result of which Japan was able to dictate her own terms. The two most outstanding military feats on land in that war were the battle of Ping Yang and the storming of the fortress of Port Arthur in a single day.

As a result of the peace conference presided over by the late Prince (then Count) Ito at Shimonoseki, the Liaotung Peninsula, Port Arthur, Talienwan, the Pescadores, and Formosa were added to the Japanese dominions. In addition, she obtained an indemnity of 200,000,000 *taels*, Wei-hai-wei being held in pledge by her until the full payment

[1] After the battle of the Yalu in May, 1904, General Kodama telegraphed his thanks to Meckel, who by that time was a Major-General, for the services rendered to the Japanese army, and ascribed the victory on the Yalu to Meckel's teaching.

had been made. Germany, Russia, and France, however, forced her to abandon her claims on the mainland of China and induced her to accept in lieu thereof an indemnity of a further 30,000,000 *taels*, the payment of this sum being assured by a loan to China guaranteed by Russia.

The hypocrisy of the three Powers, and of Russia in particular, soon became apparent, their actions during the next few years sowing the seeds of further strife in the Far East.

Amongst these was the agreement made in 1896 between Russia and China whereby the Chinese Eastern Railway was to be laid with the object of developing Manchuria, the company thus formed being under the control of the Russian Government, and a year later Russian troops occupied Port Arthur, the very place which, only a short time before, that same government had induced Japan to vacate on alleged altruistic grounds. Less than a month after the occupation of Port Arthur by the Russians, Germany landed troops at Kiao-chou and expelled the Chinese. By way of introducing a balance of power and in order to protect her own interests Britain was forced to obtain possession of Wei-hai-wei.

In 1898 these three Powers secured leases of the above mentioned pieces of territory from China, and France acquired Kuang-Chow.

The attitude of Great Britain in occupying Wei-hai-wei was purely a defensive move to counter Russian and German aggression. Apart from this she can hardly be accused of hypocrisy, as she had taken no hand in the previous dealings with Japan when that country was forced to relinquish her fruits of victory. The actions of the other three Powers, however, can only be described as perfidious, as they committed the offence of encroaching on Chinese territory without any extenuating circumstances whatever, although, under the pretext of preserving the integrity of China, they had, only three years before, compelled Japan to bow to *force majeure* and to effect the retrocession of territory obtained at the cost of blood and treasure by perfectly fair means.

Russia's action on this occasion hastened on the war which broke out in 1904, whilst the German occupation of Kiao-chou sowed the seeds of the Shantung Question.

Japan, being powerless to resist the combined forces of Russia, Germany, and France in 1895, had to rest content, noting the while the successive moves of these three Powers, and setting herself to further the development of her armed forces against the day when she might be in a position to avenge the wrong under which she was smarting.

"Nine years were given to Japan to prepare for the struggle, and of these, five were already gone when the Boxer Rebellion broke out in China, necessitating armed intervention on the part of the great Powers. The relief of the foreign legations was a military enterprise in which the Japanese showed themselves at their best, their detachment of 12,000, more than half the Allied forces, arousing the admiration of the whole world." [1]

In the meantime Russia was increasing her influence in Manchuria and extending it even into Korea. Japan, therefore, was faced with the alternatives of coming to some sort of agreement with her powerful neighbour in order to preserve her existence as an independent State, or else of forming an alliance with a third Power as a check to Russian expansion. She chose the latter course, as a result of which the Anglo-Japanese Alliance was concluded, the signing of that important document taking place on January 30th, 1902.

With the powerful assurance afforded her by the terms of this Alliance, Japan felt herself better placed to deal with the situation in Manchuria and Korea.

By this time Russia's actions in those parts had come to such a pitch that Japan was forced to make diplomatic representations, and, accordingly, she approached the Russian Government in July, 1903, with a view to reaching some amicable understanding in order to check the rapidly growing menace on land. Several notes were exchanged,

[1] From an article on the Japanese army in the *XIXth Century*, October, 1918.

but Russia assumed an uncompromising attitude, which finally led Japan to sever diplomatic relations on February 6th, 1904.

At the outbreak of the war with Russia, Japan had an army of thirteen divisions with a total strength, including reserves, of about 600,000 men, and during the war four more divisions were raised, so that by September, 1905, when peace was concluded, the Japanese army amounted to seventeen divisions in all. The combatant strength in the field at that time was about 480,000, whilst, according to official statistics, the War Department was actually feeding over a million men.

Fighting commenced in Korea, whither the Guards, 2nd and 12th divisions, were sent under the command of General Kuroki,[1] and, a few days after the forcing of the Yalu, the 2nd army under General (now Marshal) Oku landed on the north-east coast of the Liaotung Peninsula, these troops subsequently being split up into two armies—the 2nd and 3rd—the former advancing northwards towards Liaoyang, whilst the latter, under General Nogi, set to work to carry out an investment of the Russian garrison in Port Arthur, at the southern end of the peninsula.

A 4th army was landed about the same time at Takushan, a point on the coast about midway between Kuroki's army on the Yalu and the 2nd and 3rd armies in the Liaotung Peninsula, and, later on in the war, a 5th army was also added.

The earlier battles of the Yalu, Nanshan, Tehlissu, and Tashihchiao were followed on a greater scale by those of Liaoyang and the Shaho, and three months after the fall of Port Arthur, which took place on January 2nd, 1905, the Japanese army achieved the crowning victory of Mukden on March 10th.

In the war with China ten years previously an army officer had been at the head of the combined naval and military forces, and it is noteworthy, therefore, that, in the war with Russia, a precedent, which has not since been

[1] General Kuroki died in February, 1923.

dropped, was set by the appointment of two separate commanders-in-chief, a naval officer for the sea forces and a military commander for the army, whilst the Emperor himself acted as the virtual head of the combined forces.

Although, unlike the Great War of 1914-1918, but few inventions were brought out to revolutionise the science of war, it is worth noting that the use of the field telephone became universal for all arms and proved to be invaluable, as also did the telegraphic apparatus with which both the cavalry and engineers were equipped, though it was not until 1909 that the Japanese army began to investigate the possibilities of wireless for military purposes.

In 1907 two new divisions were added to the army and four independent brigades of cavalry and three of artillery were formed, the total number of divisions thus being raised to nineteen.

This was the strength of the Japanese army when the World War broke out in 1914, and Japan, with a view to assisting her British ally, opened operations against the Germans at Tsingtao. This campaign, however, only lasted two months, at the end of which the German commander of the fortress surrendered without giving the attackers the chance of storming the inner line of forts.

As the part played by the Japanese army in the late War was limited to this and to the Siberian campaign, it had little chance of either showing its mettle in warfare, as waged on the Western Front and elsewhere, or for absorbing the lessons given, and it is this lack of personal experience in the latest forms of modern warfare which is largely responsible for the lack of modern material and tactics employed. Aerial warfare, artillery and machine-gun barrage, and the employment of tanks, gas and other similar inventions have so revolutionised the tactics of the present day, that it is difficult for an individual, and still harder for an army which has had no personal experience with them, to realise fully the significance.

The year following the Tsingtao Campaign, it was decided to organise two new divisions for garrison duty in Korea—

this territory having been formally annexed in 1910—the men for which were to be recruited from the main island of Japan. By 1920 the organisation of these two divisions (19th and 20th) was completed, the total number of divisions thereby being raised to twenty-one.

In the Tsingtao Campaign a force of some 30,000 strong was employed, the main units of this consisting of the 18th division and one brigade (29th) of the 15th division. The Japanese casualties amounted to about 1500 killed and wounded.

Rather less than four years later an expeditionary force was despatched to Siberia to work in conjunction with detachments of others of the Allied countries, and, as at Tsingtao, Japanese and British troops once more faced a common enemy.

The first two divisions to be sent to Siberia were the 12th (Kokura) and 3rd (Nagoya), the commander-in-chief of these being General Otani. This campaign dragged on for over four years, during which time the two original divisions were relieved by fresh ones from home, and, by the time the last troops were withdrawn at the end of 1922, some seven or eight divisions in all—the 3rd, 5th, 8th, 11th, 12th, 13th, and 14th—had seen service there and three different officers had held the post of commander-in-chief, General Oi having succeeded General Otani in September, 1919, retaining that command until relieved by General Tachibana some two years later.

The Siberian Expedition itself is a thing of the past, but a force, consisting of a mixed brigade, still remains in North Saghalien, troops having been sent there in April 1920, in retaliation for the massacre of seven hundred of their nationals by the Bolsheviks at Nikolaievsk.[1]

The next chapter will shew that the Japanese army still consists of twenty-one divisions as its main fighting force, although the actual strength in *personnel* has been reduced

[1] Since this was written, the force in North Saghalien has been reduced to two battalions of infantry under the command of a major-general, this reduction having been carried out in April this year (1923).

lately; but, before concluding this brief history of the army, reference must be made to an important event closely connected with it, namely, the termination of the Anglo-Japanese Alliance.

Originally signed in 1902, it played a not inconsiderable part at the time of the Russo-Japanese War, as the very fact of its existence helped to deter other Powers from joining in. In 1905, and again in 1911, the terms of the Alliance were revised. Due either for renewal or abrogation in 1921, the Lord Chancellor at the Imperial Conference held in London in June of that year decided that, as it had not been denounced, it automatically renewed itself. In January, 1922, however, it terminated as a result of the decision, made at the Washington Conference, to substitute the Four Power Pact in its stead.

This is no place to discuss the *pros* and *cons* of the case, but there is no doubt that the Alliance, while it lasted, was of great benefit to both countries, and the influence it has exerted on the history of the army of Japan makes it unnecessary to apologise for mentioning it here.

CHAPTER XXVII

THE SIZE OF THE JAPANESE ARMY

PARTS I. and II. are an attempt to show something of the everyday life and customs of the Japanese army by simply quoting one's own experiences and the impressions gained during three years passed in the country, most of that time being spent in more or less close touch with their military life. Turning now from the human side or personal element, let us consider a few actualities of what may be called, for want of a better expression, the mechanical aspect.

One of the commonest questions asked by people concerning Japan is, "Why does Japan keep such a large standing army in time of peace?" Before attempting to give an adequate answer it may be as well to have before one the facts of the case. As will have been seen by those who have read the preceding pages, there were, in 1920, in addition to those in the four main islands of Japan proper, troops in Siberia, Manchuria, Korea, Shantung, Tientsin, and Pekin. In addition to these there were troops in Formosa and Saghalien also, though, much to my regret, I never managed to visit these two latter places. From this it will be seen that her main force of twenty-one divisions was scattered very considerably, though the great majority of them were in Japan itself.

Since 1920, however, considerable changes have taken place, mainly as a result of the Washington Conference. The number of divisions remains the same, but, by means of a reorganisation scheme and the disbandment of certain smaller units, the total peace-strength of the army is to be reduced by 56,000 officers and men, *i.e.* by about one-fifth, by 1925, most of this reduction having already taken place. In addition to this there has been a redistribution of troops, Hankow having been evacuated in July, 1922, and all the troops from Shantung, Siberia, and the mainland of Saghalien withdrawn by the end of that year.

The six independent battalions, which have been employed guarding the South Manchurian Railway for the past eighteen years, are also to be withdrawn and the units disbanded.[1]

Comparing the distribution of troops at the end of 1920 with what it was by the end of 1922, a table can be drawn up as under :

Disposition of Troops.	End of 1920.	End of 1922.
Japan Proper - -	16 Divisions and 4 Cavalry Brigades.	18 Divisions and 4 Cavalry Brigades.
Korea - - -	2 Divisions.	2 Divisions.
South Manchuria -	1 Division and 6 Independent Battalions.	1 Division and 6 Independent Battalions.
North Manchuria -	1 Brigade (about).	Nil.
Eastern Siberia -	2 Divisions.	Nil.
Saghalien (mainland)	Detachments.	Nil.
North Saghalien (island)	1 Brigade (about).	1 Brigade (about).
Shantung - -	4 Battalions.	Nil.
Hankow - - -	1 Battalion.	Nil.
Tientsin and Pekin -	2 Battalions.	2 Battalions.
Formosa and Pescadores - -	2 Independent Infantry Regiments with Artillery.	2 Independent Infantry Regiments with Artillery.
Peace Strength -	272,000 (approx.).[2]	232,000 (approx.).[3]
Total Units - -	21 Infantry Divisions, 4 Cavalry Brigades, Auxiliary and Independent Units.	21 Infantry Divisions, 4 Cavalry Brigades, Auxiliary and Independent Units.

The main points which will be noticed in the above table are that, although the number of the main units remains

[1] Two of these battalions have now been withdrawn and disbanded, this having taken place in April this year (1923).

[2] Figures given by General Tanaka in the Diet in 1920.

[3] Figures given by General Yamanashi in the Upper House on January 29th, 1923.

the same, they are more concentrated, whilst the actual man-power has been considerably reduced ; in fact a 15 per cent. reduction of *personnel*, which will be increased to about 20 per cent. by the end of 1924, by which time the reduction scheme should be completed.

The total *personnel* already withdrawn or about to be withdrawn from Siberia, Manchuria, Shantung, Saghalien, and Hankow, probably amounts to some 50,000 in all, and will, therefore, be about equivalent to the 56,000 by which the standing army is being reduced. That is to say that, by 1925, the total strength of the home army will be about the same as it was in 1920, though actually there will be an increase in the number of divisions in Japan Proper; in other words, the reduction is more apparent than real.

From a military point of view, of course, it is obviously more advantageous to maintain a large number of divisions in peace-time at skeleton strength (provided the strength is not too diminished) than to have an army of the same man-power with a fewer number of divisions. The former permits of greater expansion in time of war than the latter, and, after all, an army, if it is to be of any use when required, should always be trained and organised in such a manner as to be the most adaptable in the event of an outbreak of hostilities.

Looking at it from an entirely military point of view, the Japanese military authorities have done wisely in deciding on a reduction of *personnel* rather than to cut down the number of divisions. Unfortunately for them, however, this lays them open to attack from their own professional politicians as well as to criticism from those who are always on the lookout for an opportunity to accuse Japan of "militarism." They point out that, for a country the size of Japan, it is ridiculous to keep up an army of twenty-one divisions in peace-time, and that she should cut it down by at least half.

At first sight this argument may appear justified, especially when one considers that Japan's progress in communications, education, and a hundred and one other important items, is being impeded for lack of funds due to the army and navy using up such a large proportion of the national income (during the financial year 1921-2 nearly 50 per cent.). Even many of those who are most proud of their fighting forces, and most grateful to them for what they have done for their country in the past, argue on this line and point out that the military authorities, by refusing to cut down their expenses still further, are contributing to their own unpopularity. There can be but little doubt that there is much truth in this assertion, but it calls to mind the lines written by Francis Quartes, a minor ecclesiastical poet of Essex, who died nearly three hundred years ago, and apparently, in his day, found things the same in England as they are in Japan and other countries now :

> " Our God and soldier we alike adore,
> When at the brink of ruin, not before ;
> After deliverance both alike requited,
> Our God forgotten and our soldiers slighted."

The sentiment expressed in these lines is perhaps not entirely that of the present day, but there is a great deal of truth in it, for there is no doubt that the soldier in peace and the soldier in war are treated in very different ways, just as Kipling has pointed out in his famous lines on Tommy Atkins :

> " For it's Tommy this an' Tommy that an' ' Chuck
>   him out, the brute ! '
> But it's ' Saviour of his Country ' when the guns
>   begin to shoot."

The civilian, whatever his nationality, should bear in mind that the soldier knows full well who will be the fellow blamed if things go wrong when war breaks out because of lack of preparations in time of peace, and it is only natural, therefore, if he sometimes oversteps the mark in his endeavour to be ready for any eventuality.

The politician, and our old friend " the man in the street," may denounce the Japanese military authorities for insisting on the maintenance of so large an army, but if one will consider the question dispassionately, it will be seen that, apart from what has been said above, there is much to be said for the stand taken by the Tokyo Ministry for War.

In the first place, an army of 216,000 is not so very large for a country like Japan, faced with the potential power of Russia and China at close quarters and, until recently, having strained relations with America.[1] Both Russia and China are at present too much occupied with their own affairs to cause much alarm, but in ten or fifteen years, or even less, there is no saying how matters will have shaped themselves. In regard to America, the Washington Conference has happily removed the storm clouds which up to that time had been gathering rapidly. The Russo-Japanese War of 1904-5 had been brought about by the Russian land menace in the north-west, and in 1921 it looked as though a sea menace from the south-east, in the form of future naval bases in Guam and the Philippines, might lead to a war with America.

The potential menace from Russia and China still remains, especially as both have old scores to wipe off, and both, or certainly the former, are likely to rise again to power, though the latter will probably never be in a position to attack Japan unaided.

Some people in reply to this say that that is no reason for keeping an army of twenty-one divisions, a force too large for ordinary peace-time defence and yet totally inadequate in the event of war with Russia or China or the two combined; true, they admit that Japan beat Russia with a smaller standing army than she has at present, but that was because Russia never had a chance of developing her whole resources, whereas, if the two countries came to grips now, Russia would see to it that she was better prepared than she was in 1904.

All these points are superficial as compared to the ideas which are probably at the back of the minds of the War Office and General Staff, who have good reason for main-

[1] The army reduction scheme is to be completed in 1924, by the end of which year the army will have an approximate peace-strength of 216,000.

taining their stand in refusing to reduce the number of divisions.

General Yamanashi, the present War Minister, in the September (1922) issue of the *Jiyū Hyōron* ("Free Review"), put forward certain of his own views as to why he thought it would be unwise for Japan to reduce the number of divisions. Briefly, his argument was that in the long run it would be cheaper, or at any rate Japan could better afford to keep up twenty-one divisions in peace-time, each capable of considerable expansion in time of war, than to do away with half this number and then, when war broke out, have to build up and organise whole new formations. Were Japan, he argued, as rich as America, she could afford to do this, but since she is not one of the wealthy nations, she cannot afford to adopt such a procedure. He more or less drew an analogy with the man who can afford to pay down a thousand pounds for a motor-car and the man who can only afford to pay by monthly instalments. The latter in the end probably pays fifty or a hundred pounds more than the former, but, to use a very common Japanese expression, "*Shikata ga nai*" ("It cannot be helped"). He either has to pay the extra amount or go without his car, as he cannot afford to pay down the whole in a lump sum. Her army of twenty-one divisions is the motor-car which she has ready at hand for all emergencies. Unless she is content to pay out these monthly instalments, she must be prepared to do with a smaller and less reliable car which, when the time comes, is unable to bear the strain, and its owner at that point is unable to replace it with a larger and stronger one. As a result he would probably lose the race, which, in Japan's case, would be the war. That, in a nutshell, is the main reason for Japan maintaining a large standing army, and no doubt it was one of the determining factors which led the Ministry for War to decide on cutting down the size of the divisions rather than on reducing their numbers. It is highly probable that there is yet another and more pertinent reason for this decision.

It will be recalled that, in some of the preceding chapters, reference has been made to the importance attached by the Japanese military authorities to that portion of the soldiers' training known as *Seishin Kyōiku*, or "Spiritual Training." The main point about this particular branch of his education is to teach the soldier to live up to the standards of the *Bushi*—the knights of old, who ruled their whole lives according to the tenets of a code known as *Bushido*—literally, "The Way of the Warrior." This code was not dissimilar from our own "Rules of Chivalry" as they existed in mediæval times, and by which the warriors of those days were taught to practise the various so-called military virtues—honesty, bravery, loyalty, and so on. As the whole object of *Seishin Kyōiku* is to train the soldier to regard these standards of living as the ideal for which he must strive, it comes about that the army becomes a form of propaganda centre for such ideas, and that the more men it can train the greater becomes the proportion of the population imbued with these ideas, for, after all, every man who enters the army returns to civil life after the completion of his Colour Service, and the lessons learned during the period of his military training are bound to affect (in most cases) his whole outlook on life. Therefore, intentionally or unintentionally, he becomes an offshoot of this vast system of propaganda against what in Japan are known as "dangerous thoughts," for the lessons taught by *Seishin Kyōiku* are in direct opposition to those taught by Bolshevism and Socialism.

Briefly, therefore, one may assume that the answer to the question, "Why does Japan maintain such a large peace-time army?" is twofold, the first reason being that the military authorities consider that the country is better able to keep up a large skeleton force capable of expansion than a small one which would be very expensive to expand at the critical moment. The second reason is probably that it is not, as many people imagine it to be, meant for purposes of external aggression, but rather for internal effect to counteract the evils arising from industrialism and its attendant love of money and ease, which are tending to undermine all the finer qualities of the nation.

In regard to this latter point, attention has already been drawn to the way in which use is made of the annual Grand Manœuvres to show the people on what their money is being spent, and also to fire their military ardour. This may be taken by some to mean the encouragement of a militaristic spirit. In view, however, of what has just been said, it seems more probable that it is meant to encourage patriotism rather than militarism, and to be merely part and parcel of the scheme for counteracting the deteriorating effects of industrialism on the spirit of the nation.

Those who have read M'Govern's *Modern Japan* or Hector Bywater's *Sea-Power in the Pacific,* may recall that both these writers refer to Japan's army of "One Million Bayonets." It is erroneous statements of this kind, written in standard works, that are responsible for so much of the misconception of the real state of military affairs in Japan. Professor M'Govern is, no doubt, an authority on Japanese Buddhism, and probably no one will question Mr. Bywater's expert knowledge of naval architecture, but both these authors would do well to restrict their writings to matters dealing with their own particular branches of technical research. The former devotes a whole chapter to the Japanese army, and shows therein that he is totally ignorant, not only of the conditions in the Japanese army, but even of the very first principles of any military organisation, for he makes a statement to the effect that "*most* Japanese divisions have some infantry, some cavalry, and some artillery." [1] For anyone claiming to write authoritatively on such a subject, one would have thought that he would have known that *all* divisions are composed of "the Three Arms," and other branches of the Service as well, and that the proportion of each is fixed and not merely left to the whims of fate.

Leaving aside smaller points of this kind, the main thing is that the figures he quotes are grossly inaccurate and have

[1] I am quoting from memory as, unfortunately, I have not a copy of his book beside me and cannot therefore copy the exact words.

been copied direct from the *Japan Year Book*—a very untrustworthy source on such matters—without apparently ever taking the trouble to verify them by questioning anyone with first-hand knowledge. This would not matter so much if Professor M'Govern made no pretence at being an authority on "Things Japanese," but the very fact that Mr. Bywater, in an otherwise excellent book, has apparently regarded him as such and has therefore quoted him on the subject of the Japanese army *verbatim*, shows how much he, and others like him, may do an injustice to another country by writing "authoritatively" on matters about which they know nothing. No doubt, in Professor M'Govern's case, it was done unintentionally, but the effect on his readers, who regard him as an authority, is the same as though it had been purposely misstated.

Amongst other misstatements made by both Professor M'Govern and Hector Bywater is the one that the programme of the Japanese army calls for "an establishment of 41 army corps with a total strength of one million bayonets, with corresponding additions to the artillery and other branches."[1] This has unquestionably been quoted from the *Japan Year Book* in the first instance, as also have the less important mistakes that "a Japanese infantry regiment contains four battalions each of 600 men," and that "approval has been given to the constitution of each division on a three-regiment basis and the abolition of the brigade."[2] Other misstatements of fact are also made, but the first of the three is the one most likely to cause the greatest misconception as to Japan's so-called "militarism."

Anyone reading it, in any of the three books mentioned, would take it to mean that the peace-strength of the army was 41 army corps of which the *personnel* consisted of 1,000,000 infantry ("bayonets") with artillery and other

[1] *Sea-Power in the Pacific*, by Hector C. Bywater, pp. 282-3. The credit for this statement is given to Professor M'Govern.

[2] *Sea-Power in the Pacific*, pp. 283-4. In these two instances the *Japan Year Book* is definitely stated as being the source of information.

branches of the Service in proportion, which would give a total strength of some 1,300,000 or more.

The writer of the *Japan Year Book* is a civilian and, therefore, probably did not know the difference between a division and an army corps, at any rate not when translated into English, so used the latter term when he meant the former. What he probably meant was that in *war* time the army could be expanded to 41 divisions (not army corps) with a total strength of 1,000,000 all arms (not merely of infantry).

CHAPTER XXVIII

INFLUENCE OF THE MILITARY

No book professing to show something of the military side of Japanese life would be complete without mention being made of the part played by the so-called Military Party.

Without going into too much detail, it can be stated, without fear of contradiction, that the whole course of Japanese history would have been very different, especially since the opening up of the country to the outside world in the middle of last century, had it not been for the influence exercised over it by its military leaders—the word "military" being here used in its broadest sense—and by the two powerful clans of Choshu and Satsuma with which the army and the navy are so closely connected. Broadly speaking, the Choshu Clan represents the army and the Satsuma Clan the navy.

Japan is frequently accused of militarism and of carrying out a dual diplomacy, and, at the present time, no one is so bitter against the Military Party as is the Japanese Press itself, which is constantly accusing the so-called militarists of "butting into politics." The anti-military spirit, so noticeable in the Japanese Press at the present time, has been coming to the fore for some years past, but since the Washington Conference was held it has come more and more into prominence

That there is a certain amount of justification in the hostility of the Press and for its accusations against the Army General Staff—the principal object of its acrimony—for its interference in politics there can be no doubt, but in their zeal to discredit the army authorities the papers very often go beyond the bounds of reason. In order, therefore, to obtain a true perspective of how matters stand, let us look into the facts of the case.

At the time that Perry and his fleet came to Japan in the middle of last century, it was found impossible for the country to keep her doors closed any longer to foreign intercourse, the reason for this being that the Japanese had nothing with which to defend themselves, their defences being negligible, their navy non-existent, and their most modern war material hopelessly out of date and useless against the guns of the foreign war-ships.

To cut a long story short, the Japanese soon discovered that, unless the necessary steps were taken to provide themselves with the wherewithal to defend their "hearths and homes," they would soon share the fate of numerous other Eastern races and be treated by some well-meaning but undesired foreign nation as yet another bit of territory in which to "take up the white man's burden." It was for this reason that Japan decided to set to work at once to build up and train an army and navy on modern lines before attempting to carry out any other improvements commonly looked on as the requisites of a civilised nation. No one who has studied the subject can but admit that she did wisely when she decided on this course.

Although for the 250 years prior to the opening-up of the country to foreign intercourse Japan had lived at peace externally, and in comparative peace internally, she nevertheless possessed a class of men whose whole outlook on life was to fit themselves for the game of war, and these men, the *Samurai*, made excellent material for the nucleus of a proper fighting force on land, whilst the fact that Japan was an island country made it inevitable that amongst her sea coast population there would be found plenty of hardy fishermen and sailors, who only required a little discipline and training to turn them into a first-class naval force.

At that time the Japanese were split up, like the Scottish Highlanders of a hundred years before, into a number of clans, the M'Donalds, the Campbells, the M'Intoshes, and the M'Leans providing their counterparts in the Choshu, the Satsuma, the Tosa, and the Hizen clans. It was these four clans in particular which set about most strenuously to put Japan properly on her feet, but the two former gradually asserted themselves in such a way that they soon had the chief power in their own hands.

As time went on the Choshu Clan came to be regarded as the foster-parent of the army, whilst their rivals of Satsuma adopted the navy. One result of this has been that the army, even to this day, has most of its leaders belonging to the former, whilst the navy is largely composed of Satsuma men.

Apart from these two clans producing the generals and admirals respectively, they also supplied some of the foremost statesmen, though many of these latter combined that quality with that of either military or naval commander, as exemplified by such men as the late Marshal Prince Yamagata, the late Marshal Count Terauchi, and the present Admiral Baron Kato, all three of whom have headed governments of their own, the first-named having twice been Prime Minister.

From this it will be seen that these two powerful clans, and particularly their respective *protégés*, the Army and the Navy, have exercised very considerable influence on the whole history of the country, especially during the last fifty or sixty years.

Had it not been for the decision to make the building up of a strong army and navy one of the first objects to be attained, it is doubtful indeed whether Japan would to-day be occupying her high position amongst the nations of the world, so for that, if for no other reason, the Japanese should feel grateful for what their fighting forces and their leaders have done for her in the past.

It has already been pointed out [1] how the spirit animating the army and the navy, as a result of the *Seishin Kyōiku*, or "Spiritual Training," acts as an excellent antidote to the

[1] Chapter XXVII.

spirit of commercialism and self-seeking which is, unhappily, tending to destroy the finer qualities of the nation, but there is yet another side to the good done to the country by the naval and military forces.

When, in the early 'seventies of last century, Japan decided definitely that the old system of using none but the *Samurai* for military service must be abolished, and that an army and navy, trained, organised, and equipped on modern lines, and consisting of men taken from all classes of the population, must be raised, she found herself faced with the problem of either importing, at great cost, everything for equipping her fighting forces, or else of setting up new industries of her own to provide the requisite material, there being no such industries existing in Japan in those days. Thus it came about that work, in connection with supplying the army and navy with all they required, was found for thousands of her people, and new industries, such as ship-building, munition-making, woollen-cloth manufacturing, and many of the present-day key industries, were introduced and given such a golden opportunity that it is hardly an exaggeration to say that it was largely due to the requirements of her fighting forces that Japan changed, within the memory of living men, from a wholly agricultural nation to one of the greatest industrial countries of the world.

The Japanese commercial man of the present day, when he grumbles about the business and other taxes which he has to pay for the upkeep of the first and second lines of defence, should remember therefore that, were it not for them, he himself might now be living under a foreign yoke, and the very industry from which he makes his money might never have come into existence.

To anyone interested in this aspect of the situation a perusal of the work recently published by Dr. Kobayashi is recommended,[1] as in it he shows the great influence exerted by the army and navy on the present-day industries of Japan.

[1] *Military Industries of Japan*, published by the Oxford University Press in 1922 and issued under the Carnegie Endowment for International Peace.

Nevertheless it must be admitted that it is not so much the fighting forces themselves that are the butt of the attacks made by the Press and by the professional politicians as the military authorities and the enormous power wielded by them. It may be as well, therefore, to consider how this comes about.

By the terms of the Constitution it is provided that the Minister for War and the Minister of Marine must be a general or a lieutenant-general and an admiral or vice-admiral on the active list, respectively, these two positions being barred, therefore, to civilians. Not only is this the case, but it is also provided that the holders of these two portfolios have special privileges which are not accorded to other members of the Cabinet. One of these is that they both have the right of appeal to the Throne, and another is that their positions are in no way affected by a change of government. Thus it comes about that a Cabinet may fall, but the Ministers of War and Marine automatically become members of the succeeding administration. Owing to this fact it is not by any means uncommon for a War Minister or his naval colleague to sit in two or three, or even more, successive Cabinets, irrespective of the political complexion of the individual government parties represented thereby.

In addition to these two ministers, there are two other very important members of the fighting forces who hold privileged positions, and thereby help still further to invest the army and navy with what practically amounts to absolute power. These are the Chiefs of the Naval and Military General Staffs, respectively, both of whom are directly responsible to the Emperor himself, and neither of whom is in any way subordinate to the ministers of their respective services. All matters relating to national defence or strategy, as decided by these chiefs, are first of all submitted to the Emperor and, subject to his approval, are then conveyed to the respective Ministers of State for execution. It is the peculiar position held by the Chiefs of the two General Staffs in relation to the corresponding ministers, and the extraordinary privileges which the two latter enjoy *vis-à-vis* the Cabinet, that gives the military authorities power which is all but absolute.

It is this curious anomaly in the Japanese Constitution that makes it so hard for the foreign observer to understand the inner workings of the country, and it is the unique position held by these four men, and particularly by that of the Chief of the Army General Staff, that is at the root of the dual diplomacy of which Japan is so often accused.

In the case of the army you find the General Staff working independently of the War Minister in military matters and of the Foreign Office in political affairs, whilst the Minister of War holds a position in which he has little or no control over the actions of the General Staff and is, at the same time, more or less independent of the Cabinet of which he is a member. Not only can he retain his position after all the other ministers (except, of course, the Minister of Marine, who is in the same position) of the Cabinet have fallen, but he can, while a member of the Cabinet, refer matters direct to the Throne without—as others members must do—previous consultation with the Prime Minister. One has to consider facts like these, in order to understand fully the reason for the great power held by the Military Party.

Another fact which must be taken into consideration when computing the power of the military as opposed to the Foreign Office and to the Government in general is that hitherto the best brains of the nation have been absorbed by the army and navy, as must be readily acceded if one considers the number of soldier-statesmen produced by Japan, not only in recent years but for centuries past; Ieyasu, Oda Nobunaga, and Hideyoshi being but three examples of the past, whilst Saigo, Yamagata, Saito, and the present Prime Minister (Admiral Kato) may be mentioned amongst many others of more recent years.

Not only are the best brains generally to be found in the army or navy, but the pick of the former are, as a rule, taken by the General Staff and are usually more than a match for their diplomatic colleagues of the Foreign Office. This may be put into concise form by saying that the Foreign Office generally sends out men with less brains and less money than the General Staff and therefore, when it comes to the final point, almost invariably loses.

Owing to the diplomatic tangle in which Japan is apt to find herself involved from time to time, as a result of the General Staff being in a position to interfere in the foreign policy of the country, she would probably be well advised to curtail the powers of her military authorities, but, in doing this, she should exercise every precaution against going to the other extreme.

The army itself, as has already been shown, does exercise a decided influence over the country for good, and, in carrying out any reforms, care should be taken that no interference be made with anything tending to damage that influence. It should, moreover, be borne in mind that, although the General Staff of Japan may at times meddle with affairs which are not within its proper sphere, the politicians of other countries are very often apt to imagine themselves strategists and, to the misfortune of their country, meddle in matters which should be left entirely to the care of their military leaders. Such a state of affairs is just as reprehensible as, and, not infrequently, even more serious than, the action of the Japanese General Staff. Japan would, therefore, do well to bear these facts in mind if, and when, she decides to curtail the powers of her Military Party.

Hitherto, the Japanese have always been very averse from political interference of any kind where curtailment of the powers of her military leaders has been concerned, and it is quite possible that this aversion arises from centuries of study of the works of the two ancient Chinese strategists, Sun and Wu, who have already been mentioned. Sun, in particular, always refused to countenance any interference whatever from political sources, and Chinese history records that on one occasion " a certain ruler asked Sun to give a practical demonstration of his principles in the neighbourhood of the palace and entrusted him with the women of the Court for this purpose. During the operations, the leader of one of the sides did not obey the master's instructions and her execution was ordered. She happened to be the king's favourite wife, but Sun pointed out that the king's wish that her life should be spared was a case of political interference with the general in the field ; and the sentence was carried out." [1]

Such drastic measures as these are hardly likely to be adopted by any Japanese general of the present day, but the fact that successive generations of Japanese soldiers have been brought up on the teachings of Sun and Wu is bound to influence their successors of modern times. It is probable that the power of the military to-day is in part due to the importance placed in the teaching of these two old Chinese commanders, constant study of their works having helped to mould the minds of the Japanese soldiers to insist on their own omnipotence in matters concerning the military needs of their country.

[1] *The Book of War*, as translated by Captain (the late Lieut.-Col.) E. F. Calthrop, R.F.A., and published by John Murray, 1908.

CHAPTER XXIX

AVIATION AND OTHER SPECIAL BRANCHES

Occasional reference has already been made to Japanese aviation, but it seems that this subject might with advantage be touched on more fully. As, however, I was merely a "foot-slogger," it is not proposed to enter into anything of a very technical nature, as I fully realise that my qualifications for writing authoritatively on such matters are very limited in scope. The following comments on aviation in Japan must, therefore, be regarded as nothing more than a summary of personal observations and of talks with both foreign and Japanese aviators with whom I have spoken on the subject.

Although it is undoubtedly true that the military authorities in Japan are fully awake to the imperative need for the development of aviation in their country, it is equally true that the science of flying is very much less advanced in Japan than it should be and than it is in any of the other world Powers. The topographical features of the country are, of course, in part responsible for this inferiority, for a land consisting largely of mountains and paddy-fields does not lend itself to facilitate the lot of the aviator, who, in the event of a forced landing, may be faced with the alternative of "crashing" on a rocky height or of burying himself and his machine in the mud and water of a rice field.

These, however, are not the only reasons for the backwardness of flying in Japan, and amongst others that may be quoted are the mentality of the people themselves, and the fact that the machines used are very often out of date and weak in construction.

In regard to the first of these two points it may be said that the Japanese are excellent in carrying out plans which they have had time to formulate beforehand, but that, faced with the necessity of making a sudden decision, they are apt to lose their heads. Even though this state of affairs may be only of a temporary nature and, therefore, not a matter of great concern in ordinary everyday life, it can well be understood how such a psychological fact may be fatal to the pilot, who is often called on to act practically automatically if he is to avoid disaster. In Japan itself where, owing to the mountainous nature of the country, air-currents are exceptionally tricky, it is more than ever essential that the aviator should be in possession of what may be called, for lack of a better word, this " second nature "—the special instinct for enabling him to do the right thing at the right moment.

In her wars with China and Russia respectively, Japan really had ideal foes, as they always gave her time to think out her plans beforehand, and once a plan has been formulated, few people can compare with the Japanese in their ability to execute it. There are many military students, even amongst the Japanese themselves, who hesitate to express a definite opinion as to what would have happened in Manchuria in 1904-5 if she had found herself up against more active opponents. That she would have acquitted herself with distinction there is little cause for doubt, but it remains a matter of controversy whether or not she would have been able to rise to every sudden and unexpected eventuality which such an enemy would have forced upon her.

Japanese mentality in that respect is not unlike that of the Germans, who, as shown in the late World War, carried out previously framed plans with clock-like precision, until some unforeseen event occurred, whereupon, in many cases, the whole scheme fell through for lack of that particular instinct of being able to formulate entirely new and unprepared plans at a moment's notice.

The British, on the other hand, are often regarded as little short of insane (not infrequently by themselves as well as by others), owing to their lack of prepared plans and to their curious habit of somehow " muddling through," this latter point being not infrequently put down to good luck rather than to good work. If one looked deeper into the matter, it would probably be discovered that this attribute of " muddling through " is really due to the possession of this particular instinct, which appears to be lacking in both the Japanese and the German, namely, the ability to rise to any emergency that presents itself, despite the fact of having no previously formulated plans. Indeed, it is probable that the very fact of having no previously conceived ideas or hidebound plans with which to fetter their decisions may, in part, be responsible for giving them greater freedom of action and ability to form new ones for any emergency. Call it luck or instinct, as you will, but the fact remains that, in the case of aviation, it becomes an attribute in the mental outfit of the pilot without which he is liable to come to grief.

Time after time, the death of a Japanese aviator is reported in the columns of the daily papers, and, although many of these fatalities are undoubtedly due to the poor quality of the machines in use, it is certain that a large proportion is due to the pilot's lacking the instinct which makes it second nature to act the very moment something goes wrong.

Another fact which is said to be responsible for many of these accidents, and one which is, moreover, indirectly connected with the instinct in question, is that the average Japanese has not got his ear tuned sufficiently to hear whether or not his engine is running smoothly. Anyone knowing the first principles of mechanics can well understand the imperative necessity for this particular gift for the pilot in mid-air.

Despite what has been said above, members of the British Aviation Mission, which came out in 1921 under the leadership of the Master of Sempill, maintain that, given good machines, the Japanese can be made into excellent pilots if the right methods of training are adopted. Anyone visiting the Naval Aviation Station at Kasumigaura, the scene of the activities of this Mission, will see for himself that there is a considerable degree of truth in this assertion.

With all due respect to the French Aviation Mission, which came out in 1919 to organise, equip, and train the Japanese Army Air Service, and who undoubtedly put in some good work, the fact remains that their pupils, the army aviators, are below their naval *confrères*, both in efficiency and in equipment ; and the reason for this seems to be twofold. In the first place, much of the equipment which the Japanese received from the French was old and out of date, whilst, secondly, it seems that either their method of training was not suited to the Japanese, or else they left the course of instruction half completed. If the latter suggestion is correct, it may not be wrong to assume that one of the French characteristics—lack of patience—was to blame. During the War, France boasted of some of the finest flying men in the world, but, excellent fighters though they are, patience is not one of the virtues with which Nature has endowed her people, and it is an attribute of great importance when teaching the science of aviation to a foreign race whose language and customs are totally different from one's own.

Apart from much of the equipment received from the French being out of date, the Japanese military aviators are themselves partly to blame for the poor condition of many of their machines, as the pilots do not take sufficient personal trouble with them. In most countries the pilot makes a personal inspection of his machine before going up in it, so as to make certain that everything is as it should be. In Japan, however, the pilot usually leaves this work of inspection to a mechanic who is not going to accompany him on the flight. As a result, it not infrequently occurs that machines go up in very bad, and even dangerous, condition, for it is only human nature that an inspection of this kind is bound to be more thorough if it is carried out by the man whose neck is going to be risked if anything goes wrong, than it is when carried out by a ground mechanic who has no such fear hanging over him.

If Japanese do not take more care of the condition of their machines in war-time than they do in peace-time, they stand a very poor chance. They would be out-manœuvred and driven down, as they could be forced to nose-dive quicker than the greatest speed which their struts and wires would stand, with the result that, by forcing rapid turns and dives upon them, their machines would be buckled up in no time.

Talking to a Japanese officer some two or three years ago on this particular defect, he entirely agreed, and, when asked if he had ever done any flying himself, laughed and said that he had been up several times in France, but that he had never done so in Japan and did not intend to do so until he saw some improvement in the condition of the army machines. His remark was typical of others I have had made to me from time to time, and there are those who have added that officers who go into the Army Air Service do so with the fixed idea that they will be killed sooner or later, and that their carelessness as to the condition of their machines is largely due to this preconceived idea.[1]

From the criticisms made above, it will be seen that the human factor, as well as the topographical features of the country, is largely responsible for the comparatively low state of efficiency of the Army Air Service in Japan.

Another factor which may also be mentioned in this respect is that, although the naval and military authorities are fully alive to the great value of aircraft, the average civilian has never really had it brought home to him how essential it is to develop the science of aviation in Japan. The distance of Japan from the seat of the European War is probably partly responsible for this lack of realisation on the part of the Japanese, as they have never seen aircraft in large numbers, and have never experienced an aerial

[1] Japanese army aviators who are killed whilst flying receive posthumous honours, and, although it may be hard for a European to understand, it is said that there are some who join the Air Service in the hope of qualifying for a decoration of this kind.

bombardment ; yet Japan is particularly vulnerable to an attack from the air ; in fact it is virtually the only form of direct attack to which she is exposed, as her Pacific coasts are so far removed from any potential enemy that they are practically immune from a naval bombardment or the landing of foreign troops, whilst her inner, or Sea of Japan, coast is guarded by the narrowness of the inlets to this virtual Japanese lake. So long, therefore, as Japan's fleet is in being, she has little to fear from naval bombardments or military landing forces so far as her own home territory is concerned, but her air defences are negligible and it is from the air that she is most vulnerable to direct attack.

Machines despatched from the mainland of Asia could reach Japan in a few hours and unload a number of incendiary bombs on any town or city with disastrous results, as the majority of houses in Japan are constructed of wood and plaster, and burn like tinder in a very short time.

Long-distance air-raids were frequently carried out during the late War in spite of every form of obstacle, such as A.A. gun barrages, searchlights, and hostile aircraft. It is reasonable to anticipate that raids from still greater distances will be carried out in future wars, and, even granting that the Japanese maintained their hold on Korea and Manchuria, a raid from, say, Vladivostock to Tokyo itself, a distance of only 600 miles or so, should not prove impossible of execution, especially if Japanese anti-aircraft defences remain in their present undeveloped state. The destruction of the capital city of the Empire by aerial attack would indeed be a blow from which Japanese *moral* would find it hard to recover, even if the army and the fleet were still intact.

The very idea of the whole thing calls to mind the story entitled, " The Joint in the Harness," which occurs in that excellent book, *The Green Curve*, by Ole-Luk-Oie. The story, though written several years before the War, and before the science of aviation had developed to the extent of being a real military factor, tells in a most vivid and prophetic way of how a certain victorious army, with all its plans laid out to perfection against, apparently, all contingencies, was nevertheless defeated eventually because of one fatal "weak joint in its harness," which was that it had no aircraft or anti-aircraft defence scheme, and had not counted on the enemy having any. The unexpected appearance of enemy aircraft, which was able to destroy the bridges on which the hitherto victorious army had counted for its communications, brought about a defeat which would not otherwise have been possible.

Without wishing to be unduly pessimistic, this story, with slight alterations, might well be changed from fiction into fact in the event of a war in which Japan's air and anti-aircraft services were found in the same undeveloped state as they are to-day.

Some of those Japanese officers to whom I have mentioned that I was writing a book on observations made during periods of attachment to their army, have asked me to criticise them openly and not to be afraid of hurting their feelings with adverse criticism. No offence is, therefore, meant in this, or in any other, chapter in which remarks of the above nature have been made. It is written in a spirit of friendliness, and it is hoped, therefore, that it will be treated as such.

In this connection, be it said that the Japanese resent unfair criticism as much as any, but it is a mistake to think that the better type of Japanese is always searching for compliments and is averse from criticism of any kind. Probably few people ever criticised the Japanese more freely than did the late Mr. Robert Young, of *The Japan Chronicle*, yet when he died in November last, several of the vernacular papers in their editorials paid tribute to the fearless way in which he had attacked what seemed to him to be wrong, adding that, although his criticisms had often appeared unfair and too severe, nevertheless they recognised that many of them were called for ; and they preferred to hear the truth about themselves, however unpleasant it might be at times, rather than mawkish "gush" which they knew to be insincere. Criticism, provided it is constructive and not destructive, is always welcome to the best type of Japanese.

To return, however, to the subject of aviation in Japan.

Having recorded a few impressions of the *personnel* and *matériel* of the Army Air Service and of its naval sister, it remains to add a few words on the subject of the recent history and organisation of the aerial forces of Japan.

Although the Naval Air Service was established in 1912,[1] and the Army Flying Corps some three years later, but little interest was taken in Japan in regard to aviation until 1916, when a young American aviator came to Japan and gave displays of trick flying, which so impressed people with the backward state of their own aerial services that the Press started a campaign to urge the necessity of rectifying the then existing state of affairs. Partly as a result of this, the Diet started to increase the annual appropriations for improving the service and, in 1918, voted a sum of about 1½ million *yen* for the expansion of the Army Air Service.

In the following year a French Aviation Mission under Colonel Faure was lent to the Japanese Government, in order to train and organise the nucleus of the future Air Service, and, at about the same time, a Japanese Mission, consisting of about 100 officers, N.C.O's, and mechanics was despatched to Italy to study Italian methods.

In the early days of Japanese aviation, the army aviators were a component part of the engineers, but, in 1920, an Aviation Bureau (*Kōkūkyoku*) was established under the direct control of the War Minister, and an Aviation Section (*Kōkūka*) and an Aviation Department (*Kōkūbu*) were added to the War Office. The Army Air Corps is now a wholly independent "arm."[2]

[1] The first Japanese aviators were trained in France and Germany in 1909, and shortly afterwards the Government laid out an aerodrome at Tokorozawa.

[2] The *Kōkūkyoku* is no longer under the War Minister's control, but is now under that of the Minister of Communications, to whose administration it was removed on 1st April this year (1923). It deals with civil aviation entirely, though it employs a few naval and military officers as advisers.

At the present time there are four complete air battalions located in different parts of the country, and, in addition, there are two others in process of formation, a battalion being more or less equivalent to a wing.

Although there is, as yet, no Air Ministry in Japan to co-ordinate naval, military, and civil aviation, both the army and the navy train a certain number of civilians as pilots, each Service maintaining an Aviation School. As, however, these pages are mainly concerned with army matters, no further reference to naval or civilian aviation need be made, beyond referring again to the semi-official British Mission which came out to this country in the spring of 1921, under the leadership of Captain Sempill, to help in the training of naval aviators and in the reorganisation and equipping of the Naval Aviation Corps.

Before leaving the subject of military aviation in Japan, attention may be drawn to the fact that one of the air battalions now in process of formation is at Heijo (Pingyang) in Korea and that a police flying station has been opened at Ako in the south of Formosa. This latter has been created as a deterrent to the unruly savages in the interior of the island.

Leaving aside the subject of aviation in Japan and of its present under-developed state of efficiency, let us consider certain aspects of the condition of other branches of the Japanese army in which it appears to be behind the standard of what is demanded by a modern first-class army.

Even before the World War the possibilities of an air force in war-time had not been altogether overlooked, although it was left to the stern tests of actual fighting to prove the really vast importance of that arm. The War, however, in addition to this, brought out new and hitherto almost unthought-of inventions, the possession of which has now come to be regarded as a *sine qua non* for any army which may be called upon to take the field against that of a first-class Power. This refers, of course, to the use of tanks, gas, and smoke, and to the almost unlimited number of machine-guns and amount of motor transport required, let alone the counter-measures against the three former and, i matter, against machine-guns, and also for such inno as the barrage, creeping and otherwise.

In most of these matters the Japanese army is s way behind its European and American counterpar is, of course, partly due to the fact that these othei were able to develop them throughout the War l of practical experience in the field, whereas the being far removed from the seat of war, had t mainly on second-hand information, and, moreov always the case in peace-time, in all countries, mo experimental work in Japan was necessarily restricted, whereas the armies of the actual belligerents were being supplied unstintedly with all the latest devices. In this way, therefore, Japan has fallen behind other nations in the matter of modern war *matériel.*

Apart from this, however, Japanese military psychology appears to be partly to blame for the backward state of modern methods and devices, and the present is not by any means the first time in Japanese history that the army has suffered from this defect. In an earlier chapter it was shown how, at the time of the Mongol invasion in the thirteenth century, the defenders were handicapped by their lack of the modern *matériel* of those days, and how, on that occasion, they considered that the invaders were hardly playing the game, because they used mechanical devices to overcome human skill. Similarly, many of the old *Samurai*, in the early days of foreign relations, looked on the bombarders of Kagoshima and Shimonoseki as somewhat "unsporting" for taking advantage of superior weapons in order to overcome their resistance.

At the present time, of course, the Japanese army is well equipped with most of the essential weapons of war, but this characteristic of holding individual prowess as more worthy of respect than mechanical devices is still very apparent, and it was a noticeable point at the Infantry School in 1920 that the officer students took much more interest in tactical schemes of the pre-War type, and of field-firing exercises and the theory of musketry, than they did in the lectures and demonstrations on the use of tanks, smoke screens, bombing, anti-aircraft precautions, and other matters which became such a feature of the late War. They looked on gas and kindred devices as unfair methods of fighting, but, although most people will no doubt agree with them that warfare on the lines of twenty years ago would be infinitely pleasanter and more "gentlemanly," it seems a mistake to neglect the teaching of precautions against such devices, as they are almost certain to be employed in wars of the future.

The Japanese are, in fact, too prone to depend on the so-called spirit of *Yamato Damashii* to pull them through everything, and they thereby lay themselves open to terrible misfortunes in the future. No one will deny that the spirit of bravery and self-sacrifice is highly developed in the Japanese soldier, and that it is an invaluable asset to him, but in modern warfare the mechanical aspect is so much in evidence that even the bravest troops are useless unless they are as well equipped as their opponents, as otherwise they merely become cannon-fodder. The late General Nogi found this to his cost in 1904 when he endeavoured to bring about the fall of Port Arthur by force of numbers instead of awaiting the arrival of his heavy artillery. Modern mechanical devices of war have increased enormously since then, so that any army which takes the field without a plentiful supply of them is simply courting disaster.

The Japanese military authorities are, of course, taking steps to increase the mechanical efficiency of the army—in fact, the recent reduction of *personnel* was made on the assumption that increased efficiency of armaments would compensate for the decrease in man-power involved by the reduction scheme.

A programme for improvement of armaments, equipment, fortresses, aviation, etc., was drawn up in 1920, a certain sum being set apart for that purpose each year, and the completion of the whole programme being fixed for 1935. Over two hundred millions of *yen* have already been expended on this scheme during the period that has elapsed since its initiation, and there is still a sum of about five hundred million *yen* set aside for the purpose, though, owing to the present retrenchment policy of the Government, the date for the completion of the whole programme has been extended to 1940.

It will be seen from this that steps are being taken to improve the mechanical power of the army, but, even so, the year 1940 is a long way off, and much may have happened before then to revolutionise warfare still further. The present state of Japanese war material, in fact, makes one think that the military authorities do not contemplate ever having to use the army against the full strength of a first-class military Power, and, when geographical conditions are considered, it seems likely that they are right. China cannot be regarded as such, nor can Russia at the present time, whilst any other wars in which she might become involved would, for Japan, be confined mainly to naval actions. The unexpected does, however, happen at times. Prior to 1914, for instance, the *rôle* of the British army, in the event of a big European war, was never expected to be more than that of a mobile expeditionary force to be put in at one point and then withdrawn and sent to another, according to where it was most needed ; nevertheless it found itself destined to fulfil a very different *rôle* in the operations which ensued as a result of Austria's ultimatum to Serbia in July of that year. In the same way, it is conceivable that the Japanese army might one day be called upon to face an opponent who might upset their preconceived notions as to possible sites of military operations. Such an event, however, need not be regarded as a likelihood in the near future, and the Japanese army, despite its lack of some of the most modern forms of war material, is probably quite well enough prepared for all possible contingencies at the present time.

As this question of war material has already been discussed in a general way at some length, it only remains to say a few words about what, for want of a better expression, may be called the "special arms"—*i.e.* those which have of late years brought about the formation of special branches of the Service. Amongst these may be mentioned motor transport, machine-guns, tanks, and the telegraph and telephone.

As far back as 1877, at the time of the Satsuma Rebellion, the need of an efficient transport service was realised, and, as a result of the lessons learnt from those operations, the authorities set to work to perfect the system. It was not, however, until 1907 that it was decided to investigate the possibilities of motor lorries for transport purposes, and for the next few years very little progress was made, only a dozen or so motor vehicles being owned by the army at the time that Japan declared war on Germany in 1914.

At the present time there is a special Motor Transport unit, and the army gives subsidies to owners of motor vehicles who promise to lend them to the military authorities in the event of a war in which their services are required; but, owing largely to the poor condition of roads in Japan, motor transport is still in a very undeveloped state, and would be wholly inadequate for a war against a first-class military Power.

A Tank Corps and a Machine Gun Corps are both non-existent, though the army has been carrying out experiments with tanks and whippets during the last few years, and the proportion of machine-guns is to be increased shortly. The first tank, as mentioned in an earlier chapter, was brought to Japan in October, 1918, by a British officer, Major Bruce, and was of the old Mark IV. type, and since then a few more tanks and some whippets of the Rénault type have been imported, but no independent organisation exists as yet.

In regard to machine-guns, a new type of Hotchkiss (1914 pattern) was introduced into units in 1918, and, at the same time, the former establishment of 6 guns per infantry regiment (*i.e.* 2 per battalion) was increased to 12, although this increase was spread over three or four years and was not carried out all at one time. Under the reorganisation scheme formulated last year, the proportion of machine-guns is to be greatly increased by the adoption of light guns in addition to the heavy type ones of the 1914 pattern. By the time, therefore, that the rearmament programme is complete, the totally inadequate number of machine-guns, which was so noticeable a point in the Grand Manœuvres of 1918 and on subsequent occasions also, will have become a thing of the past, and a serious fault will have been rectified.

Apart from the fact that both the wireless telegraph and the wireless telephone are amongst the more modern additions to the Japanese army, no special remarks need be made on the subject of either telegraphy or telephony, as the existence of a special Communications Corps (*Tsūshintai*) has already been mentioned elsewhere in these pages.[1] This corps is a branch of the Engineers, as also are the two railway regiments; and in this connection it is of interest to note that officers of the Sappers are not necessarily, as they generally are in our own army, men of special ability. As mentioned in an earlier chapter, officers for all branches of the Service have to pass through the same institution, namely, the *Shikwan Gakkō*, or Officers' School, and there is no question of a Sandhurst for infantry and cavalry, and a Woolwich for artillery and engineers; nor is it necessary for the cadet who wishes to be gazetted to the latter arm of the service to pass out at the top of the list; in fact, the order of graduation is never made public. As a result of this, it comes about that there is no great difference between the officers of the various branches of the Service.

[1] *Vide* p. 297, where it is called a "Telegraph Corps."

CHAPTER XXX

STRATEGICAL, POLITICO-MILITARY, AND ECONOMIC QUESTIONS

In a previous chapter it was shown that the Japanese army is not, apparently, maintained at its present strength so much for external aggression as for internal effect, to counteract the so-called " dangerous thoughts " which are believed to be undermining the finer qualities of the nation. Let us, however, consider certain of the external aspects of the military situation which the army is called upon to face.

From the strategic point of view Japan is favourably placed, as, like Great Britain, it is an island empire removed from direct contact with its continental neighbours, and, with the safest form of frontiers provided by Nature, namely, the sea. Japan proper, consisting of four principal islands —Honshū (generally referred to as " the main island " in these pages), Kyūshū, Shikoku, and Hokkaidō—is so situated that its inner, or Sea of Japan, side is practically immune from attack so long as the narrow straits of its southern end, between the southern part of Honshū and the coast of Korea, are watched by the fleet, and provided that the northern entrances to the Sea of Japan are similarly guarded. The former straits are about 120 miles in width and have the island of Tsushima practically in the centre to act as a sentinel, whilst the two northern straits, the Perouse and the Tsugaru, are likewise comparatively narrow and can be closely watched. The only other entrance to the Sea of Japan is through the Gulf of Tartary in the extreme north, between Saghalien island and the mainland of Siberia, but it narrows to only a few miles in width, and could be closed without difficulty by means of a mine barrage or other similar device.

Just as the physical features mentioned above go to render the inner, or Sea of Japan, side of Japan practically immune from attack, so also is the outer, or Pacific, coast practically invulnerable to attack on a large scale on account of its distance from any potential enemy. Even if such attacks took place, most of the main points of strategic importance, such as the arsenals and ship-building yards, are protected from direct attack by the islands of Kyūshū and Shikoku, as most of them are in the Inland Sea, the three entrances to which can be guarded without much difficulty.

From what has been said above it will be seen that Japan is, in many ways, even safer from direct attack than is Britain, though, owing to its weak anti-aircraft defences, it is more vulnerable to attack from the air, and, like Britain, its chief source of anxiety in war-time would be its lines of communications on which it depends for its supplies, on account of the fact that most of its raw materials have to be obtained from abroad. Iron and steel, oil, wool, cotton, rubber, jute and chemicals of various kinds are, for example, amongst the many important items for which Japan is wholly, or mainly, dependent on other countries, and even in articles of food she is far from being self-supporting. Little wonder, therefore, that she looks on the rich and almost untapped resources of Manchuria and Mongolia, and of the Siberian littoral, with a covetous eye.

The Shantung Question was largely an economic one, as also is the whole question of Japanese domination of Manchuria. In both these provinces, resident foreigners are anti-Japanese on account of the severe business competition necessitated by their presence, and by the fact that the Japanese have not infrequently used unfair methods of competition in those parts. Without, however, attempting either to condone or justify such methods, it must be remembered that whereaş Manchuria and Shantung merely offer excellent opportunities to other foreign investors, to the Japanese the economic control of these provinces, particularly of the former, is yearly becoming a matter of increasingly vital importance to the very existence of their country. Moreover, the strategic position of Manchuria and of its railways is likewise a factor which greatly affects Japan without having any corresponding effect on the other foreign investors.

Before abusing Japan for not adhering strictly to the "Open Door" Policy in Manchuria, it should be recalled that the development of that province is largely due to the initiative of her countrymen, and that to Japan is due the credit for making Manchuria what it is.

Up to a point this is true also of California. Fifty years ago, when part of that American west-coast State was still in an undeveloped condition, no one worried about it, but now that it is so well developed, the Japanese, to whom in this case also a great deal of credit is due, are excessively unpopular, and successive laws have been enacted against them in an effort to drive them out.

In both cases the Japanese have hoped to help solve the question of their surplus population by encouraging emigration to those parts, but in the one case legislative action by the local authorities has reduced this hope to a minimum, whilst in the other the climate has proved to be a deterrent to many who might otherwise have gone there in search of a new home.

Leaving aside, however, the economic aspect, let us turn to the politico-military situation in so far as it concerns Japan.

Consisting, as it does, of a chain of islands extending nearly to Kamchatka in the north and to a point almost directly opposite Hong Kong to the south, Japan is virtually able to control all the exits from both Siberia and China, and, when accused of taking an unfair advantage of her geographical position *vis-à-vis* the latter country, she feels she is being unfairly treated. If America insists on a Monroe Doctrine for the New World, Japan sees no reason why she (Japan) should not be allowed to start a similar doctrine in the Far East. Mexico and South America, she argues, did not invite their wealthy northern neighbour, nor, for that matter, did India invite Britain, so why should these two Powers try to dictate to her if she endeavours to start a modified form of Monroe Doctrine for the Far East?

There are those who, with a certain amount of cause, fear that Germany and Russia may one day co-operate for the good of each other, the former having the organising power and scientific knowledge whilst the latter has the raw materials merely awaiting the application of both. A not dissimilar state of circumstances exists between Japan and China, the former being young and virile and well fitted to organise and administer, whereas the latter, vast in size and in resources, is too feeble and corrupt to develop them without outside aid.

Although it is the custom to decry the treatment accorded to China by Japan, it is perhaps as well for the world that these two countries are not on better terms with each other, for, if they were, it might well be that Japan would put China on her feet and strengthen her to such a degree that the Kaiser's dream of a "Yellow Peril" might become a reality. As things are, however, it is most unlikely that such a state of affairs will ever come to pass, as there is little love lost between the two nations, and, just as Britain's safety in India depends largely on the fact that the Hindu and the Mussulman hate each other more than they hate the British, so also is the world likely to be safe from the so-called "Yellow Peril" on account of the enmity between Japan and China.

China, though now weak and vacillating, is by way of being an aristocratic nation, proud of its past history, and she regards her small but virile neighbour as a mere upstart. Knowing Japan's strength and ambitions, however, she fears her just as she fears the countries of the West, but she is wise in that she realises that her own safety lies in her ability to play off one country against another—knowledge which she puts to the best advantage. Even so, however, it is a fact that, in the last two decades, China has lost about a quarter of her territory and about a fifth of her population, and has mortgaged all of her most valuable assets as security for loans.

In spite of her enormous army, amounting to about a million and a half, China cannot, by herself, be regarded as a danger to Japan, as the armed forces which go to form this total are split up amongst a number of *tuchuns*, each jealous of, and unwilling to co-operate with, the others; and the men themselves are, as shown in former chapters, little more than an armed rabble who alternate between being soldiers one day and bandits the next.

Having seen something of the relations between Japan and her immediate neighbours on the Asiatic mainland, let us now consider her position *vis-à-vis* America.

During my attachment to the Infantry School at Chiba, some of the officers used to refer to the policies of America, Germany, and Britain as the "three A's," the "three B's," and the "three C's" respectively. The "three A's" of America represented America, Alaska, and Asia; the "three B's" were Berlin, Budapest, and Bagdad; and the "three C's" were Capetown, Cairo, and Calcutta—that is to say, the linking up of the three places in each case.

It seemed that the Japanese had no particular like or dislike for the "three B's" or the "three C's," but that they were strongly opposed to America's ever trying to carry out the "three A's" policy, and that, if ever they attempted to do so by constructing a tunnel under the Behring Straits—a project which, though unlikely, has been suggested from time to time—Japan would most certainly fight in order to prevent it.

In regard to the Behring tunnel scheme, an officer once explained to me that Japan was always afraid of her "gates," which were gradually having to be pushed further and further from the main island. At one time, he said, her northern "gates" were the Perouse Straits and the Gulf of Tartary, but now they were up to the Behring Straits. If these were tunnelled by America it would, he contended, be equivalent to having "an enemy within the gates."

This talk of "gates" may sound a bit far-fetched, but one has only to look at the map to see that it is strategically true, though it will be a long time yet, if ever, before the Behring tunnel scheme materialises, and the tunnel by itself could hardly be regarded as a menace so long as no railways exist on the Asiatic side. Moreover, even if they were constructed, they would not be available for the transportation of American troops unless Russia too was at war with Japan, as the troops would have to pass through several thousands of miles of Russian territory before getting to within striking distance. Even then they could only be used against a Japanese army on the mainland and not against Japan itself, unless there was a large fleet of transports waiting at Vladivostock or some such place to take them across. Such a fleet, even if it existed, would be at the mercy of Japanese naval units, unless the Japanese navy had been destroyed in the meantime, in which case it would be far simpler to convey the troops from America direct across the Pacific.

From what has been said above it will be seen that there is not much cause for fear, even if the Behring tunnel scheme ever materialises, unless possibly from aircraft, and even then, only with Russia's consent, which presupposes Russia also being an opponent.

The chances, therefore, of America ever becoming an "enemy within the gates" are exceedingly remote, and her distance from Japan by sea is so great as virtually to constitute no military menace, though she is a dangerous trade rival in the Far East, and trade rivalry is not infrequently the precursor of war.

There are many people who laugh at the idea of Japan ever going to war with the United States, as they point out that America is her best customer, and that she could never, therefore, afford to risk losing her trade. Theoretically this is true, but such theories do not always work out in practice. The same, for instance, was said in pre-War days *vis-à-vis* Britain and Germany, but it did not prevent the world catastrophe which broke out in 1914.

Admitting, therefore, that a war between Japan and

America would be possible, the question as to how such a war would be fought naturally arises. As this question has been thoroughly thrashed out by Hector Bywater and other well-known writers,[1] it is not proposed to go into it here in any great detail, but a few points may, with advantage, be set down.

The inner, or Sea of Japan, side of Japan, as already shown, is practically, one might almost say quite, safe from attack by America, whilst the great expanse of water dividing the two countries makes it all but impossible for either country to transport an expeditionary force across the Pacific to attack the other so long as the opposing fleet remains in existence. No land warfare on a large scale would, therefore, be possible until one or other of the opposing fleets had been destroyed.

The shortest distance across the Pacific is over 4500 miles, and no large fleet is capable of covering this distance and arriving in fighting trim without replenishing fuel and other supplies on the way, particularly if there is no reasonable chance of being able to take in fuel and ammunition at some point very considerably closer than the base from which they started. In other words, "stepping-stones" across the Pacific, in the shape of fortified islands fitted with repairing dockyards and stocked with ammunition, fuel, and supplies of all kinds, are a *sine qua non* for a successful attack, either by Japan on America or America on Japan, and these preliminary essentials are absent, thanks to the provisions of the Washington Conference.

In 1921, when Hector Bywater wrote on the subject of strategy in the Pacific and the possible features of a war in that ocean, it was still possible for America to prepare stepping-stones of this description, and there were many Americans who urged the fortification of Guam, the Philippines, and other points with a view to protecting them from attack in the event of a war.

From the American point of view such a step was highly

[1] See Chapters IX. and X. of Hector Bywater's *Sea-Power in the Pacific*, published in London by Constable & Co., Ltd., 1921.

essential owing to their distance from the mother country, but from the Japanese point of view it was equally necessary to prevent any such scheme from being put into effect, as the fortification of these islands and their conversion into naval bases would have been a very real menace to the safety of Japan in the event of a war, Guam being only 1360 miles from Yokosuka whilst Manila is about 1740. Both would, therefore, have served as final jumping-off points.[1]

Relations between the two countries were very strained in 1921, and there is little or no doubt that, if America had started to carry out her fortification schemes in the Pacific —however much she might have insisted on the fact that it was being done entirely for the sake of self-defence and not with any ideas of aggression—Japan would have felt herself bound to declare war, if no other means had been found to induce America to forego her quite natural defensive measures, for the potential menace would have been too great for Japan to risk.

Now that both Japan and America have agreed to carry out no further fortification of their possessions in the Pacific, the chances of a war between the two nations have been reduced very considerably, as, apart from anything else, there is now no possibility of making "stepping-stones" across that ocean. Without these, the forces of the two nations, as already shown, would find it difficult to come to real grips. Japan, provided no other nation joined in the fight, could probably seize Guam and the Philippines without much difficulty, but this would not give her a base within striking distance of America; and, although the seizure of these islands would be a blow to America's prestige, it would have little or no other effect, except to anger the people of the United States.

If, of course, Japan could carry out the destruction of the locks of the Panama Canal, she might be able to destroy the American Pacific Fleet before the Atlantic Fleet could come to its support, and could, moreover, cut off the American

[1] Manila is about 7000 miles and Guam about 5500 from America.

naval forces from their chief bases, which are on the Atlantic seaboard ; but although the Japanese naval authorities are popularly supposed to be in possession of various schemes for the destruction of the canal locks, it is doubtful if any of them could be put into practice.

From this it will be seen that, strategically, it is difficult to see how a Japanese-American war could be fought, provided no other country came in on either side. Japan's only chance of gaining a real victory over America would be to ensure the blocking of the Panama Canal at the very outset, whilst America's only chance of winning would be to defeat the Japanese navy in Japanese home waters, a feat which would be all but impossible in the absence of the necessary "stepping-stones." Unless the Panama Canal had been sufficiently damaged at the outset, the Japanese navy could no more afford to battle with the combined forces of the Pacific and Atlantic fleets on the American side of the Pacific than could the Americans afford to risk fighting in Japanese home waters, the lack of these "stepping-stones" being the deciding factor in each case.

Nevertheless, although it is a truism to say that nothing in war-time is more likely than the unlikely, the truth of this assertion is beyond gainsaying. Although, therefore, it may be difficult to conceive how such a war, if ever it broke out, would be fought, it does not mean that it is a physical impossibility. The great advance, for instance, in the science of aviation may quite possibly alter the whole strategical aspect in a few years' time, and, further, it must be remembered that the views given above are based on the supposition that Japan and America would be the only belligerents. A war, however, between two World Powers is more than likely to spread, and if either side was joined by one or more other countries, the whole strategical aspect would be changed. Let us hope, however, that the theories as to how such a war would be fought will remain nothing more than interesting military problems which will never require a practical solution.

CHAPTER XXXI

THE JAPANESE OFFICER AND HIS COUNTRY'S FOREIGN RELATIONS

It is often said that the average Japanese officer is very ignorant of matters outside his own profession, and that he is of a class apart. In some respects there is justification for this contention, for it is undoubtedly a fact that officers of the Japanese army, as a whole, take but little interest in matters not directly connected with the science of war. It must, however, be admitted that it is not only the soldier who is ignorant of matters not concerning himself, but that the civilian is often equally ignorant; and this is true, up to a certain degree, of all nations.

One point, however, in which the Japanese officer shows particular lack of interest, as a rule, is politics, and possibly he is all the better at his own job in consequence, for the less a soldier dabbles in such matters the better it is for him, whilst the reverse is equally true, that the less the politician interferes with military matters the better it is for all concerned.

The Japanese military authorities, realising the truth of this axiom, make it a rule that neither officers nor men are to interest themselves in political matters, and, for that reason, literature of any kind which is brought into barracks by the men has to be submitted to their company commander for inspection. If it is found to deal with political controversy, its owner is duly relieved of it.

Although, however, internal politics and political creeds are barred from discussion, considerable interest is often evinced in foreign politics which concern Japan, and it is on that subject in particular that this chapter will be written.

During the three years that I was in Japan as a Language Officer, the most noticeable point in this respect was the ever-growing interest shown in the country's relations with America and the ever-increasing hostile feeling amongst army officers towards the latter. As the Washington Conference has taken place since then, and has, happily, relieved the tension, it is possible to say more on this subject now than it would have been discreet to say when the relations between the two countries were not so far removed from breaking-point.

It goes without saying that a Language Officer, while carrying out a period of attachment with a Japanese unit, is bound to overhear, or take part in, conversations which help him to form a fairly accurate estimate of the Japanese officers' outlook on the problems of the day—political, military, and general—and, as a result, he should be able to gauge the feeling in military circles in regard to international relationships and the politico-military situation of the Far-Eastern question in general. Hitherto but few comments have been made in these pages on this subject, as it is apt to encroach on dangerous ground and, in any case, it is not the purpose of this book to enter the realm of politics. It may be well, however, to show how Japanese officers, and civilians as well, feel on questions of this kind.

Looking at it from their own point of view, they see themselves confronted with the fact that their own island empire is rapidly becoming too small for their ever-increasing population. The overflow must go somewhere, but the question is, "Where?" America will not have them nor will Australia. Siberia does not want them and, in any case, the climate is too severe for their liking. China proper is already overcrowded, besides which all the other World Powers at once cry out if they turn their attention to that country or to its Manchurian or Mongolian dependencies.

What then is Japan to do? It is evident that she must either find colonies for her surplus population, or else secure for herself an assured supply of raw material with which to provide work and food for everyone within the limits of her present territory. Realising this, can one wonder that the Japanese are at times angered at the apparent indifference of the other Powers towards their needs? In the case of Australia they consider that insult is added to injury by the application of the catchword, "A White Australia," as they not only feel that it is unfair that a country of such huge dimensions should be reserved for a mere handful of men when a neighouring country (Japan) is in real need of territory in which to expand, but they also feel hurt at the reference to their colour, the expression, "A White Australia," implying to them that, owing to their colour, they are looked on as an inferior race. Politicians may try to point out that no offence is meant, but nevertheless the Japanese, knowing that, as a rule, the so-called "white" races look on "colour" as a sign of inferiority, naturally resent any reference to it.

What has been said above in regard to Australia is equally true when applied to America, especially in regard to the California question. Much, of course, may be said on the side of both these countries for wishing to keep out the Japanese, and many of the deeper-thinking men amongst the latter realise that it is mainly an economic question, and that it is merely their country's misfortune that she did not wake up in time to share in the spoils; for it was during her two hundred and fifty years of self-imposed isolation that the other Powers, more awake than herself, were carrying out the policy of "land-grab" and snatching up all the last remaining pieces of terra firma. The average Japanese, however, be he army officer or civilian, is not so stoical in his outlook, and what he feels is that his country is being grossly ill-treated by constant discrimination on the part of the other Powers. Right or wrong, one cannot help but sympathise with him in this outlook. A hundred years ago, if a country wanted to add a bit more to its territory, she could generally do so, provided she was sufficiently strong. Now, however, in these so-called enlightened days of the twentieth century, even a few square miles cannot be seized without causing a regular furore amongst half the nations of the world, and the horror-struck cries of "self-determination" and the "rights of small nations" will at once be raised in order to add a touch of philanthropy to the otherwise (probably) selfish motives of the protesting Powers.

It would not be an unprofitable matter for study to consider what we ourselves would do if we were in Japan's place, the problem resolving itself into the following points:

(*a*) No country will receive our surplus population.

(*b*) We are not allowed to seize any part or parts of another country's territory either for commercial exploitation or for colonisation.

(*c*) At the present rate of increase we shall soon have neither enough food nor enough work for everyone.

Question: What are we going to do about it?

Put down in black and white like this, it looks like the old problem of the "irresistible force striking an immovable substance."

As already pointed out, a Language Officer, if he goes about it in the right way, will have plenty of opportunity for finding out the views of his Japanese *confrères* on the subject of what may be called by the name given by Lord Curzon to one of his most interesting works, namely, the *Problems of the Far East.* The average Japanese officer does not pay much attention to European politics, but he is far from being a disinterested spectator of what is happening in the Pacific and in the Far East, and his views on these subjects are at times illuminating, to say the least of it. In the summer of 1920, even more so than in previous months, one heard Japanese officers expressing their feelings pretty freely at times on the subject of the relations between their own country and America. Grievances, imaginary and otherwise, were not infrequently aired, and feeling ran considerably higher than people at home probably realised. Happily for the world in general, the Washington Conference has taken place since then, and has undoubtedly smoothed matters down very considerably, for, prior to its opening, relations were, to put it mildly, "strained." Let us hope that, the tension having been relaxed, Japan's relations with America will never again be put to such a strain.

Although, from the very first, one had heard of the misunderstandings between Japan and America, it was not, so far as I can remember, till the summer of 1919 that I began to hear officers talking of a war between the two countries as being practically a matter of certainty sooner or later. From that time onwards, however, up to the time I returned to England a year and a half later, the subject was brought up time and again, and it was not difficult to see that such a war would have been popular, not only with the army but with the nation as a whole, in spite of the efforts of the more level-headed men to calm things down. So high, in fact, did the feeling run that on one occasion, when dining with a party of six Japanese officers, one of them drank to the downfall of America, a toast to which all but myself responded with great enthusiasm. It was the only occasion on which I was present at such an open exhibition of anti-American feeling, and it is probably needless to add that most of the members of the party were somewhat heated with *sake*.[1] Nevertheless, the very fact that such a toast was drunk goes to show that a very bitter feeling against America existed in the Japanese army during the year or so prior to the holding of the Washington Conference.

This was largely due to the numerous causes of friction which arose between the two countries—the Shantung, Californian, Yap, and Siberian questions being amongst the most serious that came to the fore, as also was the question of fortifications in the Pacific. All these, combined with the naval armament race which was in progress and also

[1] Normally the Japanese officer abstains from alcohol, none being consumed in barracks, except on special occasions. On these occasions, and at *geisha* dinners, he is, however, apt to let himself go and, as most Japanese have weak heads for drink, he soon becomes convivial and talkative if he does so. He drinks less than does the average British officer, but the effects are more noticeable.

with several matters of minor importance, were rapidly leading to a climax which was only averted by the holding of the Washington Conference. An attachment to the Japanese army at that time was, therefore, of particular interest, as not only was it the beginning of the transition stage when pre-War methods began to be dropped in favour of new ones necessitated by the lessons learnt from the War, but it was also a period during which relations with America became severely strained, and officers were wont to express their feelings more freely than at normal times.

A great deal more could be written on this subject, but enough has been said to indicate the trend of thought which was rife at that time amongst all ranks of the Japanese army.

CHAPTER XXXII

CONCLUDING REMARKS

THIS book has already run into too many pages, and only a few further comments of a general nature, mainly connected with training, will therefore be added. A certain amount has already been said on this subject, and the main points of the Japanese system may now be summarised as under :

(1) Insistence on uniformity of training.

(2) Discouragement of too much competition and of individuality.

(3) Encouragement of thrift and simple living.

(4) Importance attached to the training of *moral*, loyalty, and discipline.

(5) The teaching that, in war-time, self-destruction is better than surrender.

(6) The teaching of reticence in regard to matters of military importance.

This last point is one to which more attention might well be paid in our own army, for it is not by any means uncommon to find matters discussed in letters which, if they got into the wrong hands, might lead to very serious consequences. Not only were such matters frequently discussed in writing during the late War, in spite of a strict censorship, but also they were passed on by word of mouth from one to another, and it will be recalled how people in England often knew several days beforehand exactly when and where some particular action was going to take place and, moreover, talked freely about it in public places. The wonder is that greater disasters did not occur in consequence, and the only conclusion to be drawn from this is that the enemy, when receiving such information, could not credit the veracity of rumours discussed so openly.

One of the great features of Japanese strategy and grand tactics in their war with Russia was the secrecy observed and the false information circulated purposely. This, combined with their system of intelligence, which, both before that war and during it, enabled them to have an almost uncanny knowledge of their enemy's doings and potentialities, helped them very considerably to subsequent victory. The importance of these factors had been learnt by the Japanese as a result of generations of study of the axioms laid down by the two Chinese strategists, Wu and Sun, to whom reference has been made in previous chapters. The two outstanding points in the teachings of that somewhat disreputable couple of old warriors were that success in war depends largely on one's ability to know everything there is to know about your enemy, and to mystify and mislead him and leave him in the dark about yourself and your own doings. In carrying out these precepts the Japanese in their war with Russia proved themselves adept pupils.

In regard to the question of military intelligence, there is one point in which the Japanese have a great advantage over most other nations, and that is in their language. The written script is so complicated that, apart from themselves and the Chinese, there is probably not more than one man in a hundred thousand who can read even the printed form, whilst those who read the cursive script, which is the form normally used in letter-writing, are very considerably fewer, perhaps one in a million ; possibly not as many. Even of this number, there is probably only a small proportion who can read it with any degree of rapidity or fluency. When this fact is considered, it will be seen how greatly any nation which went to war with Japan would be hampered in the matter of censorship and in the translating of captured orders and documents of any kind.

In addition to the outstanding points in the Japanese system of training mentioned above, there are a number of points which may be defined as good and others which one has no hesitation in calling bad. Amongst the former may be classified the system of attaching officers for short periods to other units and to other branches of the Service; the system of *kengaku*, *i.e.* making officers attend and watch field exercises without taking part in them themselves, and thereby learning from the faults, as well as the good points, of others, on the principle that it is always easier to see faults in others than in oneself; the freedom and encouragement given to even the newest-joined subaltern to express his own opinions on military matters; the importance attached to giving all officers a thorough knowledge of their duties and especially of tactics, both practical and theoretical; and the encouragement given to making officers efficient lecturers.

This last point is perhaps overdone, as it results in lectures and criticisms becoming so inordinately long at times that the hearers lose all interest long before the end is reached.

Another point which deserves mention as being good is that, during his period of service in field rank, an officer must do at least two years of regimental duty. Most armies, of course, have some such regulation, the rule in the American army, for instance, being that no officer can remain away from regimental duty for more than four years at a time. In our own army, however, there is no such stipulation, and the result is that officers who have been on the Staff a great number of years are apt to be out of sympathy with the regimental officer and with regimental soldiering in general, with the result that friction is liable to arise.

In the Japanese army there are no such things as promotion examinations, although an officer may be passed over if considered to be inefficient. Staff College graduates, and those who pass the post-graduate course at the School of Artillery and Engineering, and are known as "Technical Officers," receive accelerated promotion, but in order to rise to the rank of a general officer the *p.s.c.* men, like all others, have to put in at least two years of regimental soldiering during their period of service in field rank.

While on the subject of promotion it may be said that divisional and brigade commanders are judged by their performances on Grand Manœuvres as to whether or not they are considered fit to rise further in the Service.

The Japanese officer is inclined to laugh at the idea of promotion examinations, and thinks that his British *confrère* must be a very lazy beggar who, unless he has examinations to pass, will never trouble to work. There may perhaps be a degree of truth in this suggestion, but although the Japanese officer may require less stimulus than his average British counterpart to work, there is at least one important subject which the latter comes to learn through his promotion examinations, and which the former, owing to lack of inducement, practically neglects, unless he happens to be an aspirant for the Staff College. The subject in question is military history, and it seems a grave omission on the part of the Japanese military authorities that so little notice is taken of it. Stonewall Jackson, of American Civil War fame, always maintained that " to become a master of war, one must study the masters of that science " ; and history shows, time after time, that it is the men who have studied these same " masters " who have themselves risen to positions of high command and earned for themselves the right to be classed amongst these very " masters " whose campaigns and methods they have studied.

In spite of this, however, military history is a subject that does not even appear on the syllabus of the Officers' School, and is, in fact, not studied anywhere in Japan except at the Staff College, although, of course, examples, especially those from the operations in Manchuria, are often quoted in lectures on other subjects.

This virtual omission of the study of military history seems to be classifiable as a weak point in the army educational system, and amongst other such points may be mentioned the system of " cramming," which is so prevalent at the military educational establishments ; the lack of interest and knowledge which the average officer is apt to have in matters outside his own particular duties ; and the over-confidence which the army as a whole is led to have in their own military abilities.

Nevertheless, even allowing for these and other weaknesses, there is much to commend itself in the Japanese system of training, and, before bringing this book to an end, emphasis may well be laid once more on the fact that the *personnel* of the army is about as good as could be wanted. Hard-working and keen on their profession, the officers and N.C.O's can be trusted to put their best into their work, whilst the men under them are well trained and well disciplined, are capable of withstanding the greatest hardships, and may be counted on to carry out whatever may be required of them. The main weak point is the lack of modern war material, and this, as shown in a previous chapter, has been a failure in the Japanese land forces even from very early times. In spite of this disadvantage, however, they overcame the Mongol invaders in the thirteenth century, and the same may be said in regard to the wars against China and Russia respectively. Nevertheless, the great advances made in science in late years has made "war" so much a matter of mechanical appliances that bravery and good leadership alone are not sufficient, and over-confidence on this score is more to be avoided now than at any time in the past. Provided, however, that these facts are fully realised, and that the necessary steps are taken in time, the Japanese army is likely to be as formidable an opponent in future wars as she has proved herself to be in those of the past.

APPENDIX

Present and Former British Military Attachés and Language Officers sent to Japan.

MILITARY ATTACHÉS.

De Boulay, N. W. H.	R.A.	1894-5	Retired
Sartorius, E. H., V.C.	59th Foot	1896-7	,,
Hemming, F. W.	5th Dragoon Gds.	1897-8	,,
Churchill, A. G.	12th Lancers	1898-1903	,,
Hume, C. V.	R.A.	1903-7	Deceased
Boger, R. W.	R.A.	1907-10	,,
Somerville, J. A. C., C.M.G., C.B.E.	R. Sussex Regt.	1911-14 1915-18	
Calthrop, E. F.	R.A.	1914-15	Killed in action
Woodroffe, C. R., C.M.G., C.B.E.	R.A.	1918-21	Retired
Piggott, F. S. G., D.S.O.	R.E.	1921-	

LANGUAGE OFFICERS.

(British Army.)

Rank 1922.	Name.	Regt. or Corps.	In Japan.	Remarks.
Major	Adam, W. A.	5th Lancers	1903-4	Retired
Col.	Woulfe-Flanagan, R. J., D.S.O.	R. West Kents	1903-4	
Col.	Vincent, B., C.B., C.M.G.	R.F.A.	1903-5	
Lt.-Col.	Bannerman, Sir A.	R.E.	1903-5	Retired
Brig.-Gen.	Jardine, J. B., C.M.G., D.S.O.	5th Lancers	1903-5	,,
Brig.-Gen.	Hart-Synnot, A. H. S., C.M.G., D.S.O.	East Surreys	1903-5	,,
	Yate, C. A. L., V.C.	Yorkshire L.I.	1903-6	Died of wounds
	Calthrop, E. F.	R.F.A.	1903-8	Killed in action
Lt.-Col.	Harrison, W. A.	R.E.	1904-5	Retired
Lt.-Col.	Badham-Thornhill, G., D.S.O.	R.G.A.	1904-5	
Capt.	Betton-Foster, G. H.	R.G.A.	1904-5	Retired
Lt.-Col.	Piggott, F. S. G., D.S.O.	R.E.	1904-6 1910-13	M.A. Tokyo 1921-
Major	Leader, J.	Bedfords	1905-7	Retired

Rank 1922.	Name.	Rrgt. or Corps.	In Japan.	Remarks.
Col.	Somerville, J. A. C., C.M.G., C.B.E.	Northd. Fus.	1905-7	M.A. Tokyo (twice)
Lt.-Col.	North, P. W., D.S.O.	R. Berks	1905-7	Retired
Air-V.-M.	Salmond, W. G. H., K.C.M.G., D.S.O.	R.F.A.	1905-7	R.A.F.
Lt.-Col.	Toke, R. T.	Welsh	1906-8	Retired
Brig.-Gen.	Woodroffe, C. R., C.M.G., C.B.E.	R.F.A.	1906-8	M.A. Tokyo (Retired)
Major	Cardew, A. M.	R.E.	1906-10	Retired
Major	Dixon, A. C. H.	Cheshire	1907-9	,,
Lt.-Col.	North, E. B., C.M.G., D.S.O.	R. Berks	1907-9	,,
Lt.-Col.	Stanley, F., D.S.O.	R.F.A.	1907-9	
Major	Moore, W. A., D.S.O.	R.G.A.	1907-9	
Lt.-Col.	Price, O. L., D.S.O.	R.G.A.	1908-10	
Brig.-Gen.	Leggett, A. H., C.M.G., D.S.O.	R. Scots Fus.	1908-10	Retired
Lt.-Col.	Garsia, W. C., D.S.O., M.C.	Hants	1908-10	,,
Lt.-Col.	Wyatt, G. N., D.S.O.	R.F.A.	1909-11	
	Cockburn, J. E. H.	R.G.A.	1909-12	Deceased
Major	Hulton, J. M., C.B.E., D.S.O.	R. Sussex	1909-11	
Capt.	Reddie, R. A., M.C.	16th Lancers	1909-11	Retired
	Oliver, G. B.	R.F.A.	1910-12	Died of wo
Lt.-Col.	Perkins, G. F., D.S.O.	Hants	1910-12	
	Mitchell, J. L.	R.H.A.	1911-14	Killed in a
Major	Hill, L. R., O.B.E.	R.F.A.	1911-14	
Major	Marsden, J. W.	R.G.A.	1912-14	A./M.A. T (1919-21)
Major	Simson, H. J., M.C.	R. Scots	1912-14	
Major	James, E. A. H.	R.E.	1913-14	
	Harland, R. W.	Hants	1913-14	Killed in a
	Carter, H. F. G., M.C.	Yorkshire L.I.	1913-14	Died on se
Major	Irving-Fortescue, A., D.S.O.	R.A.M.C.	1913-14	
Capt.	Bennett, R. D., M.C.	Middlesex	1917-20	
Capt.	Kennedy, M. D.	Cameronians	1917-20	Retired
Lieut.	Withers, A.	R.A.	1918-21	Deceased
Capt.	Alms, G. F. H.	R.E.	1919-22	
Major	Hill, D.	R.A.	1920-22	Retired
Capt.	Saunders, E. G.	Gordon Hrs.	1921-	
Major	Smith, R. H., O.B.E.	R.A.S.C.	1921-	
Lieut.	Delamain, C. B. H., M.C.	R.F.A.	1922-	
		(Royal Air Force.)		
Flt.-Lt.	Wanless O'Gowan, L.	R.A.F.	1918-21	
Flt.-Lt.	Bryant, W. E. G., M.B.E.	R.A.F.	1922	
		(Indian Army.)		
Lt.-Col.	Cheyne, R. E.	8th Cavalry	1906-7	Retired
Brig.-Gen.	Bateman-Champain, H. F., C.M.G.	9th Gurkha Rif.	1906-7	,,

(Indian Army.)

Rank 1922.	Name.	Regt. or Corps.	In Japan.	Remarks.
Lt.-Col.	Steel, R. A., C.M.G., C.I.E.	17th Cavalry	1906-7	Retired
	Moore, C. M., M.D.	I.M.S.	1907-8	Deceased
	Simpson, W. H.	93rd Burma Inf.	1907-8	Killed in action
Lt.-Col.	Dopping-Hepenstal, M. E., C.B.E., D.S.O.	1/3 Gurkha Rif.	1907-8	
Lt.-Col.	Wallace, E. C. L., D.S.O.	30th Punjabis	1907-8	
Major	Jolly, G. A.	I.M.S.	1908-9	
Major	Delme Radcliffe, S. A., O.B.E.	87th Punjabis	1908-9	Retired
Major	Hogge, L. R.	47th Sikhs	1908-9	
	Blair, G. L.	36th Sikhs	1909-10	Deceased
	Wood, P.	89th Punjabis	1909-10	Died of wounds
Lt.-Col.	Nangle, M.C.	92nd Punjabis	1909-10	
Lt.-Col.	Combe, S. B., D.S.O., M.C.	47th Sikhs	1910-11	Retired
Major	Barr, J. H. V.	109th Infantry	1910-11	
Major	Walter, E., C.I.E.	S. & T. Corps	1910-11	Retired
Major	M'Neight, A. A.	18th Inf., I.M.S.	1911-12	
Lt.-Col.	Kirby, J. T., D.S.O.	S. & T. Corps	1911-12	
Major	Lecky, J. G.	119th Infantry	1913-14 1920-22	
Capt.	Langhorne, C. C.	24th Punjabis	1918-21	Retired
Capt.	Morgan, K. S.	19th Infantry	1919-23	
Major	Woodward, R. F.	130th Baluchis	1920-23	
Major	Smith, Y. E.	66th Punjabis	1920-22	
Capt.	Russell, R. W.	9th Gurkha Rif.	1920-23	
Capt.	Whitworth, D. E., M.C	2nd Lancers	1921-22	
Capt.	Fuge, T. L. M.	130th Baluchis	1921-22	Retired
Capt.	Mullaly, B. R.	10th Gurkha Rif.	1922-	
Lieut.	Wards, G. T.	84th Punjabis	1923-	
Lieut.	Dicker, B. P.	83rd Wallajabads	1923-	

INDEX

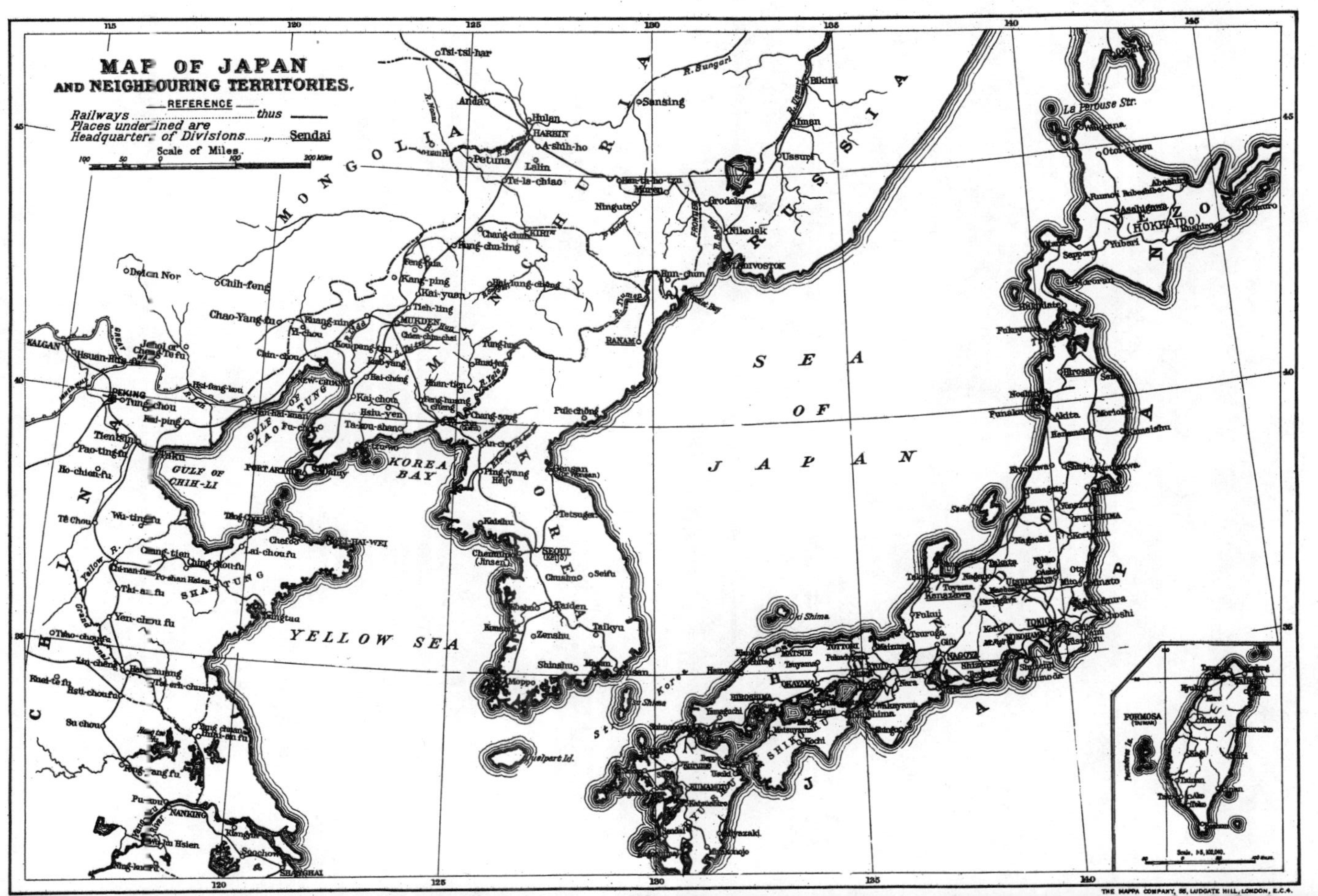
MAP OF JAPAN
AND NEIGHBOURING TERRITORIES.
REFERENCE
Railways .... thus
Places underlined are Headquarters of Divisions ...... Sendai
Scale of Miles.
MONGOLIA
MANCHURIA
RUSSIA
KOREA
SEA OF JAPAN
YELLOW SEA
KOREA BAY
GULF OF CHIH-LI
GULF OF LIAO TUNG
SHANTUNG
La Perouse Str.
YEZO (HOKKAIDO)
Oki Shima
Quelpart Id.
Sado
FORMOSA (TAIWAN)
Pescadores Is.
Tsi-tsi-har
Harbin
Sansing
Mukden
Kirin
Peking
Tientsin
Port Arthur
Seoul
Vladivostok
Nanking
Shanghai
Sendai
Tokio
Yokohama
Nagoya
Osaka
Hiroshima
Kumamoto
Sapporo
THE MAPPA COMPANY, 35, LUDGATE HILL, LONDON, E.C.4.

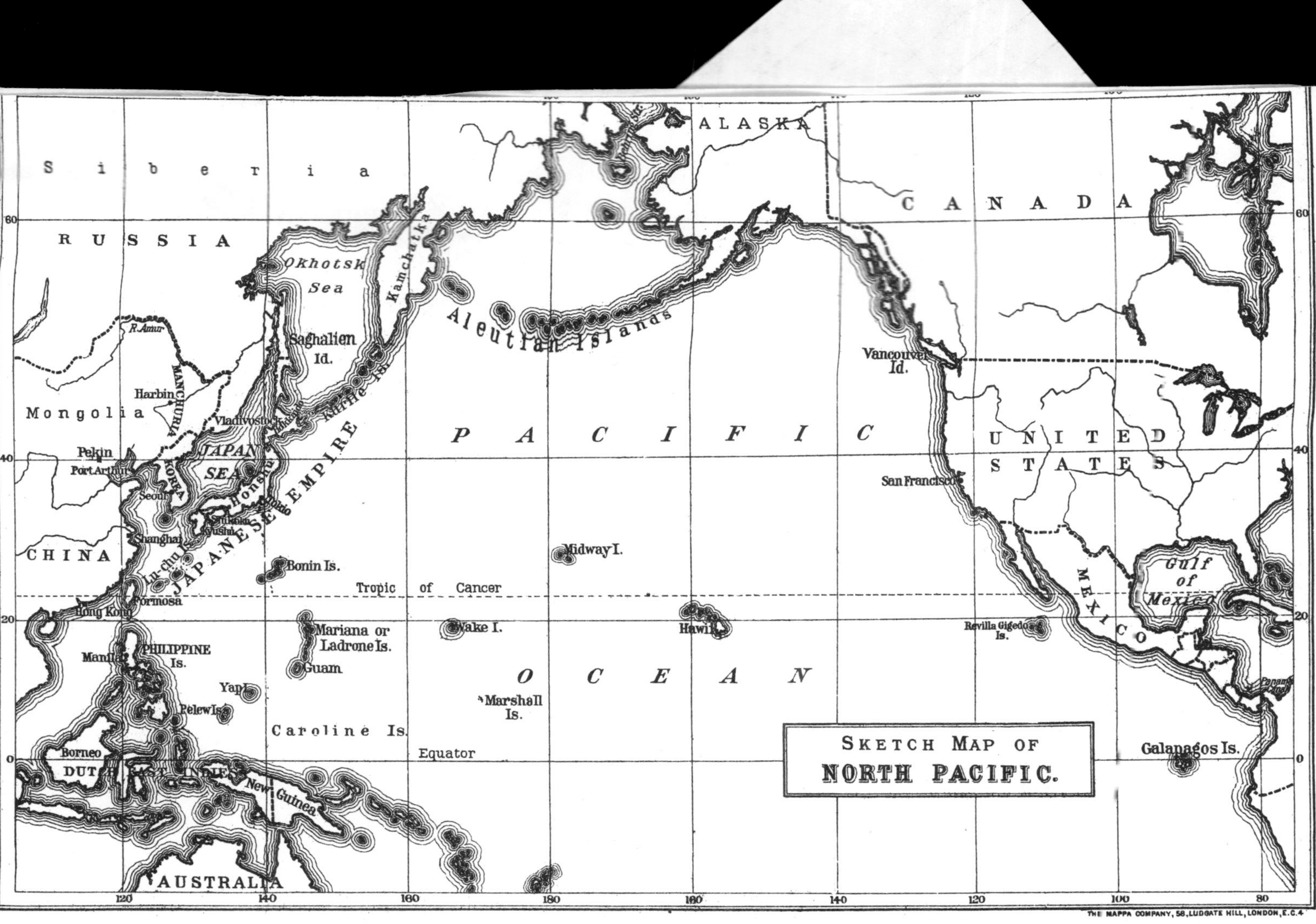
SKETCH MAP OF
NORTH PACIFIC.
Siberia
RUSSIA
Okhotsk Sea
Kamchatka
Saghalien Id.
R. Amur
MANCHURIA
Harbin
Mongolia
Vladivostock
Pekin
Port Arthur
KOREA
JAPAN SEA
Seoul
Honshu
JAPANESE EMPIRE
Kurile Is.
Shanghai
CHINA
Lu-chu
Formosa
Hong Kong
Manila
PHILIPPINE Is.
Yap I.
Pelew Is.
Borneo
DUTCH EAST INDIES
New Guinea
AUSTRALIA
Bonin Is.
Mariana or Ladrone Is.
Guam
Caroline Is.
Equator
Tropic of Cancer
Aleutian Islands
ALASKA
CANADA
Vancouver Id.
PACIFIC
OCEAN
Midway I.
Wake I.
Marshall Is.
Hawii
UNITED STATES
San Francisco
MEXICO
Gulf of Mexico
Revilla Gigedo Is.
Galapagos Is.
THE MAPPA COMPANY, 58, LUDGATE HILL, LONDON, E.C.4.